New Careers and Urban Schools

A Sociological Study of Teacher and Teacher Aide Roles

William S. Bennett, Jr.
Western Michigan University

R. Frank Falk
University of Denver

HOLT, RINEHART AND WINSTON, INC.

New York · Chicago · San Francisco · Atlanta
Dallas · Montreal · Toronto · London · Sydney

New Careers
and
Urban Schools

Preface

This book is about two different but complementary movements in the American schools: the *teacher aide* movement and the *new careers* movement. Our goal is to provide a sociological analysis of both movements and to further indicate how the two are inextricably linked on the contemporary scene. The book clearly takes a position of advocacy toward the new careers concept as a highly workable solution to a wide range of educational problems. Nonprofessionals are being used in large numbers in the American schools. At the same time, there is the start of a strong move on the part of the poor and the nonwhite to have a genuine say in running their own schools. The strongest "say" will come through having community governing boards and teachers of the same cultural and economic experience as the children. The teachers (at least some teachers in any inner city school) must speak the language of the children. This book is, then, about where these teachers will come from, how they will be recruited, and how their careers will fit with the present models of professional training. We are strongly convinced that the present methods of training and, to some extent, the present role structure of teaching must change, especially within the urban schools.

One should not, of course, be naïve about the realities of the situation. To a great extent the present goals of professionalism in teaching are in conflict with the goals of community control and community participation in education. The practical and realistic thing is to seek solutions that will allow us to have the best of both values. But as events of recent years (for example, the Ocean Hill–Brownsville crisis and the resulting teachers' strike) indicate, these solutions are not easily come by. The book is a sociological analysis of the complex relationship between advancing professionalism in teaching and the need to bring more people from the community into the schools.

We take the position that one important way to tie teacher professionalism with community ambitions is to *link* the wide-spread use of teacher aides with the less widely understood new careers concept. As will be indicated, this is not an easy matter, but it is a route that *does seem possible* if both sides (those who urge professionalism and those who urge total community control) look at the practical alternatives and are willing to plan for the long run. We attempt to analyze the changing nature of teaching and to look at this as providing certain positive advantages toward obtaining community control of schools. If teachers are seen as more than drill masters, there is room for persons with less training to do important jobs in the school and to use this experience toward recognition as fully certified teachers. Alternatively, it may be possible to have different ranks of teacher aides organized into a career ladder so that one may climb from the bottom to the top (that is, become a teacher) with a combination of experience and formal education. These general goals imply that all institutions having anything to do with teacher training and employment must change in fundamental ways. The universities, the junior colleges, the professional organizations, the schools, the state departments of education (and other certifying agencies), and the U.S. Office of Education must all change or adapt to changes. One of the problems in engineering any large societal change is ignorance (or naïveté) about the fact that these big changes usually depend on many little changes and many little steps taken by a large number of different institutions.

The difficulty of obtaining real change in teaching and teacher training will be illustrated by this book via an analysis of the contemporary teacher role, its relationship to the use of nonprofessionals, and the present attempts to develop what has been widely called the new careers concept in education.

Chapter 1 is a topical introduction to the concept of new careers and its relation to the urban crisis. Chapter 2 is an historical review of the use of nonprofessionals in the schools. Chapters 3 and 4 focus on the present role structure of teaching and make an attempt to pull together the most useful sociological observations on contemporary teaching. This section focuses on the differentiation and specialization of teaching and implies that changes in teacher function will soon force major changes (especially a continued decline of the generalist) in the organization of the teaching profession. Chapter 4 is directly concerned with the role that nonprofessionals play in the *new* role structure.

Chapter 5 deals with the new careers concept at some length. Starting with the teacher aide role, the chapter illustrates how the new careers concept is really a major alternative among several different patterns of teacher aide use. It focuses on the recruitment and training of teacher aides according to a new careers model. Chapters 6, 7, 8, and 9 deal with aspects of the new careers concept. The four chapters go together as an attempt to describe the three major dimensions of new careers (as seen by us) via a detailed account of the attempts to build a new careers type of aide program in one city: Minneapolis. Chapters 6 and 7 deal with building a career ladder (in the schools and in training, respectively). Chapter 8 deals with the use of new careers to bring about a personal change in low-income adults recruited to work in the schools. And Chapter 9 deals with the improvement of educational quality through the use of nonprofessionals.

Chapter 10 takes a step back from the situation to look at some of the more mundane problems of teacher aide use; and we hope this will be of use to those not wanting to move at full speed in the direction of new careers. Finally, Chapter 11 provides an epilogue that points out the salience of the new careers idea within the crisis of urban education.

A closing word about our experience with teacher aide programs and new careers programs is perhaps appropriate. The senior author was for eighteen months program coordinator for the training component of the Minneapolis new careers program. He has since been consultant to both the Grand Rapids, and Kalamazoo, Michigan, teacher aide programs. The junior author was the research director of the Minneapolis new careers program and during 1968 to 1969 was the principal investigator on a Labor Department research contract for research into new careers. Both of us went to work on a new careers program as "outsiders." We are both primarily sociologists and not educators or antipoverty workers. We see ourselves as attempting to apply a variety of sociological theories and observations in analyzing the chaotic urban educational scene and especially in using these observations to make predictions and policy recommendations for the future. This practical orientation is seen by us as an appropriate (perhaps the most appropriate) role for a sociologist in these troubled times.

We would like to acknowledge the 206 new careerists in Minneapolis who through countless encounters taught us a great deal about the problems and hopes, the needs and ambitions of low-income adults in American society. Beyond this we are in special debt to Frederick Hayen and Esther Wattenberg of the Minneapolis public schools and the University of Minnesota, respectively. Many of the ideas in the book and certainly many of the programs discussed in the later chapters were the conceptions of these two talented applied social scientists. Acknowledgment is also due to Frank Riessman for original inspiration, for a criticism of the manuscript, and for the use of materials available only through his Center for the Development of New Careers at New York University. Comments made by Bruce Biddle, Richard Wisniewski, and Gordon Klopf were also very helpful. We did not always take all the advice offered, but the wide-ranging criticism was invaluable.

Kalamazoo, Michigan   W. S. B., Jr.
Denver, Colorado   R. F. F.
March 1970

Contents

New Careers and Urban Schools

1   Introduction

To the impartial observer American education must seem a picture of feast and famine. It is a scene of growth, affluence, and creativity; yet there are mean and vicious pockets of poverty. This is true both literally and metaphorically. Cost per pupil has been steadily rising throughout the postwar era; more children graduate from high school each year, and teacher training is becoming increasingly sophisticated. Yet at the same time conditions are such as to make possible Jonothon Kozol's (1967) tragically accurate account of the "destruction of the hearts and minds of the Negro children in the Boston school system." It is a time when more masters degrees in education are awarded than ever before, yet teacher turnover in slum areas is higher than at any previous time. It is a time when high-powered new curricula are being introduced in all of the major school systems and yet is a time when a ghetto classroom may have as many as 100 days of substitute teaching a year. Poorly trained, peripatetic, and unwilling personnel attempt to interpret these high-powered curricula to those most in need of them.

In the United States today, education is one of the great growth industries. Yet a very persuasive argument could be made that this is "growth" in middle-class schools, for middle-class students, by middle-class teachers. It is not a growth that can be said to be shared equally among all sectors of American education. In the great egalitarian American school system, many are considered to be "more equal" than others.

Similarly, American education places great emphasis on numbers and on efficiency of operation. Not nearly so much attention is given to the problems of individual differences or of the relationship of the school to the community or of the quality of instruction in general. This is particularly apparent in the schools in economically disadvantaged neighborhoods.

Teacher Aides and New Careers

This is *not* a book, however, about poverty and education per se. Rather, it is a book about some important changes in the role structure of American schools. These are changes that have a direct bearing on the relevance of education to the poor, the Black, or the disadvantaged. It is a book about two major trends in the development of instructional staff: the growing use of teacher aides and other auxiliary personnel in the schools, and the concept of new careers for the poor, especially the teaching profession.

If education in general has seen great growth in the 1960s, the use of teacher aides is probably the single most dramatic growth. In 1968, 80,000 teacher aides were at work in American schools. This alone represents an increase of 800 percent over 1960. More impressive still is the estimate that there will be 175,000 aides by 1970 (Gaylord Nelson, 1967a). In some ways these aides have simply sneaked into the schools; very few educators are aware that there are this many auxiliary personnel employed in the schools. Many educators are totally unaware of the federal legislation that made most of this growth in teacher aides possible, and fewer still are aware of the dimensions of proposed legislation that will vastly expand the position of this group within the schools.

Who Is a Teacher Aide?

Teacher aides are essentially noncertified persons who directly assist the teacher in his instructional role. This description is totally inadequate, however. Aides are in fact assuming a wide range of educational tasks. Some school systems are distinctly creative in their use of aides, others are following a highly conservative line that emphasizes the menial and housekeeping functions of aides. There is little systemization regarding aide use; and individual programs are growing up in an uncoordinated fashion. Even administrators of aide programs are not well informed about developments elsewhere in the country.

This book is an attempt to develop fully the concept of the teacher aide. It will look at the connection between the rapid growth in the teacher aide role and the advancement of the ideas of *new careers* for the poor (Riessman and Pearl, 1965; Riessman, 1966b; Bowman and Klopf, 1967). The latter concept emphasizes the vital role that poor people, minority group people, or even educationally disadvantaged people can play in American education.

The new careers concept involves linking the school with the neighborhood and the group of people whom it serves. It makes this link by hiring the poor *themselves* into the schools and by using this approach to recruit much larger numbers of low-income adults into teaching itself. The new careers concept questions the notion that all teaching is technique and insists that education is part of a community process involving both children and adults from the *same* community. In its most audacious forms it argues that Black should have a role in teaching Black, that the poor should have a role in teaching the poor. It also suggests that if these people do not have the credentials for teaching, perhaps something is wrong with the credential requirements rather than with the people and that maybe these people should be allowed to do some teaching regardless. At the same time, the new career aide will be encouraged, in the ideal program, to pursue further education with the goal of joining teaching ranks. The person pursuing the new career in education will work (and to some extent teach) in the schools at the *same time* that he is obtaining the proper credentials. Ideally, the teaching credential will be obtained in a program that is accelerated and more focused than that typically pursued by the middle-class person in his preparation for teaching.

Obviously, the teacher aide role and the new careers concept are closely linked. But not everyone has seen this connection, and many teacher aide programs have little resemblance to the new careers ideal. Most administrators approve the use of teacher aides, but many are skeptical of new careers proposals. The latter programs are troublesome, politically involved, and, at points, inconsistent with the tradition of American education. The new careers concept, especially in its most radical form, is often in conflict with some of the deepest values of an older generation of school administrators. This is a generation that fought hard to assure professional status and recognition for teachers, and for whom certification procedures, controlled by the profession, represent the culmination of a century-long struggle.

Importance of Sociological Analysis

We will try to look at the total scene and attempt to bring to the analysis of it as much of the sociological imagination as possible. However, we do not claim to be unbiased, because we have been involved in the day-to-day conduct of a teacher aide program. We have left a little blood behind in a number of battles concerning the introduction of teacher aides into a major metropolitan system, certification of aides (as "career aides"), and the generation of a new careers style program. However, as professional sociologists we will try to view these changes in the role structure of the schools in the widest framework possible and will look especially at the developing role of the teacher and relate this to the emerging role of teacher aide or assistant teacher. We will also take a long look at the internal social structure of American education in terms of general organizational processes, especially differentiation, integration, and role conflict; and we will attempt to place the teacher aide development in this broader context.

Without an extensive review of the sociology of poverty and race, which is already dealt with by many other authors, we will examine the application of the new careers idea to education. This will be done by looking at numerous alternatives for the recruiting, the selection, and the training of teacher aides. It will be seen that the new careers idea is simply one set of alternatives for recruiting, training, and using aides in American schools. Ambitious proposals to recruit teachers themselves from among the poor by use of a new careers program will also be examined in some detail and discussed in terms of experimental programs that have been used to test this point.

Finally, a report will be made on one operating program. This program is the teacher aide program carried out in the Minneapolis school system in conjunction with the University of Minnesota. The discussion will focus on the radical portion of this program—the part that has emphasized the building of new careers in education. We will examine the complex jobs of building career ladders in education and of altering educational opportunities for those beginning a new career. There will also be a brief preliminary review of some research on what happens to individuals who penetrate these educational frontiers.

Dimensions of Teacher Aide Use

It must be re-emphasized that the teacher aid—new careers picture is multifaceted. It is impossible to set neat boundaries to the discussion. The use of aides involves complicated changes in the structure of the schools themselves. The employment of teacher aides under the guidance of a new careers concept involves changes in the teachers' role, the emergence of new roles in the schools, and a much closer integration of the school with the neighborhood in which it is located. It involves new patterns of communication and authority.

We are seeing here the new face of American education. It is to some extent a face that reflects two simultaneous developments that are in many respects in conflict with one another. These are, on the one hand, the growing professionalism of teaching and, on the other, the growing concern that a school have roots in the *real* community whose children pass through its doors in the most important socialization experience of their lives. A brief look at one of the more radical proposals for using teacher aides and for integrating school and neighborhood may serve as the best general introduction to our subject.[1]

Returning the School to the People

For thousands of years the young received their education in small, isolated communities: pastoral bands, agricultural villages, or

[1] It should be made clear to the reader that this description is being offered as an appetizer. It is meant to stimulate thinking and to provoke questions. It is not typical of teacher aide programs; the following sections describe an experiment in which teacher aides are used in a ground-breaking way and as such may give a sneak preview of the schools of tomorrow. The remainder of the book will remain somewhat closer to current events.

raw cities eking out a civilized existence on a narrow margin of economic surplus. In the vast majority of these communities children learned of life from older brothers or sisters. Older kinsmen played a role on special or ritual occasions and nonkinsmen played an educative role on only the most holy or ceremonious occasions such as the critical *rites de passage* (Wilson, 1966).

Western society lost touch with this educational tradition a long time ago. Out of necessity the schools have become increasingly differentiated from the family and other socializing institutions. The school, in American society, and especially on the frontier, actually replaced the family in order to assure that every child, whether immigrant or atheist, had an "equal opportunity" to learn the Bible or to cope with an uncertain market economy (Bailyn, 1960; Smith, 1966). In recent years the increased sophistication of educational methods, combined with barriers of race and language, has significantly isolated school from community for a surprisingly large group of Americans. Even middle-class schools have become autonomous islands in their communities. Most commentators see the autonomy of the middle-class school as a positive step forward, providing needed protection and opportunity to teachers and other educational specialists. But the isolation of the urban or ghetto school from the community may result in an evolving tragedy: a noble but inflexible cause leading to disaster. Many doubt that any amount of high-powered educational hardware or teacher preparation can effectively tell the poor, or the Black, or the psychologically disadvantaged child that the school is really for him; or that the school is preparing him for a part in his society. It must seem to many of these youngsters as if they were being prepared for a trip to a foreign land.

The San Jose Program

The perception of this problem is at the heart of several highly innovative programs for returning the schools to the people by the use of teacher aides and a totally new structure for teaching. One of these is a proposal, not yet fully operative, designed by Eldred Rutherford (1967), a psychologist at San Jose State College. Rutherford would quite literally tear down the schoolroom walls and start all over again. He proposes the breaking up of the schools into smaller, more autonomous and self-contained units. His experimental program involves using five or six large older homes for five or six ungraded schools. Each school would be a self-contained educational environment for a small number of students. These small groups of students of mixed age and mixed educational ability would receive a great deal of their education within this new "one room" schoolhouse.

The major part of Rutherford's proposal is not concerned with buildings or the size of classrooms but rather with people. Rutherford perceived the tremendous gap between the middle-class teachers, even the well-meaning and well-trained teachers (not to speak of the others), and the underachieving Negro or Mexican-American youngsters in San Jose, and proposed that a great deal of the actual teaching of these kids be done by noncertified personnel. These teaching nonteachers would be college students (and others) of the same ethnic or racial background as the pupils. They would be young adults who have grown up in the same ghetto neighborhood.

> *The concept.*[2] Our idea is neither new nor is it original. But it is radical in its implications for the education of minority youth from the ghetto. The critical phrase is a "new, all-encompassing culture of learning." It suggests, first, that the program's sole purpose for being is educational, in the broadest, most all-inclusive sense possible . . . that the school itself will be a culture providing students with the basic experiences from which will emerge their growth towards maximum intellectual, social and economic competence. Second, it suggests that present public school settings are failing to provide students with such a culture—that in fact public schools too often occupy themselves with non-educational tasks (e.g., caretaker functions) which are detrimental to real learning. And third, it suggests that experiences obtained in this culture will be directly relevant to experiences occurring in the daily lives of the students. . . .
>
> It is proposed that a new, all-encompassing culture of learning can be created for minority students from San Jose's eastside neighborhoods by establishing a special instructional program. . . .
>
> The students, whose characteristics are described in a subsequent section will be enrolled in a program that has these general features:
>
> a. Total emersion in a corporate, self-governing life embracing the academic and social life of the school affairs in the life of the community from whence they come and, most importantly, the communal life that they create for themselves within the program itself;
>
> b. Immediate contact with and guidance from instructors who are of racial-ethnic backgrounds identical to the students

---

[2] All of the following quotation is from an unpublished manuscript written by Eldred Rutherford (1967). Reprinted by permission of the author.

and who as part-time regular college students are themselves experiencing pressures toward growth similar to those of the students;

    c. Less immediate, but extremely valuable, contact with and guidance from faculty and regular students (of all backgrounds) at the college and from persons in the community; and,

    d. Economic arrangements by which students earn money sufficient for their daily needs which while working on tasks will teach them skills transferable to profitable jobs elsewhere.

But who will teach in this program? . . . In contrast to virtually all instructional programs found within American public schools, the present program will not use formally trained experts (i.e., teachers) as its primary instructors. Rather, the program's instructors will also be students—regularly enrolled college students at San Jose State who work part-time in the program as instructors . . . [and] like the students will be of Afro- and Mexican-American backgrounds. . . .

Pupils. Fifty Mexican-American and fifty Afro-American youths (girls and boys) ranging in age from (approximately) 15 to 18 years who are presently doing average-to-below-average work in school and 100 young men and woman of similar racial-ethnic background who have dropped out of school but who indicate a desire to obtain an academic education, will be enrolled in the program. Except for certain obvious limitations (e.g., those based on age), their enrollment in the program will entitle them to partake of all aspects of school life available to regular students. . . .

Few criteria will be used in selecting the youths for the program. Reversing procedures typically used in setting up special programs, the present program will not enroll students who, on the basis of their present academic records, show promise of being admitted to college. Rather the focus will be on youths who, under present standards, are very poor candidates for college admission. Students will not be excluded for histories of emotional disturbance, being "educationally handicapped," legal difficulties or the like. . . .

From a pool of names of youngsters with poor academic histories in eastside schools, 100 students will be selected randomly; school, parental and student permissions for enrolling them will be obtained and arrangements for their enrollment the following fall will be completed. Arrangements for obtaining the older (dropout) students will be made through the use of social agencies in the Bay Areas (e.g., job-retraining programs). Again, from a pool of such names, students will be selected on a random basis and arrangements made for their entering the program the following fall and for providing them room and board at the college when they arrive.

Student Instructors. Sixty Mexican-American and 60 Afro-American male and female college students who have completed at least one year of college will be hired as the primary instructors for the program. These student instructors will carry a maximum of 6 units of college credits during their tenure as instructors. They will be recruited from the student body and San Jose State and from other colleges in the state (e.g., San Mateo Junior College). Where necessary, admission standards at San Jose State will be waived to permit them to enroll as regular college students. Apart from their involvement in the program they will receive special assistance as needed in their regular college course work. They will be well paid for working as instructors and will receive room and board at the college during their tenure as teachers. . . .

Their recruitment and selection will employ the minimal standards of racial-ethnic background as demanded by the program (50% Afro- and 50% Mexican-American); sex (50% male and 50% female); and an expressed desire to enter the program. Past histories will *not* be examined. Following their selection, the necessary arrangements will be made for their enrollment at college and in the program, for their room and board on campus and for their arriving on campus at the beginning of the summer prior to the program's initiation in the fall.

Program Coordinators. Three faculty members from the college and two adults from the community (one Afro- and one Mexican-American) will be hired to plan, initiate and coordinate the many activities of the program. In addition to their duties as coordinators (these are spelled out later), the coordinators will conduct seminars on campus on problems relevant to the program's operation and on educational theories and practice.

The coordinators will work full time on the program for a minimum of two years, thereafter (if they desire) reducing their commitment to half time. Hopefully (to reverse typical developments), as the program develops the teachers will become less dependent on their services. One of the coordinators will act as program director.

Criteria for their selection will include a minimum of two years' college experience; a history of working effectively with young people and of following through on projects or programs; an ability to speak Spanish fluently; credibility with the relevant people in the college and community (especially with leaders of the progressive elements in the Afro- or Mexican-American populations); experience with group-oriented approaches to problems;

and an intense desire to see this program work. All five coordinators will receive the same salary, an average of the present salaries being paid to the three college staff members.[3]

Basic Teaching Units. These [basic units] . . . are the major all-important units of the program. The effectiveness with which these units achieve their primary objective of forming close-knit, self-governing units capable of educating one another [*sic*] of their members will determine the extent to which the program attains its goals. . . .

The students will be assigned in groups of ten (5 Afro- and 5 Mexican-Americans, men *and* women) to small, vertical (varying ages) basic units. Each unit will have three Mexican- and three Afro-American part time college students assigned to it as its primary instructors. Thus, each basic unit will include 16 members, and the entire program will be made up of 20 basic units. One program coordinator will be assigned to five basic units and the fifth coordinator, the program director, will act as a consultant to these coordinators and as a trouble-shooter for the program as a whole.

Though a massive volume of research findings have been reported on the functioning of small groups, it is extremely difficult to determine ahead of time the exact number of persons one can expect to function well together in pursuit of common goals. The nature of the goals, the kind of resources available and the conditions under which the groups will operate are critical factors in this determination. Consequently, "educated guesses" about the optimum numerical size of the basic units had to be made for this program.

The size of sixteen—ten students, six instructors—was selected because such a number seemed large enough to insure sufficient diversity of viewpoint, talents and background, to permit the development of internal structures within each unit—i.e., "natural" divisions of labor on different tasks—and the emergence of leaders among students and instructors in each unit capable of ably representing their unit's interests; and *small enough* to guarantee that frequent face-to-face contacts among unit members will occur easily and to facilitate each coordinator's task of forming effective working relationships with his (or her) units.

The large number of six instructors per unit was chosen

[3] The one radical aspect of the present program with which we strenuously disagree is the exclusion from the staff of the San Jose program of all certified teachers. While the program is obviously a frontal attack on the present school system, the total exclusion of trained secondary teachers seems going a bit too far. It does, however, point up the complete return of the school to the community advocated by the Rutherford proposal. Nothing could be clearer.

mainly for the purpose of providing conditions by which the instructors will be able to receive optimum support from one another in their difficult decisions and tasks. Hopefully, as instructors gain experience and confidence, this number can be reduced, with perhaps certain instructors breaking off to form the nuclei of new units as the program begins to expand its operations.

An essential structural dimension of these basic units is the "little red schoolhouse" feature of including students of widely varying ages in each unit. Except perhaps for a few country schools still in operation, most public schools rigidly adhere to class groupings based on chronological ages of the pupils. California law even prescribes the exact age at which this lock-step process must begin. The issue here is not whether this system works in general—obviously many youngsters pass through it with presumably some benefit to themselves—but whether, for the purposes of this program, it is more adequate as the basis for forming primary teaching units than is a system in which students of varying ages are grouped together. . . .

The San Jose program grants great autonomy to the basic units. It is unequivocal in its adherence to the principle of local control, to a degree that will be surprising, if not shocking, to most American educators. Despite the strong national adherence to local control over education, this concept has rarely meant real control by those actually involved in education, that is, the teachers, students, and parents. Rutherford proposes what must be the logical extreme of classroom autonomy.

The education of its own members is the primary goal to which the activities in each unit will be directed. In the last analysis, students and instructors in each unit will define the terms of their own education—the extent to which they want to concern themselves with problems not typically considered within the school settings (e.g., learning various techniques of self-presentation for use in different social situations), the priorities they want to give to such matters as the roots of their own cultural identity, and the nature of the political process as it operates in their community (e.g., they might conceivably decide to devote several weeks of effort, working as a unit, on some particular political campaign in the community); and the manner in which they make use of the educational resources available to them both on and off campus. The coordinators and other personnel at the college and in the community may—and should—attempt to influence individual units in what they do, but the ultimate authority for deciding what the units actually do will always remain with the units themselves.

This is an unabashedly radical proposal, and it is radical in several ways. From the standpoint of the present volume on teacher aides, the most dramatic aspect of this proposal is the extensive authority and responsibility granted to noncertified teacher personnel. Obviously this is no mere proposal to increase the supply of teachers through lowering requirements or to shore up administrative needs against teacher professionalism. This proposal has its own rationalization in its desires to return the school to the community and to reduce the social distance between classroom teacher and pupil. It derives directly from a concern with the inability of the middle-class teacher to reach the poor or minority group youngster. It is saying that teaching involves more than a learned pattern of didactic performances.

This is a basic theme that will be examined closely in later chapters and will be a thread running through the general discussion of teacher aides. It goes to the very heart of the logic involved in what will be referred to as the "new careers" concept in education. Although outlandish in some details, Rutherford's is the most innovative new careers proposal of which the authors are aware, and it functions as an admirable introduction to the wide-ranging topic of new careers in the public schools.

2 Historical and Legislative Background

The Historical Perspective

Before turning to a discussion of current events in the area of teacher aide development and new careers, we must discuss the history and legislative background of the idea. Things are changing so rapidly today that history may seem like an ill-afforded luxury. But some educators are unfamiliar with the idea of teacher aides and the changing role structure of the schools, so a brief review of the historical background is appropriate.

The teacher aide movement is a recent phenomenon. The new careers movement is even newer. Little was heard of teacher aides before 1960. There are no references to teacher aides in any educational index until 1956. There are early references to various kinds of volunteers: lay readers, tutors, and unpaid housewives helping out in various capacities. There are references to homeroom mothers and unpaid fathers filling in as coaches. But one looks in vain for any use of paid nonprofessional help in the classroom before the 1940s or any discussion by educators until about a decade later.[1]

Volunteers in Education

There was a time when practically all teachers in American elementary schools were volunteers. Many were farmers who taught school part time or women who took children into their own home or, more often, young men or women who taught for a short time in their mid-twenties before plunging into marriage or a more "serious" occupation. That day, of course, is long gone, vanishing with the general emergence of the common school and compulsory public education. Since the mid-nineteenth century, teaching has gradually become a professional career.

One of the little remembered early forerunners of the common schools, however, was the messianic school societies, like the Public School Society of DeWitt Clinton's New York. These societies were designed to provide a free, or nearly free, education to the poor in rapidly growing urban centers such as New York, Baltimore, and Philadelphia. This included teaching basic literacy. At the same time, they provided a heavy dose of Bible reading and Protestantism to urban "street arabs," many of whom happened to come from Roman Catholic parentage.

The societies, like urban schools in the 1960s, faced a severe manpower problem. If they were to teach the little "heathens" to read and to write and to love the Bible, they needed teachers and disciplinarians. They could not rely on the folk spirit of the small town to coerce the youngsters into the paths of education; indeed that was their entire problem: the children were not socialized by family or neighborhood in a suitable way. They solved the problem, to the extent that they did solve it, by the first use of teacher aides.

The Public School Society of New York, soon copied by a half dozen offspring organizations, adopted what was variously known as the Lancaster Plan or the Monitorial System. The Lancaster Plan was apparently devised by the British socialist Robert Owen for use in his own progressive community with its system of free public edu-

---

[1] Of course, one must note that for many states it was not until the 1950s that a clear majority of full-time teachers had four-year degrees.

cation. The plan called, in brief, for several of the largest one-room schoolhouses on record. Often operating in a loft over a store or tenement, an entire elementary school, numbering perhaps 150 students, was crowded into one room. Squarely facing the manpower question, the societies generally assigned only one teacher to this one room. This teacher presided over the gathering as general administrator, disciplinarian, and possibly sermonizer. The actual drill with alphabet, reading, and numbers was carried out by older boys, called monitors, who were responsible for a single row. The monitor would sit on a high stool at the end of the row, keeping a wary eye on his 10 to 15 charges (grouped according to ability and/or size) and calling them singly or in groups for recitation. The recitation assignment was made by the teacher, who maintained himself on a podium in front of the room.

The public common school ended the societies and their fervor for mass indoctrination.[2] The growth of normal schools, begun in Massachusetts in 1845, ended the use of the monitorial system. The specially trained two-year teacher replaced both amateur and monitor. Later, by the 1950s, the four- or five-year teacher had replaced the two-year instructor.

Now, American schools find themselves faced, somewhat ironically, with a similar passion (now secular) for rapid improvement and change in urban education. There are some similarities in the response. Again there is a call to bring irregular personnel into the schools to assist in many ways. There is great concern that educational resources will not be equal to the task. It is hoped that one hundred years of education science will allow the present generation to handle the situation in a less awkward fashion.

Recent Forerunners of Teacher Aides

Although the development of the teacher aide movement and new careers has been rapid in the past four years, the initial efforts began in the 1940s and 1950s. In the United States an organized program based on similar concepts was begun under the National Youth Administration (NYA). The NYA emphasized the employment of out-of-school youths as well as potential dropouts. These youngsters were trained and placed as nonprofessionals in the human services. In its

[2] The common school movement was aided in several states by political opposition to the school societies.

1940 annual report, the NYA indicated that more than 13,000 young people had been trained for nonprofessional jobs in the fields of health, education, recreation, welfare, corrections and the arts. However, only about 12 percent of the jobs were in education, with a much larger portion in health and recreation (Bowman and Klopf, 1967).

Unfortunately, NYA was mainly a white-collar WPA (Works Progress Administration). It had no programmatic follow-up in terms of long-run use of auxiliary personnel, nor did it include provisions allowing young people to obtain professional credentials while in the program. The NYA was formally liquidated in 1943, leaving only the experience of an attempt to use nonprofessionals in the human service.

In 1953 the first major experiment in the utilization of teacher aides was undertaken in Bay City, Michigan, with funds from the Ford Foundation. This program was the first conscious attempt to improve classroom performance by freeing teachers from the huge amount of busy work. The Bay City program was considered successful and has continued to this day on local funds. There followed two similarly financed studies: the Yale-Fairfield (Connecticut) Plan and the Rutgers (New Jersey) Plan. These programs, also financed by the Ford Foundation, were designed to assist administrators in preserving quality education in the face of severe personnel shortages. It is interesting that the emphasis was placed on *maintaining* instructional quality rather than on improving or changing it.

The latter problem may point to a major tactical error on the part of those interested in developing the teacher aide concept today. The teaching personnel in the latter programs raised several objections to the concept. The hub of the objections seems to have been that resources for educational expenditures were scarce, and that these resources could be spent in better ways. Salary levels in education were incredibly low in the midst of the broad inflation following World War II, and teachers felt that new money, even experimental money, should be spent on them first. Bowman and Klopf (1966) have commented that it was the emphasis on budgetary considerations in the programs (Bay City program included) that retarded progress in the development of teacher aides for at least a decade. This may be partly true. In fact, however, it seems fairer to say that the *un*professional treatment of teachers and the miserable wage levels of the 1950s made it difficult to discuss using assistant professionals in a field that could not afford to pay regular professionals in the first place. This situation was altered somewhat in the 1960s.

Berkeley Program

Another important and recent foreunner of the teacher aide idea was the use of college students as aides and tutors to school children in economically deprived areas.

In 1961 the Berkeley California School System, in cooperation with the University of California YMCA, asked university students to join their teaching staff as volunteer teaching assistants. Students were assigned to subjects closest to their major. The success of the program was never documented, but if the impressions of the teachers and college volunteers are valid, the program was effective.

One of the authors of this book participated in the program, and this discussion of the program represents his recollections. Recruiting for the program was selective, because only university students were asked to participate. Beyond this, however, there was no further selection. The volunteers were then assigned to teachers, who were completely responsible for their duties. Generally the teachers made use of the volunteers by having them act as interning teachers. The volunteer was asked to take over the class, tutor individuals who were either advanced or behind the class, and perform supportive services such as making up displays.

Several aspects of the new careers idea were present in the program. Supervision and administration of this program were decentralized. There was an institution of higher education associated with the program, although there was no attempt to innovate new courses for volunteers or supervisory teachers. Neither was there an attempt to recruit the volunteers into the school system as a permanent cadre of assistants. The administration merely hoped that the program would encourage college students to become teachers. This parallels the new careers goal of recruiting the poor to educational careers.

Legislation of the 1960s

The major breakthrough in the funding of teacher aides came from two pieces of federal legislation passed in the mid-1960s. The first, and by far the most important with regard to education, was Title I of the Elementary and Secondary Education Act of 1965 (ESEA). ESEA was, of course, a break with many American traditions, because it was the first general source of federal funds for the public schools.

Most commentators on ESEA believe that it was passed in part because of the great pressure to improve education in disadvantaged neighborhoods. This certainly was the impetus for Title I, symbolically placed at the head of the bill. Title I ticketed substantial sums for improving education in low-income schools. Monies under Title I are available for direct payment to teachers and for direct support of instruction as part of an antipoverty strategy.

One of the aspects of Title I, least commented on in 1965, was the provision of about $75 million for teacher aides. All of these aides were to be used in low-income areas and were to be proportioned out between elementary and secondary education. However, nothing was said about the recruitment of these aides or the general administration of the program. Nor was any comment made about hiring the poor to teach in their own schools. All this was left to the discretion of local administrators, creating the general impression that some kind of semivoluntary system would emerge in which people would come from various walks of life to help out in the badly beleaguered inner city schools. There was little sign of the new careers idea.

The second boost for teacher aides has come from the Scheuer Amendment to the Economic Opportunity Act. The Scheuer Amendment provided about $40 million in 1966–1967 for the development of demonstration programs in new careers for the poor. About 30 cities in all have received money under the Scheuer program. These local programs have taken a wide variety of forms. In southwestern Ohio, a broad six-county program called Supporting Council on Preventive Effort (SCOPE) sponsored a multipurpose new careers program in which 100 aides work as aides in education, housing, engineering, community development, child welfare, and law enforcement. In Kansas City about 80 aides are employed in half a dozen different health fields. In Minneapolis, 11 different human service agencies (representing education, social work, and corrections) are employing 207 aides. Two thousand residents of the south Bronx are employed in educational and welfare positions. This is the largest individual program under Scheuer funds.

Administered through the Labor Department, the Scheuer program is viewed as an antipoverty strategy and, more specifically, as a manpower program. Under recent administrative changes, the program has been integrated with the Labor Department's Concentrated Employment Program (CEP), which is seen as a comprehensive attack on the whole range of employment problems in a community. From the total pool of unemployed, *those with the proper background and interests* are spun off into new careers programs. This has placed qualifications (for example, education) on the recruitment to new careers and has displeased some of the main advocates of the new careers idea. Although some people have tended to identify new careers with the Scheuer bill, this is a fundamental error; and, as indicated, some feel that the Scheuer program has only partly borne out the promise that was held for it. This is as good a point as any, then, to make the distinction between *new careers* (lower case *n* and *c*) and any particular governmental program that may bear the title *New Careers*. The specific programs may be far removed from the ideal. Later chapters of this book will develop this distinction.

Education Professions Development Act

The third major piece of legislation affecting new careers is the Education Professions Development Act (EPDA) of 1968. EPDA authorizes the most comprehensive training program ever launched in any human service area. It has authorized some $240 million for colleges, state and local education agencies, and nonprofit private agencies to identify and assist capable youth in secondary schools who may be interested in careers in education. It also attempts to utilize local community people in part-time or temporary teaching and to provide training for teachers, teacher aides, and administrators (*New Careers Newsletter*, 1968).

Office of Education guidelines emphasize concentration of resources in areas of high impact and encourage comprehensive programs that combine several funding resources. Preschool programs for the urban economically disadvantaged have top priority. While the first set of proposals for EPDA funds are just being submitted, the signs are good that teacher aide programs will get significant support under the act. The EPDA guidelines identify the use of nonprofessionals as an area of special concern and indicate that at least 5 percent of the funds are to go to these programs. Likewise, it is important that Don Davies, formerly the director of the National Commission on Teacher Education and Professional Standards (NCTEPS) has been appointed the administrator of EPDA. Davies chose "the teacher and her staff" as the theme of the 1967 national conference while he was NCTEPS head.

Under the impetus of this legislation [3] the use of teacher aides

[3] A short list of additional sources of federal funds that might be used to support teacher aide programs is as follows:

    Higher Education Act (Title IIB), Library Research and Demonstration

    Public Library Services and Construction Act (Titles I, III, and IV)

    1963 Vocational Education Act, George-Barden Act, Smith-Hughes Act

        in Vocational Education

and the development of new careers programs have grown rapidly. In most cases these have been kept distinct from one another. In only a few cities, like Minneapolis, have Title I teacher aide programs operated side by side with Scheuer new careers programs. Both programs are related to the attack on poverty. However, the direct support to teacher aides is the simpler of the two strategies, concentrating on providing additional manpower to beleaguered school systems. It is reasoned that the additional hands in the classroom will make better schools and improve instruction regardless of specific use. The Scheuer program and other new careers ventures are clearly more complex. They combine a number of goals in one rather elaborate manpower proposal. As one of the authors of the Scheuer legislation wrote in another publication:

> New Careers is, without question, one of the most sophisticated and promising of any manpower in human service programs ever legislated by Congress. It has the potential to deeply affect public policy, the manner in which public agencies and their professional and nonprofessional staffs supply services to the public, and the way educational and training institutions perform their roles in society. Even more important, new careers focuses directly on the potential of the human being to be trained and educated in the context of work within and on behalf of the community. (Cohen, *New Careers Newsletter*, 1968)

New Careers and Teacher Aides

This book will be an attempt to elaborate on relations between the teacher aide idea and new careers. As indicated in the outline provided earlier in the first chapter, the idea of teacher aides will be discussed in the context of the changing role of the teacher and the structure of American education. Following this, the discussion will turn to an elaboration of the new careers concept, which, as Cohen notes, is a complex and politically potent subject.

The authors will make no attempt to hide their position in this issue. They generally support the idea that, at least in the inner city schools, teacher aides should be employed according to some aspect

---

Manpower Development and Training Act (Title IIA, B, C)
Adult Education Act (Title II)
National Defense Education Act (Title V)
Elementary and Secondary Education Act (Titles III, IV, V in addition to Title I)

of new careers. The remaining chapters will attempt to point out a number of compelling reasons why new careers should be a major aspect of inner city school policy. These reasons reach into almost all areas of community-school relations. Without completely prestating the case, it can be pointed out here that new careers is a major part of a process by which the inner city schools are being returned to the residents; this is completely consistent with the venerable tradition of local control of American schools.

Summary

The concern for urban education goes farther back in American history than many realize. Since the early nineteenth century there has been a history of sporadic attempts to marshal educational resources for the urban poor. This has usually involved efforts to use nonprofessionals in the schools. But it was not until the present decade that adequate funding has been available for teacher aide programs.

In the 1960s, three pieces of legislation gave a strong boost to the use of nonprofessionals. Title I of the Elementary and Secondary Education Act (1965) has paid for a large infusion of teacher aide assistance into low-income area schools. The Scheuer Amendment (1965) to the Economic Opportunity Act provided for demonstration programs in new careers. There have been a great variety of nonprofessional programs sponsored under the Scheuer Amendment, and a large proportion of these have been in education. Finally, the Education Professions Development Act (1967) has provided funds for training and for innovative programs using nonprofessionals. Additional legislation is currently being proposed in Congress by Senators of such different political positions as John Tower (R., Texas) and Gaylord Nelson (D., Wisconsin).

3 New Roles for Old: An Analysis of Teacher and Teacher Aide Roles

The use of teacher aides in the schools is inextricably tied into the evolution of the teacher role itself. In 1966 to 1967 the NCTEPS program sponsored what came to be called "the year of the nonconference." In this year, no national convention took place. Instead, a conference was held linking many cities by telephone hookups. As we have mentioned, the theme of this mass long distance phone call was "The Teacher and Her Staff." In making his initial statement to the nonconference, Don Davies referred to the essential part played by the nonprofessional within the new concept of a teacher and her staff (Davies, 1967). A sociological analysis of this phenomenon will be pursued in the next three chapters.

For many years, at least since the disappearance of the monitorial schools of the early nineteenth-century cities, the teacher has been a behavioral isolate in performing his professional duties. He has worked alone in classroom or shop, in reading group or physical education class. One author has gone so far as to see the isolated nature of the teacher as an extremely important dimension of the profession itself and as a dimension that is deeply involved in the recruitment process for teaching (Neubacher, 1965). The isolation of the teacher from other adults and even from other professionals during most of his actual workday attracts certain people into the field and repels others who might under different circumstances be attracted to the field. In any case, isolation is an important aspect of the daily rounds of the teacher. It can not help but have an effect on someone spending many years in classroom teaching.

It is clear that a number of recent movements have begun to break into this isolation of the teacher. Team teaching in secondary schools, the so-called dual program in elementary programs, the expanded use of student teachers, the integration of other professional services into the schools, and other trends are moving the teacher out of the single-adult–many-children role orientation. The teacher is moving into a situation in which interaction with other professionals is a routine experience. Moreover, interaction with other professionals is of an egalitarian nature. It is a distinct change from the previous dependent relationship between teacher and principal. In some schools the high status of certain teachers (master teachers, specialists, or team leaders) puts the teacher on an equal footing in many of his relations with the principal. There is no doubt that the old educational stratification patterns are breaking down and new forms—generally more democratic (and professional)—are emerging. At the center of this shifting of patterns is the notion of a staff for a teacher. Although there are numerous variations on this theme, the main type of staff in use today is a staff of nonprofessionals or paraprofessionals.

The Nonprofessional

It has long been recognized that a great many classroom chores are what may be called "dirty work" or "scut work." It is equally obvious that for generations these tasks have been done by regular teachers. Because much of the dirty work is essential, even if menial (for example, taking attendance, putting on wraps, and cleaning book shelves), the dirty work has often taken many minutes, even hours, from the time devoted to the most elementary educational tasks. Not so obvious is the fact that such dirty work will expand to meet almost any amount of free time any normal teacher would have for reflection and diagnosis of complex pupil problems. It is a rare teacher who can give careful thought to upcoming lessons when engrossed in the chaos of collecting money, distributing milk, or wiping running noses. A few are perhaps capable of such divided concentration, but most will find themselves dragged down by the large group of menial chores that the classroom requires.

The nonprofessional teacher or classroom aide was originally employed to carry out the routine chores that brutally consume the teacher's short hours. For years, isolated school systems have used volunteers to perform the function of a teacher aide, but only in recent years have school systems begun to employ such personnel on a regular basis. Although a good deal of the impetus for this movement has come from the federal government (as discussed in chapter 2), the evolving definition of the teacher has a great deal to do with the emphasis. It is, of course, not impossible that the expanded definition of teacher role may itself be subtly generated by the experience of teachers with a staff of at least one nonprofessional.

It seems obvious that the nonprofessional role cannot be defined without reference to the definition of teacher role itself. Anyone interested in teacher aides must at least briefly address themselves to the question of teachers and teaching. What is a teacher? What defines teaching?

The surgeon has finished his job when the patient is sewed up and is on his way to recovery. When is it that the teacher has finished his job? This question is not easy to answer. But the public is beginning to expect comparable performance from teacher as from physician. Recently malpractice suits have been filed against teachers in one Eastern city. With or without malpractice suits, it is, in any case, clear that expectations for teacher performance are being heightened. But what are the behavioral dimensions of teaching to which these expectations are related? This takes some careful consideration of recent academic folklore concerning teaching as well as other sources of "soft" data concerning teacher role. After a discussion of these sources, this chapter will conclude with an attempt to define the "new" aide role in relation to the "new" teacher role.

The Teacher

Role Analysis

In answering the question of what a teacher is in the context of discussing the proliferation of staff in the schools, it is necessary that one stick to an analysis of the way things are *today*. It will not really help us to speculate about the platonic idea that *teacher* may conjure in the minds of some theorists. Nor does a strict behavioral analysis of what teachers do get directly at the matter either. *Rather, what is called for is some understanding of what normative expectations the teacher meets in his day-to-day activities* (see Gross 1958; Biddle, 1966). What are the current versions of teaching for the majority of practically minded schoolmen? What does the educational establishment say in the colleges of education throughout the nation? What do sophisticated and active community leaders expect of teachers right now in the 1970s? How do most teachers view themselves? This is what will be meant by the current teacher role.

There is, of course, no single answer. There are some real differences of perspective. Nor do we have the "hard" data on this normative picture. A few isolated studies limited in implications to several communities (for example, Kansas City) indicate some surprises; for example, that school administrators have more limited goals for teachers than do teachers themselves or that noneducation students have a clearer picture of norms held for teachers (Biddle, 1966) than do education students. But in general there is considerable uncertainty about current norms or anticipations for teacher roles.

Four Dimensions of the Teacher Role

Professional

Some things come through loud and clear, however, from the monograph and article producing educational leaders. Besides being expected to be a generally upstanding citizen—a norm that carries over from the days when a teacher was to be a paragon—several dimensions of teaching seem emphasized above others. He is also supposed to be a *professional* in his performance, meaning (if anything explicit) that the teacher has a relatively esoteric set of skills that the community needs and that only a properly prepared teacher can be trusted to know or to be able to use. This is, of course, an old story. Professionalism has been pushed for a long time. What may be somewhat new is the emphasis on special skills rather than on special responsibilities or special status. As Willard Waller points out (1932) in one of the classic analyses of the teacher role, the professional status of the teacher of yesteryear was asked for (and to some extent granted) arbitrarily in an honorific process. In past years a teacher was called "Doc" or "Professor" but in fact was treated as a somewhat immature social and political citizen. Today the teacher is not usually greeted in the same manner, but he is more confident of a set of skills —with or without an honorific title. The public's confidence in these skills is perhaps the key point. These skills lacked specificity until the postwar era.

Whether colleges of education are doing a better job today or whether the breakthroughs in educational science have been that great since 1930 will remain a moot point here. What does seem clear is that the public and educators themselves by and large *believe* that this training is better, more important, and so on. The public is willing to view the teacher as a skilled craftsman and not as a combined nanny and camp counselor. There seems to be very widespread acceptance of the idea that four years of college (and possibly more) are absolutely prerequisite to entering the classroom. California has moved in recent years to require five years of college for entry into the classroom.

Specialist

Secondly, and perhaps less consensually, the image of the teacher is becoming that of the *specialist*. Here we witness the first stages of broader movement to identify teaching with more highly skilled specialities. At present most of the emphasis on specialization appears to come from the academic establishment. Local administrators are less likely to emphasize specialization. But at the national level one is aware of increasing movement in the direction of teacher specialization, either in particular academic subjects (for example, reading, mathematics, and music) or as especially versed in the lore of human behavior so as to function as a counselor, a test specialist, or a diagnostician of special educational needs. Conceptual clarity is still a bit ragged on this point. Many still see counseling or diagnostic specialities as somewhat divorced (physically and in terms of communication) from the classroom and the teacher. Others see the future of these specialities lying in the close integration of these roles into the *ongoing* classroom situation. A prime example of this movement is the dual program that clearly extends subject matter specialization far down into the primary grades (Stoddard, 1961). The dual program envisions a "master teacher" or a "home teacher" (the latter is the preferred term for obvious reasons) as responsible for a homeroom, or homeroom complex, consisting of perhaps 80 children. The home teacher is responsible for the general flow of students into and out of the classes of numerous subject matter specialists. The home teacher is responsible for everyday kinds of test evaluation and general planning. He is the master of an integrated team. He is highly trained in testing, counseling, and the general pedagogy relevant to the age level at which he operates.

Child Psychologist

The third dimension of teaching today is that of *child psychology*. It is increasingly assumed that the teacher of today is skilled in certain of the mysteries of modern psychology. He is not an expert in this area but, rather, is seen in an image that successfully merges the old image of Cub Scout leader and substitute parent with the glitter of the psychiatrist's mantle. Parents are more likely than ever before to suspect that teachers may know (or be able to find out) things about their children that may not be obvious at all to the parents.

These observations of teacher qua psychologist may pose some threat to the parents. The idea is increasingly accepted that the eccentricities of the parents are visited upon, and are quite visible in, the children. This is not a totally original observation about human behavior. But it is certainly a more commonly held, and at the same time more scary proposition in the post-Freudian era. Teachers share liberally in the mixed prestige, fear, and skepticism that attends the present-day psychological practitioners. Again, this is nothing new to educators; educational psychology has been strong in the colleges for nearly 50 years. What is new within the past two decades is the increasing acceptance by the public of this point of view. The psychological training of the colleges may not have changed much, but the convictions of the public and perhaps the more general run of schoolmen themselves have changed. In a world that is frequently defined as sick or disorganized or troubled, the teacher is seen as healer, perhaps a low-grade healer among more high-powered (and more threatening) colleagues, but a healer nonetheless.

Supervisor

A fourth dimension of teacher role that must be more tentatively advanced is that of supervisor of other personnel. Somewhat akin to the marginal acceptance of the teacher as a specialist that one might have found with a national poll *circa* 1935, there is today a growing but limited recognition that in the school of the future, teachers will assume more and more leadership chores. This will definitely involve an image of a teacher and his staff, an image that is not easily evoked today except within certain advanced circles. It is an image that also meets resistance in many places. There is a distinct lack of consensus on this aspect of teacher role.

Most of the thinking concerning the teacher as a supervisor seems to be taking place in the colleges. Jerome Bruner, a psychologist with a growing reputation in education, has pointed out (1960) how underutilized experienced teachers are in training new personnel. In education, even more than in medicine, training is left to former teachers or nonteachers attached to the universities. After this essentially amateur training, the fledgling teacher is thrown immediately into the classroom to take his place among the pros. The new teacher can learn from these professionals but only in an informal and haphazard way.

Bruner hits directly at the organization of the American schools as "somewhat less than imaginative." He notes that the communication among teachers is nearly always informal and crisis ridden. It typically concerns educational problems and problem children. It is exceptional when the more general educational strategies are comprehensively discussed by young teachers in consultation with their more experienced colleagues. Young male teachers seem especially unwilling to discuss their teaching with older teachers, who preponderantly are older women.

Closely related to the training of novice teachers is the question of teachers training nonprofessionals and the broader problem of the teacher aide role. Bowman and Klopf (1967) have discussed at some length these problems of teachers and teacher aides. The thrust of their argument is that the nonprofessional is most useful in teaching the economically disadvantaged. These authors have reviewed 15 teacher aide programs sponsored by the federal government. These studies deal with a rich variety of types of nonprofessionals including low-income college students, high school dropouts, and low-income (generally AFDC) mothers involved in a series of pilot programs.

Bowman and Klopf are carefully nonideological in their conclusions; but they do come up with some general observations and recommendations based on their own experience and the 12 pilot programs that were studied during the training periods. They conclude unequivocally that "low-income auxiliaries with minimum education appeared to be capable of assisting with the learning-teaching process in the classroom with benefits to pupils, particularly when the auxiliaries were carefully selected and trained." They also conclude that many teachers who participated in the programs "perceived their own roles in new perspective after working with aides in the classroom. . . ." They found that these teachers who experienced the use of low-income nonprofessionals placed more emphasis on diagnosis, planning, and coordination of classroom activities than upon the traditional dimension of teacher-pupil interaction. The new role, however, was additive for the teacher; it was not seen as a substitute for the old style classroom patterns.

The effects uncovered by Bowman and Klopf went beyond the classroom situation to involve administrators and others in the new instructional system. "A salient outcome was that all concerned—administrators, supervisors, teachers, and ancillary personnel [counselors, curriculum specialists, and others]—had to rethink their roles and relationships when aides were introduced into a school system."

This is reminiscent of concern expressed at one workshop on the use of paraprofessionals organized for school administrators in the upper Midwest. A recurrent theme of the meeting had to do with the fact that the administrator had to delegate his supervision. Not all of the actual instructional staff was directly under his wing. The assumed total responsibility of administrators came out in numerous ways. There was special concern about admitting low-income people to jobs in the schools when they (the principal or superintendent) could not keep a watchful eye on them. Some administrators seemed quite taken aback at the idea of a chain of command in the school, despite the fact that such a form of organization is ancient history in other kinds of institutions.

The Teacher and His Staff

Don Davies, director of NCTEPS in 1966 to 1967, has frequently propounded the idea that professional staff ought to be used to coordinate the activities of a less skilled junior staff. His theme has been that the sophistication of teachers is not used in creative ways, especially in regard to educational planning and curriculum design. Davies has emphasized the double loss involved when people become full-time administrators with responsibility for curriculum development. The schools suffer in terms of day-to-day activities, and Davies feels that the curriculum itself may suffer in numerous instances. Davies has stressed four lines of attack on the present system (Denemark, 1966; Davies, 1967). These are (1) the infusion of large numbers of teacher aides and other types of paraprofessionals into the system, (2) the use of educational technology and hardware in a sophisticated way, (3) an emphasis on the close cooperation between specialist and teacher, and (4) the creation of a permissive environment for teachers where creativity can be encouraged and innovation can actually take place outside the usual confusion of school politics. Davies sees all of these, but especially the first, as heralding changes in the teaching role. He recognizes the fact that many teachers are not prepared either by temperament or by training to work with another adult on a professional basis. But he insists that it is this kind of occupational inhibition that has perpetrated the vicious cycle of low wages and low professionalism in education today, one feeding inexorably into the other. He conceives the use of teacher aides and the teacher's staff concept as a major way to break out of this box.

Anderson (1964, 1966) proposes essentially the same theme but treats the idea of a staff for teachers in a more systematic fashion. He draws a distinction between at least three categories of aides: the preprofessional, the nonprofessional, and the paraprofessional. Into the first category fall various arrangements for gradually exposing college students to the teacher role through an apprenticeship served under a teacher's supervision. Note first that this is not student teaching in the traditional sense (these are *pre*-education people) and, second, that the supervision is under a teacher, not (even in part) under someone from a university. Anderson also supports plans that call for the teacher to be assisted by older or brighter pupils in some formal way.

The use of nonprofessional aides includes arrangements in which people who do not necessarily intend to follow a teaching career and who often have no college education serve in an assistant's role. This role would call for little or no formal training. Any training that would take place would be on-the-job training. This role is what will be called an "entry level" position in the next chapter.

Anderson's third category is referred to as paraprofessional, indicating that they are in some part professional. These kinds of aides will have some type of formal training and will be competent to take over "tasks that might otherwise have to be performed by a regularly certified teacher." In Anderson's own words, "The term is used to cover a rather wide range of talents, some of which have more economic value than others." This somewhat obscure characterization of the paraprofessional is intended to open up the possibility of an alternative position(s) between the unskilled novice and the certified teacher. To the reasons for developing such a junior colleague that have already been mentioned, Anderson adds the notion that very few teachers can do everything well and that judicious assignment of aides can help to fill these natural gaps in a teacher's ability. For example, the teacher completely devoid of musical sense (a not unusual phenomenon) could utilize an aide for this portion of his class.

This view of Anderson's is different, then, in the sense that the paraprofessional (not the nonprofessional) would be competent to take over *completely* the teaching function in certain kinds of situations. This is an interesting variation on the theme and one with a great deal of logic behind it. But it is also one that confuses the issue that most commentators are clear on, that is, that a noncertified teacher can never assume the actual teaching duties, but must always be supervised. In numerous confrontations in several states, teachers and other school people have been firm on this point. We will have more to say about this critical issue later on.

The Anderson position, if carried forward from the minor point it occupies in his commentary, raises many important questions about the supervisory responsibility of the teacher. It implies that in some areas the aide may be more competent than the teacher, in fact would be useful only *if* he were more competent. Anderson probably does not realize the implications of this particular point of view on aide use. He does, at another point in his account, specify that there are some educational tasks which only the certified teacher, indeed only a superior teacher, could be expected to perform.

Anderson points out one somewhat overlooked barrier to creative aide (nonprofessional or paraprofessional) use. This is the fact that many teachers and administrators, according to Anderson, derive satisfaction and comfort from clerical and housekeeping functions. "They [clerical tasks] are usually discharged with relative ease, and, when they are carried out with accuracy and efficiency, they often bring disproportionate rewards. . . . By contrast, to solve a real educational problem is usually far more difficult. . . ." In short, some teachers may resist the supervisory role in order to retain the chance to do menial tasks in which they can experience real competence. To the extent that this form of resistance does actually exist, rational discussion of aide use and the movement of teachers into supervisory positions is impossible.

The Evolution of Teacher Aide Roles

Once the teacher role has been identified, one can come closer to a definition of the teacher aide. Expectations for aides develop in close conjunction with the changing set of expectations that define the teacher role. Also, aides are an important element in the broadening conception of teaching. The changes are as inseparable as Yin and Yang.

Just as one must look at the comments and opinions of representative educators to locate the teacher role, one must examine a small body of literature—most of it in out-of-the-way state and local educational magazines—to determine what the present state of the teacher aide role is. Most of this commentary is brief, specific in reference, and redundant. There is very little systematic thinking about teacher aide use. What little there is has already been mentioned previously in the discussion of teacher role or will be discussed in Chapter 5 under the new careers concept.

Generally speaking, however, three characteristics emerge from discussions of aide use, and these dimensions seem to define the teacher aide role as it exists in 1970. The three characteristics will be referred to as *technical, supportive,* and *supplementary.*[1] Most discussions of aide use tend to emphasize some combination of each of these role elements, and most at least pay lip service to all three.

Technical Assistance

The most common feature of the aide role is the technical assistance dimension. Most discussions of teacher aides begin and end with concern for the technical assistance that can be provided to the teacher. This view of the aide is in a sense the most primitive in that the aide is seen as a third arm for a harried teacher. Aides are to "pitch in," with all the busy work connotations of that phrase, and help the teacher wherever necessary. The next chapter will discuss this aspect of aide role as the main feature of what can be called the entry level job, implying that this is a *beginning* stage of aide work and is preliminary to advancement to more difficult tasks. It must be admitted, however, that many educators see the entire teacher aide role as composed of technical assistance. They are not always aware of alternatives.

Kinds of Assistance

The kinds of performances that can be included under the heading of technical assistance are really innumerable. They include al-

---

[1] The only other comprehensive analysis of the teacher aid role is a brief discussion of "behavior" of aides in Bowman and Klopf, 1967, pp. 47–48. These authors deal with two of our three categories—the "technical" and "supportive." They do not clearly conceptualize the "supplementary" dimension.

most any dirty work that the teacher wants to assign to the aide. However, several areas are commonly mentioned. These include monitoring hallways, getting children in and out of the classroom (with coats, hats, and other paraphernalia), doing routine class record keeping, running errands, baby-sitting with a class for brief periods of time, helping to assemble materials for classwork, running audiovisual equipment, and cleaning up the classroom. The major unifying theme connecting these tasks and the wide variety of other odd chores is that they can in no way be defined as educational.

To illustrate the difference that is (theoretically) made between noneducational dirty work and other low level tasks that are to some extent educational and, therefore, not included under this technical assistance category, it may help to look at a couple of problem cases. Supervising study hall or even playground duty have a marginal status in this scheme of things. Some (a minority of teachers probably) define study hall duty as a teaching job and therefore to be done *only* by a certified teacher. To these teachers, aides are not qualified to supervise study halls. Some questions raised by pupils during study hall or the very organization of pupils' activities in study hall may call for professional judgment, or at least so this argument goes. Another marginal case is the use of aides to help with artistic activities. Some feel that this can properly be supervised by a teacher with an aide actually handling the art session or the music session. Others maintain that the face-to-face instruction going on here must involve a teacher. At some point in each of these concrete cases the argument becomes a matter of words and the rhetoric of pedagogy. (But, as has been emphasized previously, it is this kind of rhetoric that is the stuff of which roles are made.) In any case, these concerns are relevant only if the teacher aide role is limited to the technical dimension.

Supportive Role

The supportive aspects of aide work are somewhat harder to define. This part of the aide role requires the aide to do supportive educational functions under the supervision of the teacher. Once beyond the level of technical assistance, the supportive opportunities of the role develop rapidly. At some critical point the idea is accepted or the position is taken that aides can "teach." As long as he functions under the supervision of a certified person, a wide range of classroom activity becomes possible. The aide can take reading groups, he can carry out number games with groups of children, or he may undertake to help a child with some special problem on a one-to-one basis.

One program (Minneapolis) has explicitly defined teacher role in such a way that the certified personnel is given the responsibility for diagnosis and prescription of student needs but is permitted wide latitude in assigning instructional activities to a paraprofessional. This position is made possible by a precise definition of what a teacher is and by placing no specific teaching job in his hands beyond the supervision of someone doing the actual teaching.[2] Great freedom of judgment is left to the teacher in this situation. On his own, he must determine the competence and reliability of his aide. Given proper assurances, the aide can be assigned nearly any classroom task. Although in practice teachers in this system exercise the opportunity conservatively, the door is wide open.

Closely connected with the idea of the aide as supportive in the sense just described is the notion of gradually increasing responsibility for an aide through a series of formal step-by-step advancements. This will be discussed in more detail in the next chapter, but it may be noted that very few school systems have actually introduced any kind of career ladder for the aide. Thus, the teachers have very little but their own judgment (and possibly training records) to go on. Therefore, a great deal of responsibility is given to the teacher in determining what aide, or when an aide, is ready for a supportive staff role. At least one study has raised the question as to whether any teacher should be burdened with such a decision (Emmerling and Chavis, 1966). It is clear that such a burden will make the teacher tend to be conservative in his judgment and generally inhibit the use of aides in a truly supportive way.

Supplementary Role

A third and even less common dimension of the aide role is that of supplementing the work of the teacher. This view of the aide casts

[2] The following is the critical section of the Minneapolis Public Schools "Guide for Teachers": "The professional teacher is trained and certified to perform certain functions in the education of children. The responsibilities that are reserved for teachers involve (1) analyzing the instructional needs of his pupils, (2) prescribing educational activities to meet the pupils' needs, and (3) certain supervisory responsibilities consistent with established school policy and directed by the school principal. The teachers working with nonprofessional helpers . . . must rely on their own judgment when assigning duties. . . . These duties should not infringe upon the responsibilities of the teacher, but nonprofessionals may assist the teacher in meeting these responsibilities." This was written in 1967.

him as one who, for a number of reasons, has something special to add to the teaching situation. This addition to the class is above and beyond anything the teacher himself could bring.

A classic example of supplementary role performance (from the senior author's own experience) is the case of an aide who brought a somewhat unique musical ability and love of song to a series of elementary classrooms. When engaged in playground duty or in cleanup tasks, this aide often inserted her purely poetic sense directly into the class situation by leading the children in a spontaneous song—a Christmas carol, or hymn (probably in violation of Church-State separation), or a bit of a pop tune.

The children usually responded eagerly. The aide was a neighborhood resident who knew many of the families of the children. Her breaking into song was a singular example of her closeness to the children and her ability to get them to engage in an important educational activity with surprising spontaneity. But the point is not really that she had a unique way of teaching music. In terms of the current discussion it is, rather, that the aide brought something to the situation that very few teachers (or other aides, in this case) would have brought. She was *adding* something to the total class experience. The class would have been much less of a class (although probably quite adequate) without her.

Two Supplementary Activities

From a somewhat broader perspective, there are two general types of supplementary activities provided (or potentially provided) by teacher aides. These are special personal abilities (like musical talent or athletic ability) and neighborhood contact. The musical ability so prized in the American Negro community and nurtured even in very poor ghetto families is, therefore, probably higher in a cross-section of AFCD mothers than in a typical group of urban elementary school teachers. Or, again, many Indian aides can teach nature lore in a way far more productive of learning than the sterile science project that is characteristic of this stage of the American education system. Even when good scientific habits are taught, the nature lore may be a vital supplement.

In many classroom activities, special groups or special individuals can supplement the skills of almost any teacher at almost any level of the educational ladder, including the colleges and universities.[3] However, far more commonly referred to is the supplementary service provided by the aide as (typically) a neighborhood resident. Although certainly not a recognized part of aide use in all sectors, the use of neighborhood people, closely linked to the new careers for the poor concept, is of increasing interest to those concerned about the creative use of aides.

The aide as a neighborhood person is, in most instances, a vital supplement to the teacher's effort to know, understand, and communicate with the child and his family. This works on two levels. On the individual level each child is different and every teacher struggles with the effort to know each child in his individuality. Both teacher and aide are at a disadvantage in not being a member of the child's family and in not being an intimate part of the family circle that produced the child. The teacher, especially the teacher in an area to which he is a stranger because of race or ethnic background, finds it difficult to communicate with the child's family. The aide has a distinct advantage in almost every case where a positive contact with a family is needed. The aide (whether classroom aide or home visitor aide) generally has a better chance of gaining admission to homes or of being able to talk to the parents about personal problems. In many neighborhoods teachers are afraid to walk the streets and are even more hesitant about knocking on doors. In most cases this is unwarranted and based on fantasies, but nonetheless, it is a fact of life of inner city teaching. In these cases the aide can be an indispensable bridge or channel for information about the child and the reasons for his behavior in school. An aide can sometimes come close to being the advocate of the child against the irrationalities or inflexibility of the system.

The Case of Aaron

An impressive example of the latter occurred in one urban middle school, in what may be called a case of school neglect. In this not so unusual case, a boy whom we will call Aaron was identified as incorrigible to school discipline. Aaron, a thirteen-year-old Black, was insulting and (in one case) threatening to several teachers; he refused to follow class routine except when and where he wanted to; he would leave class without permission; and he would be truant for

[3] The University of Minnesota has recently inaugurated a program of having "professional aides" work with regular university faculty. These aides will actually work into a position where they will deliver a number of independent lectures in university classes. This program began in January 1969.

days without any home excuse. All this took place despite the fact that Aaron's parents did urge him to attend school and did punish him for truancy. It also occurred despite the fact that the boy was recognized as bright and clever. If a piece of class equipment (for example, a movie projector) broke down, Aaron was often able to fix it; he was nearly always able to do work if he "took a mind to"; and he was reading at about grade level despite his erratic attendance for more than three years. The school had become thoroughly exasperated with Aaron, and finally his threat of physical abuse to a teacher stimulated the school (which had, in fact, a heavy compensatory program for education of the disadvantaged) to recommend Aaron to Juvenile Court for removal from his family and institutionalization at a detention center. It seemed to be clear that if Aaron's family could not control his behavior then (unfortunately) correctional custody was called for. The school officials began this process of referral unwillingly but in their own minds without any alternative.

Aaron's case would have ended there, and nearly did, if it had not been for Mr. Brooks, a home visitor aide assigned to the case. Brooks intervened at this point by bringing up several obvious considerations that had not been given much attention by the supervising social worker or several other professional staff in their decision to refer Aaron to court.

The crux of Brooks' argument was that there was no evidence that Aaron had any serious problem at home or that the family was in any way unsupportive. In fact, the family seemed to have closer relations and greater parental concern than the typical family of this neighborhood. There was no divorce, the mother worked part time but was regularly at home, and Aaron himself was proud of his family. He was completely enraged at the possibility of having to leave home. The parents were equally distressed.

The aide went on to point out in a series of tense meetings with the social worker and the principal that Aaron was actually rejecting the school, not his family. It was the school that Aaron did not like. He was hostile toward his predominantly white teachers and one Black teacher in particular whom he openly called Uncle Tom. One person, a young Black female teacher had, however, had a good relationship with Aaron the year before. The aide went on to point out that Aaron was only a more extreme, and admittedly very troublesome, example of a pattern becoming increasingly apparent among militant Black youth in the community. He pointed out that two years earlier the schools had at his parents' request bussed Aaron to a suburban school as part of a sporadic attempt at integration. Brooks explained that this experience had upset Aaron and that his more open hostility had begun at that point. He had not liked the nearly all-white school where he had been placed and had begun a pattern of fighting and disobedience that led to his being "recalled" to the neighborhood elementary school. It was pointed out that outside school Aaron was being regularly exposed to the rhetoric of militant Negro groups and that his own father had become increasingly involved in these activities. Aaron's behavior was a part of a new web of activity burgeoning in the neighborhood.

In short, the aide pointed out a number of harsh realities to the handful of professionals deciding Aaron's future; many of these "realities" related to recent changes in attitude throughout the neighborhood. He pointed to new social forces impinging on Aaron to which the principal and social worker were not yet "tuned in." Most importantly, he pointed out that it was in many ways not a case of parental neglect but was a case of school neglect, in that it was the school that had the bad relationship with this boy. It was this school that was the major problem for him, not other neighborhood institutions, and most especially not his family. Brooks pointed out that there were steps that the school could take that, although not necessarily assuring success, might stand a chance to end this pattern of neglect, at least in Aaron's case. The school, with some trepidation, then embarked on this latter course following some of the suggestions made by the aide. At this writing the experiment is still in progress.

The Teacher Aide as a Bridge to the Community

On a slightly different level a teacher aide can function to interpret an entire area or community to a teacher, especially a young teacher new to the local "turf." This interpretation can sometimes extend to the entire staff. A common example of this kind of interpretation is found in the efforts of a home visitor aide in a large urban secondary school. This aide regularly asked teachers to take kids back into their class after expulsion; this involved making up work after school. The return of the student to the class (not always accomplished) was usually accompanied by a systematic explanation of why after-school punishment was unfeasible for this type of student. Many of the pupils had jobs after school that they needed to keep; several had to look after smaller children at home in the absence of parents. The aide would interpret the apparently incorrigible attitude of these kids in regard to after-school work in the light of their family expectations and their pressing job needs. Each case was somewhat different, but the aide's consistent purpose was to bring each one to the attention of the teacher (where relevant) explaining pupil needs not understood by the staff.

On a somewhat less dramatic level there is the example of one ghetto school principal who ran a week-long (one hour after school) orientation session for his new teachers using aides as the total staff of the orientation program. This program included an introduction to the economic conditions of the neighborhood, the argot of the people, and the kinds of situations that the kids found at home. Teachers appeared to have found this reversal of role quite helpful, although reaction was admittedly varied among the participants. Several teachers were even angered and probably vaguely threatened by this unique orientation.

Nor is the anger of these few teachers a completely unique example. The supplementary use of aides, as opposed to the technical assistance or supportive role dimensions does have seeds of conflict. The structuring of the role relationships deviates sharply from the more comfortable one of supervisor and subordinate to the more complex problem of professional collaboration. There are certain areas always somewhat ambiguously defined, in which the expertise of the aide is greater than the professional. The case of Aaron involved a professional social worker taking the expert advice of a neighborhood aide in regard to a range of community pressures that she was not in a position to directly assess herself. Even temporary resolution of this case demanded that the professional alter her judgment in a critical matter on the advice of an aide. One does not have to be a sociologist to see the charged nature of this relationship. Nonetheless, it is this admission of a certain amount of professional egalitarianism to the teacher (or social worker) and aide relationship that is at the heart of allowing the aide a genuinely supplementary role. Its problems and its potential must not be ignored in assessing the future development of the teacher aide role in American public schools.

4 Sociological Analysis: Aides in the Changing Social System of the School

The emergence of the teacher aide role in the public schools is part of much broader structural developments occurring in the educational systems of highly industrial nations. Some authors have placed these phenomena in the postindustrial era; others have termed this period the cybrocultural era.[1] In any case, there is little doubt that the emergence of aides is linked to broad changes taking place in education and society.

[1] These somewhat grandiose references tend to imply that the emergence of the teacher aide role is part of a widespread process in which demand for human services is increasing more rapidly than any other kind of economic demand and in which the concomitant differentiation of human services is quite rapid. Society is giving greater attention to art, leisure, and human service in a way that will see future developments dwarf the already considerable change in these occupational sectors.

In a room in an old school in the Bedford Stuyvesant area of Brooklyn—one of the world's noisiest, dirtiest, and most violence-ridden slums—there is a series of soundproof booths. In each of these booths is a large unusual-looking typewriter with colors on the keys and a screen hovering above. Children periodically enter these booths and work for a period of time in an autonomous fashion, prompted only infrequently by an adult manning a control panel, also located in the room. Every now and then this adult at the control panel will rise and enter the booth with the child to give a direct, non-electronically mediated, suggestion or answer a nonacademic question from the child (such as, "Can I go to the bathroom?").

These are the much discussed talking typewriters (or Edison Responsive Environments), first introduced by the sociologist O. K. Moore. The children are the poor and often emotionally unstable products of one of the nation's worst ghetto slums. The adult, sometimes a man, sometimes a woman, is an educational assistant (or teacher aide) doing the hour-to-hour monitoring of the typewriters. He or she is quite likely black, and a resident of the same Brooklyn ghetto. This is a teaching situation, but the teaching here is done by a team of typewriter and aide, supervised by a regular teacher, who herself must have special training in the use of this sophisticated educational hardware.

The job of teaching reading is being done as always. But the presentation of this instruction has altered radically. Where originally there was one instructor responsible for coaxing the child into literacy, now a team of three is coordinated to accomplish the same task. Teacher, educational assistant, and talking typewriter work together to get the job done. This is the face of change in American education.

Differentiation, Integration, and Social Disturbance

In 1896 Herbert Spencer completed his *Principles of Sociology*. In this book Spencer traced an evolutionary theory of the development of society. In fact, he linked this process into a general theory of evolution. "All life," asserted Spencer, "proceeds from a diffuse, unintegrated homogeneity toward a specific, integrated heterogeneity."[2] Spencer indeed meant *all* life. For Spencer this statement approached axiomatic status in that it was a postulate applying to the universe, to

---

[2] This is a popular paraphrase of a more complex passage from Spencer.

the earth, to animal life, and to human society. Each of these evolutionary developments was, for this nineteenth-century philosopher, simply a manifestation of one overreaching principle. If it was true of the universe and if it was true of animal life, it seemed only natural that it should also apply to social evolution.

Very few, if any, people today would buy Spencer's postulate in its baldest form. Nonetheless, a respectable number of anthropologists and sociologists have recently returned to an interest in evolutionary theory (White, 1959; Childe, 1951). This renewal of interest has probably been generated by the obvious phenomenon of momentous changes occurring in Western society under the impact of industrialization, as well as the newer phenomenon of modernization (really, the struggle for industrialization) in the non-Western world. Sociologists have definitely turned to the study of social change, and a good bit of this interest has been invested in modified evolutionary models.

These evolutionary models characteristically conceive of society as a system of interrelated institutions. These theories also tend to view technological change as the major instigator of change in all other parts of the system. The widespread changes attributed to higher productivity levels and to a greater concentration of energy have surprising similarities to the theory of Spencer. In particular, *differentiation* and *integration* are seen as inherent in any technological change that leads in the direction of greater total productivity (Mott, 1964). Put very simply this implies that with the great increase in per capita productivity characteristic of modern industrial society there will be a complementary increase in the number of roles in all the other systems of the society as well as increased integration of all these roles. As the number and diversity of roles increase, there is a similar increase in the number of relationships involved in any institution. This proliferation of relationships and all the attendant problems is what integration means.[3] The more parts there are, the more problems occur in relating these parts to each other. Caplow (1964) has a particularly good discussion of this general problem. Leslie White (1959), an anthropologist, talks of the elaboration of culture as being a direct function of the increase in available energy. Smelser (1966) outlines the major factors in modernization as differentiation, integration, and social disturbance. Although, it is perhaps worth noting that while Smelser carefully indicates how these processes act

[3] It probably would be wise to distinguish (for nonsociologists) between the more limited use of the term *integration* in regard to relations between majority and minority groups and the broader use of the term to refer to *all* types of social relations.

in political systems, family systems, and religious systems, he does not discuss similar processes in educational systems. This gap is apparent elsewhere in the literature.

Corwin (1965), in a well-received recent textbook, discusses the increasing problems of specialization and coordination—merely a second set of terms for differentiation and integration. He places these among the focal problems of a sociology of education—although he does not adopt an evolutionary perspective. Corwin tends to relate the growing specialization in the schools to a concomitant growth in bureaucracy in the schools. "The degree of specialization and the extent to which authority is centralized . . . are only two of several bureaucratic characteristics." This perspective is adopted because Corwin, like many others, sees the "integration" problem as being handled through growing centralization of authority represented by traditional bureaucratic patterns. In a later work (Lane, Corwin, and Monahan, 1966) he does begin to distinguish between "professional" and "employee" principles of organization—a very fruitful redirection in this area.

From among these discussions, this chapter will choose Smelser's lead and treat the role changes in the school system as involving the three processes that he outlines: differentiation, integration, and social disturbance. These trends can be recast slightly into differentiation, integration, and role conflict. This is probably the most general scheme for relating the vast social changes (in education or elsewhere) made in response to technological advance. The reasons behind the three processes are reasonably clear, but perhaps some general discussion is warranted.[4]

Differentiation: More Parts in the System

Differentiation, or the increase in the number and functions of parts, of a system is obviously a response to the increased complexity of technology. On top of a vast increase in the amount of know-how needed to operate an advanced technology there is the wide ranging and complex development of jobs in the service area. In modern industrial nations the service sector of the economy is the most rapidly growing part of the economy. This is basically premised on increased leisure time and higher per capita income in real wealth terms. The

---

[4] This dicussion is not meant to be a definitive explication of these complex terms but rather a brief definition of terms for the sociologically uninitiated.

supply of teachers, psychologists, social workers, doctors, and so on is falling farther behind demand every year. Furthermore, training of these service sector people requires additional differentiation within education. And so it goes throughout all the subsystems of a society.

The parallel tendency for increased integration is deducible directly from the fact of differentiation itself. The more parts there are, the more relationship problems there are. Caplow has brilliantly discussed the way in which the increase in the number of relationships is a geometrical function of the number of parts in an organizational system (1964, pp. 29–36). When there are three parts there are 6 relationships including all possible coalitions; but when there are 10 parts there are 29,268 potential relationships with which to contend. As indicated, bureaucracy has been the predominant response to the necessity for integration; but it does not necessarily preclude other responses. One sociologist has pointed out how the current hippie vogue of "doing your thing" is an attempt to have the specialization (in craft, service, or art) required of modern society *without* bureaucracy or (one might better say of the hippies) *with* a plea for the absence of central authority integrating these efforts. Be that as it may, integration as a problem must be dealt with in some fashion whether it be by bureaucracy or by hippie communes. Their function in the broader scheme of things has some similarities.

Finally, Smelser talks of social disturbance as the third major concomitant of technological advance. This is premised on an inevitable lag between differentiation and integration. Differentiation of parts is continually running ahead of the ability of the system to develop new and successful means of integration. An example from modern American education is the somewhat less than uniformly successful integration of rapidly expanding federal projects into slow changing school systems. No clear-cut mechanism has been developed for plugging these federal programs into local, ongoing programs without friction, sometimes deeply disruptive friction. One major integrative problem is the failure of line educators (teachers, building principals, and so on) to view the new power of federal project administrators as wholly legitimate. There is in some systems a state of mind bordering on a palace-revolution mentality. The line instructor feels the federal administrator has usurped power, or is trying to usurp power, that legitimately belongs to the teachers.

In any case, Smelser posits that the very process of differentiation and lagging integration brings on social disturbance. He has a certain "faith" in the rigidity of human institutions. This chapter will look at a subcase of social disturbance. It will focus on the *role con-*

flict generated by the processes of role differentiation in the American schools, only one example of which is the development of the teacher aide or educational assistant role.

Differentiation within the educational system will be basically role differentiation. The role structure of American schools has changed to a limited extent in the recent, post-Sputnik decade; but the most dramatic changes are undoubtedly still to come. If teachers are to teach, if reading specialists are to diagnose problems, if language teachers are to have time to upgrade their own skills, as well as to pass them on, if talking typewriters are to be programmed by people who are teachers as well as technicians, and if dozens of similar jobs are to be done with appropriate finesse, then much greater differentiation of role is going to take place. The subject matter specialists, the professional educational psychologists, the captains of educational hardware will not have the time, indeed will not be physically available to help children with number games, to organize field trips, or to prepare an exhibit or school pageant. These latter tasks must be undertaken by other people working under the supervision of the teacher-specialist. The latter group in turn will not have time to supervise lunchrooms, to police halls, or to prepare materials for classwork, especially as these materials increasingly involve programmed instruction and electronic equipment. It seems obvious that future increases in educational personnel will take place along lines of increasing differentiation in which the present omnibus role of the teacher, especially the elementary school teacher, will disappear.

The roles of teacher aide and educational assistant are already developing at both the elementary and secondary levels. It is, of course, the business of this book to present a discussion of the teacher aide role and to a lesser extent the concept of new careers. But it might be well in this chapter on theory to take a brief look at two comprehensive programs that involve the use of aides as only one component. These programs are what we will here refer to as the *dual program* and the *Carnegie Experiment.*

Dual Program

The dual program concept has been known for some time. The term was coined by George Stoddard (1959) but has been proposed in various forms by several commentators. The essence of the dual program is the responsibility on the part of one home teacher for more than one schoolroom of about 25 children per room. The home teacher is responsible for registration, counseling, and (depending on the program) teaching reading and/or social studies. In a radical version, the home teacher would do no classroom teaching except, perhaps, reading work with grade level or above children.[5] All other direct instruction would be left to subject matter specialists (art, music, mathematics, science, and physical education) or an educational assistant working with programmed instruction or workbook activities.

In Stoddard's moderate plan the home teacher would occupy one room, while the specialist teachers would have a second group in a second room under general supervision of the home teacher. Subject matter specialists would rotate in and out of the second classroom according to a wide variety of schedules. Any class might spend as much as 50 percent of their day under the immediate supervision of a teacher aide or educational assistant. This aide could handle nearly all drill, workbook time, and recreational activities. A second version of this system (and one closer in line with present educational mythology about teacher duties) would have the aide merely available to help subject matter specialists or the home teacher with individual drill with problem cases.

In the more radical plan a drastic change in the ecology of the school is proposed as a parallel to major alteration of role structure. In this latter version the home teacher would control as many as five or six classrooms from an office-control center. From this center he would orchestrate the daily activities of as many as 80 to 100 youngsters and numerous subject matter specialists, who would take individual classrooms for varying periods of time. The control center could include a small room for reading groups taught by the home teacher, as well as office space.

The home teacher, as illustrated by this brief description, is neither teacher nor principal as these roles exist under the present system. The home teacher is one specially trained in psychology, educational theory, and, possibly, reading methods. Generally, a pupil's grade standing will be determined by the home teacher. His rate of advancement will be controlled by him. Combining consideration of the child's social maturity, his achievement level, and his raw ability, the home teacher can advance any student to a higher grade level in any particular subject at any time.

[5] One obvious problem with the radical withdrawal of the home teacher from the classroom is the undetermined extent of need on the part of lower grade youngsters for a substitute mother in the classroom. Some people have argued with considerable rationale that a child in grades K to 3 needs a single mother surrogate for at least half a day. However, no one has perceived any serious problems along this line for grades 4 to 8.

An additional part of the dual program as discussed by Stoddard is the fact that, because the home teacher concentrates on knowing as much of the whole child as possible, he is also in reasonably close touch and is reasonably knowledgeable about home difficulties and family problems that might affect a child's performance. Here again the aide, especially the indigenous aide functioning as a "home visitor" and responsible directly to the home teacher (rather than to an administrator), could be an important part of the new structure.

Carnegie Experiment

The second illustrative example of differentiation in American schools is not a description of a plan but is a description of a single local experiment. This will be called the Carnegie Experiment, after the source of support for the program. The Carnegie Foundation sponsored a program in teacher training in Minneapolis in the summer of 1967. This experiment had a number of goals, including both the ostensible goal of developing new ways of supervising student teaching and the latent goal of experimenting with team teaching.

In this program a number of middle school English classes were selected and assigned student teachers (as part of a regular university training program). These classrooms were then broken into groups of four or five classes and each group was placed under a single supervising teacher. This embodied two major departures from typical teacher training procedures. First, a cluster of classrooms was placed under the direct supervision of another teacher, and second, the supervising teacher was not a university staff member (with no real authority in the school system) but, rather, a member of the school system on joint appointment with the university.

The upshot of this arrangement was that both the development of new student teacher training techniques and the ongoing conduct of a seventh- or eighth-grade English class had a certain amount of direct guidance from another, supervisory, teacher. As previously indicated, this was both an attempt to find new and better ways to structure teacher training and an experiment in a team arrangement in conducting class activities. The supervising teacher planned lessons for the benefit of the student teacher and entered into the prescription of educational needs for the junior high students in the classroom. In a way not too dissimilar to the dual program model just described for primary grades, this individual was orchestrating a series of activities in a number of classrooms. He was having some impact on the educational activities of three different types of classroom personnel: aides, student teachers, and regular certified teachers. He was free to move into any classroom any time, and indeed most of the supervising teachers did a great deal of this. At the same time they had extensive discussions with both regular teachers and student teachers about teaching tactics, selections of materials, and handling of special problem cases. They were aware of the different teaching styles of the five teachers involved and were authorized to move students from one class to another if they thought that one teacher might do a better job with a particular pupil.

This latter option was an innovative grant of authority to the supervisory teacher and was in fact used infrequently and only with great discretion. It is clear that this kind of authority to shift children on an academic basis, although theoretically open to the principal, has never been a real possibility due to the removal of the principal from the ongoing instructional process. Class changes by principals usually occur only in disciplinary cases, and the initiative for change generally comes from the teacher. The supervisory teacher in this situation was empowered to intrude into the situation on the basis of his legitimate knowledge and participation in what was actually going on in the class.

At the same time, the supervisory teacher was empowered to coordinate relationships between student teacher and teachers. This situation would have been only slightly different if the trainees had been teacher aides instead of university students. And, in fact, several of the classrooms had teacher aides as well as student teachers. The supervisory teacher was an experienced classroom teacher, as well as an individual who had had experience with supervision, generally through the Minneapolis teacher aide program. He was therefore in a good position to offer indirect assistance in the business of supervision as well as direct support for the student teacher. The supervisory teacher was sought out by trainees for special advice on technical teaching problems. Topics such as a student's reading problem, psychological problems that seemed to be burdening the student, and ways to handle special assignments made by the teacher were some of the subjects on which the trainee came to the supervisory teacher for help. In almost all cases this advice seeking was on referral from the regular classroom teacher (the first line supervisor of the trainee), and it was generally expected that any serious consultation with the supervisory teacher would follow this route. However, in a few cases the trainee sought out the supervisory teacher on matters that directly or indirectly pertained to the trainee's relationship to the teacher.

Integration: The Problems
of Relationship

The dual program and the Carnegie Experiment are just two examples of rapid differentiation, or experiments with differentiation, within the American school system. A reader can see for himself, even without a complete chronology, the increased problems of integration inherent in this process. In the dual program an entire new set of relationships emerges between teacher (whether home teacher or subject matter specialist) and the pupil in the classroom. If nothing else occurs, the subject matter specialist is freed from the need to provide emotional and personal support to individual pupils. At the same time, the home teacher must learn to relate to the subject matter specialist in a way that is supportive of the teaching efforts at the same time that his psychological training (and experience) is used to individualize instruction. Both home teacher and subject matter specialists must learn to relate to teacher aides or other auxiliary personnel in a way that will allow aides to function, at least part of the time, in an independent manner and to carry out the assignments of their supervising teacher(s). In short, differentiation of this sort produces a vastly more complex social system than exists in the self-contained classroom.

Integration can involve many subtleties of human interaction. For present purposes, however, we would like to emphasize two major dimensions of the integration problem: that of *authority* and that of *communication*. Both are relevant to the present structural changes occurring in the American schools (as any teacher can testify), and both relate to problems of instituting the use of teacher aides. Some authors, in fact, have seen them not as independent problems but as alternatives; that is, in a complex organization, integration occurs either through a communication solution or through a restructuring of authority. In short, one can structure an indeterminate situation either by talking to the parties involved and getting broad agreement or simply by hitting people over the head until they get the idea. Gouldner (1954) has called the former kind of integrational pattern *representational* bureaucracy, to distinguish it from the more classic kind dependent on authority from the top. The latter is called *punishment centered* bureaucracy by Gouldner.

In the schools, of course, the real problem is vastly more complex than this somewhat analytic distinction can communicate. It is no secret that certain traditional authority patterns have been undermined in recent years. The most obvious of those trends involves the erosion of power or the shift of power to the staff officer (curriculum specialist, director of school social work, or director of federal projects), away from the local building principal. The principal of today may have a larger budget, but he has decidedly less autonomy than his predecessor of past generations. This undoubtedly leaves him with a feeling of constriction and in some cases with a sort of diffuse frustration.

Integration and Authority

The authority problem is more clear-cut when it comes to the problem of integrating teacher aides into the classroom. At the present stage of thinking in regard to teacher aides, the problem is totally one of delegation of authority. All teaching is construed to be the responsibility of the teacher. It is so construed by all those who count: teachers, administrators, and school boards, even though teacher aides, pupils, parents or people in general may not necessarily see things this way. As will be indicated in later chapters, militants and moderate residents alike are now making themselves heard on the subject of inner city education. Even as this book goes to press, the influence of these new leaders seems to be growing; and they do not necessarily share this view of teacher responsibility. All professional associations that have discussed the problem, however, have been unequivocal that teaching is the sole responsibility of teachers and that teaching covers nearly everything that happens in the classroom. If social norms were not clear (consensual) on this point, state law would require acquiescence to this point of view in most states. All responsibility, hence all immediate authority, lies with the certified teacher.

The question then is just how much of this total authority does the teacher delegate to the aide. Here is where agreement breaks down. Only a handful of experimental programs have actually turned classrooms over to teacher aides, even for a short period of time (Rutherford, 1967; Rademacher, 1968). In most of these cases (for example, Rademacher's experiment using ex-Upward Bound enrollees to prepare high school dropouts for an equivalency examination), the aide has remained under the indirect supervision of a certified teacher. But within the classroom just how much authority is delegated to an aide or educational assistant? Does supervision by the teacher require that he always be physically present? Does it require that he be explicit in this delegation of authority and spell out exactly what it is that the aide is to do for the teacher? It is in this area that considerable disagreement exists.

An important distinction, also, must be made between the formal definition of the role and the actual movement of the aide into the role. One group of researchers looking at highly innovative new careers type programs found this to be a problem even in a context where supplementary activity on the part of the aide was highly approved. Even in a permissive context there was great variability in the actual amount of authority delegated to aides.

> The principal dilemma appeared to be the conflict between *role definition* which was recognized as necessary to institutionalization, and *role development* which was a dynamic of each classroom situation where auxiliaries were utilized. The degree of responsibility assigned to an auxiliary is dependent upon the interaction of a particular teacher and a particular auxiliary operating within a given structure and responding to the special needs of individual pupils. A delicate balance seems to be required in order to provide the specificity that means security along with the flexibility that promotes growth (Bowman and Klopf, 1966).

Delegation of Authority

Succeeding chapters will deal with the actual working relation between teacher and aide. However, without a description of any ongoing program, certain general considerations are clear on the basis of logic alone. First, the delegation of authority in any given program bears a direct relationship to the amount of training and/or skill possessed by the typical aide employed in that school system. This skill is in turn related to several variables, most importantly the recruitment policy and the training program developed by the system. The training question is relatively simple: the more training and the better the training, the greater the delegation of authority to aides. Teacher resistance to delegating authority to aides and resistance to employing them at all are presently most closely tied to the amount of training or lack thereof that the aides possess. Greatest teacher resistance has been encountered where the use of aides has begun hurriedly with little preparation available for the new recruits to these positions.

Second, recruitment is also clearly related to delegation of authority. At first it might seem that the more aides that are selected from within the population of a total school district, the greater the willingness to delegate authority. But there is a serious hitch in what may seem like elementary logic. This is mainly due to the fact that the open entry recruitment policy (see chapter 5) with its planned lack of selectiveness and its reliance on neighborhood people (when it is given time to work itself out) may increase teacher willingness to delegate authority.

This is true for two simple reasons. First, neighborhood people, even those with little formal education, may, as described in the preceding chapter, be able to provide leadership in the classroom in vital areas where family or personal background of the pupil is a factor in a learning problem. It may also be true where the aide's ability to communicate with a pupil may give the aide greater leeway in carrying out some specific assignment (for example, playing a spelling game) than would accrue to a better-trained person to whom the children were just as "foreign" as to the teacher. A confounding factor here has to do with the real possibility (suspected by many social psychologists) that recruiting from low-income, neighborhood groups via an open entry policy will produce a group with higher native ability than the alternative recruitment of bored housewives who were college dropouts at an earlier period of their lives.

For these reasons the authors tentatively advance the hypothesis that within any given system delegation of authority to aides may be *increased* by the open entry recruitment policy and a general new careers approach. But it must be admitted that this is distinctly hypothetical at the moment and should be the object of serious study.

Putting the above considerations on increased delegation of authority together into a single theory, it may be tentatively proposed that, within any given system, delegation of authority will increase in direct proportion to the amount of in-service training and extent of "open entry" allowed in a city-wide program. The better trained the aides and the more open the recruitment, the more organized will be the movement to grant responsibility to aides, under appropriate supervision.

Communication Problems

As previously indicated, the communication problem is closely linked to the authority problem. Working with an aide, a teacher is faced for the first time with the problem of communicating directly to another adult instructions involving what to do in a classroom. Teachers are not trained to do this, and it has been suggested that to some extent teaching has been selected by many individuals for the very fact that they do have freedom from this communication problem that is so important a part of the day-to-day performance of many other professionals (Neubacher, 1965). The teacher has been more free to behave (or view his behavior) as an artist than other professionals. He typically has not been required (after finishing student teaching) to formulate the principles governing what he is doing so that another adult can carry out part of the job for him. Nor is adjustment to these new communication requirements as easy as one might expect. Teachers will often complain that "It is easier to do it myself" than to explain a task to an aide. Although there may be some situations in which this is true, it seems that in many cases this is pure rationalization. The investment of a certain portion of time early in a year to explain some technique to an aide will often save dozens of hours in the long run. This might be called the "reticence problem" in teacher aide use.

On top of the reticence problem, there is an additional communication problem that may affect teacher–teacher aide relations. This is the difference in styles of communication possessed by teacher and aide. Although these differences do not always follow predictable lines and cannot be dealt with in any systematic way, there is a frequent pattern that will bear close attention. This is the situation in which a talkative, brash, somewhat "crude" lower-class aide is paired with the more sensitive, literary, and middle-class teacher. The aide can in fact threaten the teacher on any number of levels, sometimes including professional competence and extending to sexual adequacy. One might say that in a situation like this the aide "must go," that certainly some other aide would fit better the style of the teacher, who after all is the boss, and that a quick substitution should be made.

However, two things should be kept in mind. First, sometimes this kind of aide, a little pushy, a little brash, a little bit of the hustler, is exactly the kind of person needed to lend a hand with those rough kids whom the more sensitive teacher cannot reach. In other words, despite initial problems, the aide and teacher may complement each other and make an effective team. Second, a brash or aggressive aide may be a useful means of socializing the teacher to a low-income area. If he and the teacher can begin to understand one another, it is possible that the teacher will be better able to understand the kids, especially the problem kids, and their environment. This can be an important postgraduate learning experience for the young teacher intellectually committed to teaching in a disadvantaged area, but not quite emotionally or communicatively prepared to do so. At the same time, the aide may learn something from the teacher about gentler ways of handling people. He may be less likely to frighten the more sensitive kids in the class or to engage in rough banter with more sensitive youngsters after watching the teacher handle these less aggressive pupils. The fact that not all inner city children tend to hostility or aggressiveness or delinquency and that apathy and fear are sometimes more pervasive seems often forgotten in the process of sociological stereotyping. Both types need attention in the inner city school.

Pairing Aides and Teachers

The point seems to be that the rough aide and the sensitive teacher, or the inverse arrangement, may allow for a better team performance. It is certainly a question that will bear researching in the face of overwhelming evidence that very few, if any, teachers feel competent to deal with all (or even a decent majority) of children in their classes and that this situation is intensified in the inner city classroom with its extremely heterogeneous student body (Smith and Geoffrey, 1968). It is seriously proposed, for the first time as far as the authors know, that research and attention be directed to the ideal of *pairing* appropriately incompatible aides and teachers or at least looking at the latent function of putting two different communicative styles together in the classroom. The payoff from such a seemingly alarming partnership may be high in any number of areas. Pupil, teacher, and aide may all benefit in the long run, and there may be a distinct advantage to an entire future generation of students who will be taught by this teacher or that aide.

Role Conflict

As should be clearly indicated even by this brief discussion of integration and differentiation, these latter processes lead, almost inevitably, to social disturbance. If we focus on role differentiation, this implies role conflict. This chapter has already noted several examples. After role differentiation in the schools, people will not agree on the appropriate definitions of the new roles, norms will vary widely, and role behavior will be inconsistent and somewhat unpredictable. This is as true of the teacher aide role as it is of the other new roles in the instructional process. There is never full agreement about any role in modern complex societies, but a new role will very likely give rise to greater inconsistency and more conflict than an old one. This is a rule of thumb that has been helpful in understanding change in numerous institutions.

Agreement on the Aide Role

The greatest problem of role conflict in regard to educational aides is the obvious one: there is great variety in definitions of the role and in the social expectations held for aides. There is variety among teachers and there is variety between teachers and administrators. Administrators, in some places, are suspected of wanting to use aides as a form of "cheap" teaching. And in some limited number of cases it is possible that this is part of the expectations held by administrators. A handful of penurious administrators may, indeed, hope to decrease the direct costs of instruction by employing aides.

Aides quite frequently disagree among themselves as to the proper role for aides, and often these disagreements parallel those that divide teachers. Aides are about as likely as teachers to feel they should be given greater responsibility or should take a more dynamic role in class proceedings. The majority appear to be conservative; a minority look for increased opportunity to "teach" on their own. This parallels a conservative teacher majority and a progressive minority, the latter encouraging more creative aide use.

Conflict on Aide Training

A second critical point of disagreement has to do with the nature of aide training. There are those who propose that all aide training be accomplished within an in-service program. This approach to aide training emphasizes the acquisition of specific skills: clerical, arts and crafts, audiovisual, and so on. The proponents of this approach to training see the needs of the aides and the utility of the aide role bounded by the carrying out of relatively mechanical tasks in relation to specific classroom assignments. From this perspective the aide is very much a technician, quite distinct from the teacher, and therefore does not require any introduction to psychology, sociology, or pedagogical theory. These proponents would hold that a little learning in these areas might be a dangerous thing and in any case would be a gross waste of money, for either the school systems (if they were paying for training) or for the aide (if he bore the costs of training himself). This position would also emphasize that there are hidden costs in time and energy (for example, time spent in traveling to college campus) in addition to those payable in cash.

The conservative point of view on training would emphasize in-service work with the rationale that this permits training to be more flexible and to be much more responsive to the particular needs of the schools. It would place the immediate needs of classroom and supervising teacher clearly ahead of any long-run goals, such as the development of a permanent cadre of trained aides capable of undertaking a variety of instructional tasks.

The alternative to this point of view is, of course, that which emphasizes collegiate level work for teacher aides. This will be discussed in a later chapter under problems of training and the new careers concept. Although few would propose that college should be required for entry-level teacher aide jobs, many hold that such general training, combined with in-service work, should be a prerequisite for advancement to higher level positions (with or without new titles).

From the sociological perspective the interesting thing about this conflict over training and the aide role is that the advocates of collegiate level training are most often found among the national level staff of professional organizations or among "outsiders" to the schools: education professors, poverty strategists, and social scientists in general. In some cases, then, the conflict is between grass roots organizations and national ideologists, with a large group of local level administrators wavering in between. In some cases, there is even conflict between local organizations (most often branches of the United Federation of Teachers) and the parent organization. Several state education associations have also equivocated or opposed the idea of higher education for teacher aides, despite the fact that the NEA (National Education Association) has been strongly in support of such programs.

Role Conflict among Aides

The second dimension of this conflict over training is among aides themselves. This usually occurs between the aides who, either before or after entry into the job, orient themselves to using the role as a means of upward mobility. This group is predominantly made up of the young and the poor. These are the ones most interested in using aide work to get a better aide job, to advance to teacher status, or to obtain another human service occupation. Arrayed against this group is a larger group of aides who are "work" oriented in the aide role. These are largely housewives to whom collegiate education is expensive in time and money and who feel that they can perform aide work quite competently without this aide training. Their interest lies with a paying, interesting, but relatively nontime-consuming job, and thus they find the notion of higher educational requirements somewhat threatening. This group probably composes a majority of the current roster of teacher aides.

Conflict over New Careers

The greatest degree of role conflict undoubtedly exists over the question of whether teacher aide programs should be cast in the new careers mold. This question basically has to do with whether aide programs should allow for increasing responsibility following job experience and/or whether the use of aides should be used as a means of recruiting large numbers of low income adults to teaching. The latter would ordinarily be done by providing a massive, college-linked educational opportunity for the aides who want to take advantage of it.

Few people would argue that all teacher aides should be cast as new careerists or that all aides should be encouraged to pursue a B.A. degree. But there is wide disagreement over just how much of the national effort should go to support new careers type aide programs. There is considerable disagreement about just how much of a role the local schools should or could play in this development. It would be poor sociology to hide the fact that, again, much of the discussion opposes the national leaders of the teacher aide movement against the grass roots. A later chapter will, however, show just how important the local institutions and their readiness to respond are to implementing new careers. At present, the picture is very much one of national figures and organizations urging institutional changes at the local level that will make the new careers ideal possible. The response is mixed and uncertain.

Summary

Changes are occurring very rapidly in American schools. In this chapter we have attempted to elaborate on this truism by applying a broad sociological framework to the complex of events involved in this change. We have especially tried to place the protean teacher aide role within a broader picture.

The major social changes in the schools follow the general pattern of role differentiation, integration (or the lack thereof), and role conflict. The emergence of the teacher aide role is a major (but not the sole) example of this role differentiation. The teacher aide represents a fundamentally new three-party interaction (pupil-aide-teacher) in the classroom where originally there was only pupil and teacher. This immediately creates new problems of relationship for the teacher. How does he work with another adult in the classroom? How does he carry out supervision? How much of a personal relationship should be developed with the aide? Should the relationship be formal and authoritarian or informal and democratic?

To the extent that these relationships are unclear in wide segments of American education or to the extent that they are unstable, it is proposed that (as in many similar emerging roles) there will be role conflict (loosely defined as lack of consensus over what a teacher aide should be and do). The conflict seems most severe over questions of training, proper relationship with the teacher, and the new careers concept in general. There appears to be very low national consensus on these questions, and a major split appears between national organizations and grass roots educators, with the former pushing for more adventurous and experimental use of teacher aides.

5 Recruitment, Training, and New Careers

The teacher aide role has been described and has been placed in the context of broad changes affecting modern educational systems. It is now time to turn to consideration of some of the more specific problems of aide use. Among these are the problems of recruitment, training, and the new careers concept. These problems are closely intertwined, but for the sake of clarity they will be discussed independently. Since 1965, when the Elementary and Secondary Education Act (ESEA) moved many school systems quite rapidly into the teacher aide business, a large number of personnel have entered American schools in paraprofessional positions. This rapid influx of a "new breed" in the schools has created massive recruitment, training, and promotion problems. Because these problems have not always been met with clear policies and sometimes have been dealt with in almost offhand ways does not lessen the existence of the problems. As indicated earlier, conflict over the teacher aide role has increased rapidly.

Recruitment

A discussion of recruitment to teacher aide posts requires attention to several major questions. Where do aides come from? What are their educational backgrounds? What is their previous occupation history? How (since most of them are women) are their spouses employed? How do they view long-run employment as an aide? And, what are their future occupation expectations, if any?

Open versus Selective Recruitment

Even though it has not been so in the past, recruitment of teacher aides is going to become an increasingly self-conscious procedure. Where certified school personnel are concerned, the problems of recruitment have been removed from the schools. Within limits, the colleges and universities decide who shall be a teacher and who shall not. School systems do discriminate among applicants. College grades, sometimes length of hair, politics in a few cases may all affect secondary selection by school personnel departments. But the primary selection of teachers remains with the colleges. They are the watchdogs on entry into the teaching profession.

None of this pertains to teacher aides. There is no pre-employment training program to weed out the undesirable. There is no testing program to pick the desirables. There are few formalized recruitment policies anywhere, and certainly there are no national criteria for selection of nonprofessionals. Thus, there is great variety in local recruitment policies, most of it without philosophy or direction.

Nonetheless, some polarization in recruitment policy is apparent. There is a tendency for a system, on the one hand, to move toward what will be called here the *open entry* recruitment policy or, on the other, to reject open entry and adopt a *selective* recruitment policy. These alternatives, open entry versus selective policies, are the anchoring points for a continuum on which any recruitment policy could be placed. The following is a brief discussion of these two alternatives as they are represented by two operating teacher aide programs in the upper Midwest.

Minneapolis and St. Paul:
Two Policies in the Twin Cities

Both Minneapolis and St. Paul, the two largest communities in Minnesota, linked together in the Twin City metropolitan area, began teacher aide programs in 1965 with funds under Title I of the ESEA. Both cities have restricted the use of aides to low-income neighborhoods (as required by Title I) and both have moved into the program in an ambitious way. In 1967 to 1968 St. Paul employed about 370 aides, and Minneapolis employed nearly 400 (110 under Labor Department funds). Both cities have a city-wide coordinating office for the teacher aide program and both have appointed experienced administrators to run their programs. Yet the recruitment policies of these two cities contrast in a way that illustrates the selective versus open entry recruitment policies already noted. That these two cities, separated only by the Mississippi River, should have such radically different recruitment procedures is symbolic of the contrasts appearing on a nationwide level.

St. Paul Program [1]   Of the Twin Cities, St. Paul comes very close to having a picture-book illustration of the selective recruitment policy. Beginning with 250 aides in 1965 and moving up to 370 in 1967 (before all Head Start aides were dropped in the federal cutbacks of late 1967), the St. Paul program is a conservatively run program. About 50 percent of all aides work in the public elementary schools, 30 percent in public secondary schools, and 20 percent in parochial schools. The latter figure is high by national standards and may reflect the heavily Catholic composition of St. Paul.

The great majority of aides in St. Paul, as elsewhere, are housewives in early middle age. All personnel in the program are women, the median age is 43, and 85 percent are married or are divorced with children. Of the 15 percent who are unmarried, all but two are college students who do aide work as a part-time job, typically to see if education would interest them as a career. The population of aides in St. Paul is definitely not characterized by economic need. All spouses are reported as employed. And only 11 percent of the married aides list their spouses' occupations as semi- or unskilled workers. Eighty-nine percent are married to men with jobs at the skilled-worker level or higher.

[1] Most of the data reported in this section come from the 1967 to 1968 report of the St. Paul teacher aide program (Manchester, 1968).

The St. Paul aides are oriented to the aide role with little aspiration to other forms of work or mobility. Only 9 percent of the group expressed any interest in teaching as a future career. Fifty percent hope to continue their work as aides indefinitely. The salary of the aides is $1.50 per hour, and 85 percent reported that they were happy with that salary. This somewhat surprising lack of financial aspiration indicates either that the aides do not need the money but are working for the "fun of it" or that the level of occupational ambition is practically nil. It is likely that both factors are operating. In any case, there seems to be only a minority who object to not being paid a living wage.

St. Paul aides overwhelmingly express their satisfaction with working in the program. Many are obviously in the program for the intrinsic rewards of working as a teacher aide. Fifty percent are high school graduates, and an additional 37 percent have some college work. They are a relatively well-educated group, especially considering the age range involved. Ninety-five percent of aides report enjoying doing what they are doing very much. Sixty percent report that their main motivation for working is in what they can do for the schools, or the children, while only 40 percent indicate any "selfish" motivation, either income or experience. When one puts these figures together, the St. Paul program begins to look very much like a volunteer program. Its teacher aide ranks are largely composed of educated housewives whose children are in school and who have free time.

St. Paul Recruitment Policy The nature of this population of teacher aide recruits is directly related to the type of recruitment policy and the selection procedures that St. Paul follows. Because the St. Paul recruitment policy is similar to the majority of the nation's aide programs, it is not unreasonable to assume that the characteristics of the St. Paul aides are very close to the national population of aides. Nationally, the typical teacher aide then is probably a middle-class housewife with children in school who is willing to devote 20 or 30 hours a week to assisting teachers in low-income or overcrowded schools. The concentration in low-income schools is, of course, because a majority of all aides are employed under Title I of ESEA and therefore must serve poverty areas; it does not necessarily reflect the choice of aides.

The St. Paul recruitment policy is a highly centralized one. It is also consciously selective in nature, relying heavily upon the self-starting motivation of people interested in doing something in the schools. There has been no formal recruiting or advertising for the St.

Paul aide positions. The news of these $1.50 per hour openings is left to word of mouth, using the regular school personnel as the initiators of this grapevine effort. The approach is apparently quite adequate from the standpoint of quantity in that over 600 applications have been filed since the beginning of the program. There is usually a waiting list of about 20 ready applicants at any time.

All applications are filed directly with the city-wide director of the program. He then makes a preliminary review of applicants. The director matches the applicants with the openings around the city and picks the applicant seemingly best qualified for each position. When an applicant is found qualified for a position, he is then referred to the school principal for approval. The principal retains a veto over the appointment, and, if he does not approve of the applicant, the director refers another person on the list for this position. In the absence of a ready candidate for the job, he begins the selection process all over again by reviewing the waiting list.

The principal thus retains some control over the aide positions. He may bring one or more teachers in on the decision, but there is no formal policy on this, and, in fact, it appears that there has been relatively little teacher participation in selection. Aides are typically shared by several teachers, and there is not the close relationship between one teacher and aide that is found in some aide programs.

The recruitment policy of the St. Paul program is highly selective, as well as centralized. The program director has considerable latitude in his decision on referral for aide slots. Although no civil service exams are involved and although there are no legal or formal requirements for the position, the director has made it a general policy not to refer people without a high school diploma (or equivalency certificate) for any aide position that involves direct contact with children in a classroom. Educational experience counts highly in selection and college experience is preferred. Applicants who have not been graduated from high school are referred only for clerical or menial-type aide positions. There is a distinct but informal attempt made to assure that all teacher aides working in school offices have lower status (and, of course, lower pay) than do the civil service staff to whom they are generally responsible. This informal arrangement is an astute adjustment in regard to the politics of civil service. St. Paul undoubtedly has avoided some of the conflict that has arisen between teacher aides and civil service personnel in other programs— including the Minneapolis program.

All aides in the St. Paul school system are funneled through a careful, if largely informal, central selection process. When possible the aides are referred back to schools in their own neighborhood. But this is not possible in most cases because the aides live outside the low-income target areas served by the program and unfeasible in other cases because the best candidate for a particular position is unlikely to live in the neighborhood. In a city of 450,000 the laws of chance assure that few people will find their way back into their own neighborhood school under such a recruitment policy. Most aides will be as "foreign" to their school neighborhood as are the teachers.

Minneapolis Program If the St. Paul program approximates the typical selective approach to recruitment, the Minneapolis program is a good example of the open entry approach. Minneapolis has no prerequisites whatsoever for beginning teacher aides. It has been publicly commented by the director of the Minneapolis Program that all that is needed for employment is "a clear chest X-ray" (the public health requirement).

Development of the Minneapolis Aide Program Although the open entry approach has been (under a number of names) advanced by numerous national figures, the Minneapolis program seems to have developed its position on the basis of local decisions concerning the needs of the school system and without regard to high-level ideological disputes. The Minneapolis teacher aide program had its beginning with a local (pre–Office of Economic Opportunity) poverty program partially funded out of the federal Office of Juvenile Delinquency. This was in the summer of 1964, when a part of the Minneapolis summer school program was developed under the umbrella of this poverty program (Youth Development Program, YDP), and teacher aides were used experimentally in the YDP classes. This program was coordinated by Frederick Hayen, who has been director of the Minneapolis teacher aide program ever since.

Under the original YDP program, all aides had to be from the school neighborhoods. They did not have to be low-income people, but the fact that the program dealt only with target area schools and that the aides had to come from the local population made it a strong likelihood that an aide would be a low-income and/or minority-group person. That fall (1965) Minneapolis entered into a teacher aide program during the regular school year under Title I of ESEA. In this they were joined by many schools across the nation. Like the local YDP program, the Title I funds were earmarked for poverty areas, and it seemed natural for Minneapolis to continue the program of local hiring begun under YDP in the previous summer. Although it was not required to do so, the Title I program (employing 245 aides) in Minneapolis did continue the policy of neighborhood hiring.

Minneapolis Recruitment Policy   Almost without realizing it, Minneapolis had instituted one of the more original aide recruitment programs. The recruitment and selection of aides was left entirely up to the principal and (in most cases) the teacher scheduled to use the aide. No school was prohibited from hiring outside the neighborhood school district but, in fact, out of 325 aide positions only 13 were filled by people living outside the district in which they served. The middle schools and the senior high schools, of course, had a wider selection than did the elementary schools, but all schools adhered closely to the principle of neighborhood hiring. And, most pertinent to the present discussion, none of this would have taken place if it had not been for the open entry procedure that also carried over from the previous summer.

The key role played by open entry followed a somewhat simple logic: with either educational or work experience as a criterion for employment, the neighborhood hiring would not be possible. The Minneapolis program dispensed with both kinds of qualifications. The program set no formal requirements (and no informal ones) other than those set by state public health statutes.

This provided great freedom for the principal in his selection process. He could hire virtually anyone who applied. A few people on the scene at the inception of the Minneapolis program feared that this might lead to a form of local school patronage that would be open to all sorts of preferential treatment. It was felt that the principal might play favorites among local groups or cliques or even dispense the jobs on an ethnic or racial basis. But support for the open entry prevailed. Recognizing possible abuses in this procedure of local control and open entry, those directly responsible for the Minneapolis teacher aide program maintained that the potential benefits to all concerned were worth the risk of principal favoritism. The situation was to some extent formally controlled by the directive that teachers were to participate in the selection of aides, thus making the principal's selection subject to a kind of local veto.

From the vantage point of two years experience, the administrators of the Minneapolis program believe that their decision was the correct one. There have been few if any complaints of favoritism in the selection of aides. In only one school are we aware of any friction. This occurred between a small group of mothers selected as aides and another group (mainly mothers of children in school) who felt that the aide-mothers went too far in defending the principal against PTA-sponsored criticisms. It does seem that this particular principal co-opted certain mothers and other community people into his camp (as aides) in a deliberate attempt to blunt community criticism— which came anyway!

This process of co-optation, or any other form of favoritism, has not surfaced anywhere else in the Minneapolis program. However, a general discussion of recruitment policy should not ignore the possibility of such a sequence of events occurring. It is likely that a school system adopting a system of local recruitment and selection might want to institute some form of checks and balances against such potential abuse. One possible system of checks could involve regular review of selections by central administration personnel, giving them a veto over selections after some reasonable and impartial review in questionable cases. The mechanism for such a review may sound a bit clumsy and somewhat out of character with the general permissive attitude of open entry procedures, but these checks could be used sparingly and would be so used by any wise administration.

Potential Problems

There is no doubt that there are other problems inherent in open entry recruitment. Training of aides may be a serious problem. The first reaction of people unfamiliar with open entry is usually skepticism about allowing people with no more than elementary school education and possibly only marginally literate (to take the extreme case) to function as aides. When one examines the facts, however, Minneapolis has had no trouble arising from the use of aides with low educational background. In Minneapolis about 6 percent of the aides have only an elementary school education, and 25 percent lack a high school diploma. The educational background, of course, distinctly affects the kind of work the aide can do for the teacher, especially at the beginning. Education partly determines the aide role that the individual recruit can assume.

In-service training, combined with use of the adult basic education facilities that every major school system operates, can usually remedy literacy deficiencies very rapidly. Also, the predominant remedial problems lie in a different direction. Minneapolis has experienced problems with aides not being trained in practical skills that individual teachers have desired (for example, skills with audiovisual equipment or typing skills). There have been no serious complaints about lack of general literacy skills. It has also been found that the aides who have tried it have rapidly made up deficiencies through specially programmed work in adult education. This is true despite the fact that during the first two years of the program (1965 to 1967) there was very little pressure placed on the aides to take general education work.

Undesirables

Another potential problem frequently alluded to in regard to the open entry approach is that of getting "undesirables" into the schools. To many school people, in many sections of the nation, the idea of really poor people (or people without the appropriate life styles of middle-class America) working in the schools is virtually unthinkable. Quite literally they cannot conceive of this person in a school. They cannot see the image of this person in the school context. And this is wholly consistent with many aspects of American education. The school is, perhaps, America's most explicit institutionalization of the "average." The image of the school is that of a building, people, and an organization neither too efficient nor too inefficient, neither too sophisticated nor too crude, neither too expensive nor too cheap. Traditionally school personnel are not expected to be flashy, eccentric, dirty, or exotic. Some low-income aides may be all these things, especially in the eyes of the middle-class taxpayer or parent.

Although school officials generally look deeper than skin or clothing, there is no guarantee that they will do so. As one Iowa school administrator put it to a regional conference on paraprofessionals in the schools: "We don't want any red-necks in our school." This blunt and unfortunate remark was directly stimulated by a brief description of the Minneapolis open entry system presented by another participant in the meeting. The general concern about "undesirables" is probably a totally irrational one; even an open entry system tends to pick the residents of a target area who share the middle-class values and appearance of the school. (The greater concern probably ought to be how to bring *more* so-called undesirables into the schools, especially if *undesirable* is really a euphemism for *typical resident* of the neighborhood.) [2] No one should overlook the gut-level objection to the hiring of people who not only are poor but also have the misfortune to look that way. This will undoubtedly be a basis for resistance to an open entry system. The emotional reaction can be doubly difficult to deal with in that even when people do consciously

---

[2] Of course, no one would advocate the hiring of psychotics or hard-core criminals at any level or in any capacity in the school system.

feel this objection (like the assistant superintendent from Iowa), they (unlike the Iowan) are likely to be too embarrassed to state their feelings openly.

The general objection to using low-income people in schools can range from a blunt emotional revulsion with poor "types" to a more "sophisticated" ideological opposition to giving people an unearned chance or "break." This latter argument is most often encountered when the open entry approach to recruitment is explicitly linked to a means of recruiting low-income people to the teaching profession by giving them a steady work opportunity in the schools while they chip away at the difficult task of getting through a teachers' college. From our impression it seems safe to say that a distinct majority of teachers and administrators have at least initially negative reactions to the latter proposal. They are very skeptical of anything that may look like a "cheap" or "back door" route into teaching. We will return to this mare's nest of resentment and skepticism on the part of teachers in the latter two sections of this chapter that deal with the new careers concept and training problems.

Two Dimensions of Recruitment

At this point it might be well to summarize some of the problems involved in recruitment. Great emphasis has been placed on the distinction between "open entry" and "selective" recruitment policies. This seems to be the major issue in recruitment. The question of local versus central recruitment has also been introduced. The previous discussion has loosely assumed a high correlation between type of entry and degree of centralization. The exigencies of central office decision making will usually make centralization of recruitment a correlate of a selective recruitment. Likewise, local recruitment will tend to be associated with open entry. But this connection is not an inevitable one. Theoretically, at least, open entry selection might be associated with centralization. One part of the Minneapolis teacher aide program, that funded under New Careers (U.S. Department of Labor funds), has an open entry recruitment policy (with the exception that the recruits must be low-income people) but at the same time has the administration of the selection highly centralized. Low-income recruits selected by the local CAP office are referred to the school central administration for final approval. Only as a third step are the recruits sent to the local schools for final placement. It has been only by nimble administrative footwork that the some 100 school aides employed under the new careers program are still predominantly residents of the school neighborhood. It is not clear that the line can be held on this in the future.

In any case, open entry and local selection do not have to be found together. They may vary independently. A somewhat simple table can be constructed (see Table 5–1) indicating the independence of these two important dimensions of recruitment policy. Illustrative examples have been placed in three cells of the table. It would also be of great interest to know what the national breakdown would look like in terms of this classification scheme. What percentage of programs can we expect to find in each cell?

Table 5–1   Chart of Teacher Aide Recruitment Policies by Degree of Centralization and Nature of Education Prerequisites (Type of Entry)

Education Prerequisites	Centralization	
	Centralized	*Decentralized*

Selective	Cell I
	
	Example:
	    St. Paul Program
	
	Estimated
	    National = 56%
		Cell II
		
		Estimated National = 8%

Open Entry	Cell III
	
	Example:
	    Minneapolis Program
	    (New Careers Component)
	
	Estimated
	    National = 34%
		Cell IV
		
		Example:
		    Minneapolis Program
		    (Title I Component)
		
		Estimated
		    National = 2%

There is currently no up-to-date national survey or study that can give us hard figures on this question. The most recent figures are from the 1965–1966 National Education Association survey of the 217 school systems (National Education Association, 1967). The figures from this early study indicate that about 90 percent of the programs had a centralized selection procedure. At the same time about 36 percent of the programs had no rigid educational requirement.[3] Therefore, by extrapolation based on splitting the open entry programs

[3] This figure is arrived at by looking at the programs that would employ people with only an elementary school background.

equally between centralized and decentralized programs, we arrive at a highly tentative estimate that 56 percent of the nation's aide programs is of the Cell I variety, having selective and centralized recruitment policies. The next largest percentage of programs is estimated to be 34 percent in Cell III, which is open entry programs with centralized administration.[4] Cell IV, which represents ideal type of open entry plus decentralization and is best illustrated by the Minneapolis Title I program, is estimated to typify only 2 percent of the nation's aide programs. Although these percentages are five years out of date, the general run of commentary at both the national and local level would indicate that they are still representative.

New Careers Concept

Overshadowing the practical considerations of recruitment policy and centralization of administration is the broader national debate over the new careers concept in teacher aide use. The new careers idea became popular in the early 1960s and was discussed in some detail in 1965 by educational sociologists Riessman and Pearl. In part new careers is a formalized version of the open entry and neighborhood hiring policy discussed previously. It emphasizes innovative career opportunities for low-income people in the human services. The human services cover a wide ill-defined territory ranging from school social work to industrial relations. Education, however, is the largest human service institution in the nation today and has received the most attention from the new career ideologists like Pearl and Riessman.

Three Goals of New Careers

The new careers concept embraces three broad goals. These are (1) the provision of new career lines (as opposed to jobs) in the major human service agencies of our society, (2) the provision of a new opportunity for people caught in the cycles of poverty to move out of poverty status either through the new career line or through some alternative mobility channel opened up by the experience and education of the new career, and (3) the improvement of the level of

---

[4] This is probably slightly overestimated because of the fact that other criteria besides education may be applied in selection (for example, a personality test).

human services, especially the delivery of these services to low-income or minority groups.[5] It is clear, then, that new careers is a complex concept involving considerable innovation in recruitment, employment, and training in the human services. There has been great controversy surrounding the appropriateness of the new careers idea. The question of providing new careers opportunities in the schools has been close to the center of this maelstrom of activity.

The three major goals of the new careers concept, as already noted, are usually linked together and seem closely dependent on one another. However, it is equally clear that they are not inevitable concomitants of each other. They can vary independently, and most new careers ideologists tend to emphasize one or the other, thus providing an implicit ordering of priorities in any attempt to operationalize new careers.

New Careers and the Delivery of Human Services   Of surprise to some is the fact that the kernel of the new careers idea seems to have originated with the much older and somewhat shoddy image of the ward healer. It was argued, originally by S. M. Miller and Riessman (1961) that what was missing from many low-income areas was the once vital institution of the political machine and the ward boss. The political vacuum created a need in two ways. First, it reduced a major mobility opportunity for lower-class youth, especially those too bright or too tough to play the game by middle-class rules. Second, it removed a bridge between the low-income neighborhood or ghetto and the new white middle-class professional agencies. The complexity of modern urban life, as well as the controls and reforms instituted in the political system, made the old ward healer concept outmoded. A new type of role, legitimate[6] within the context of modern society, had to be found. If new careers were not developing naturally, they would have to be invented. Thus, the term was coined and a somewhat diffuse yet energetic movement began to develop new jobs in human services.

Riessman and Pearl (1965) and (Riessman 1967a) have called these jobs "new careers for the poor" (a phrase that has annoyed some) and

[5] This goal model has been devised by the authors in an attempt to synthesize a large body of literature (see especially Riessman and Pearl, 1965; Bowman and Klopf, 1967; Effhirm and Aronowitz, 1968; Haber, 1968; and Riessman and Gartner, 1969).

[6] The term *legitimate* is used in its broader sociological meaning of "acceptable to all participants," not in the more limited sense of "legal or according to law."

have placed great emphasis on the way in which these new nonprofessional personnel would help the human services overcome their middle-class biases and recruitment programs. The new careerist is seen as a person who accepts the basic goals of the agency, whether it be distributing welfare payments, teaching preschool youngsters, or providing medical services, yet he retains his basic personal and ethnic ties with the neighborhood being served. He is a translator of the agencies' goals into the "language" of the community and is simultaneously an interpreter of the community to the professional. In some cases he can simply replace the professional, in other cases he can act as a go-between in initiating service, and in still other cases he will tell the agency how it should change its operations to become relevant to local conditions. The new careerist is a sort of ombudsman for the people and *of the people.*

The new careerist can make home visits for the agency, he can accompany the professional on difficult assignments, he can be involved in community surveys, and he can also be an effective community organizer. His job is an extremely varied one that can be adjusted somewhat drastically to build whatever bridge required between agency and neighborhood.

One of the more dramatic experiments with new careers, and one that emphasizes the delivery of services to a ghetto community, has been the Lincoln Hospital (New York) psychiatric aide program. At Lincoln, psychiatric patients are used as social work aides and community organizers. Adhering to the belief that many mental health problems in the ghetto are connected to the powerlessness and alienation of residents, program directors have made a dramatic move to reinject patients into the political process as a form of therapy. The community itself is poor and powerless; the residents (patients in this case) are suffering the alienation connected with this pariah role; the agency is locked in its middle classness and its whiteness and is equally powerless to help people or community. The new careers concept becomes the bridge.

Another example, more closely related to education, is the Howard University program in which high school dropouts (or under-achievers) were used as teacher aides in classes with younger children —the next generation of dropouts. The expressed purpose of the Howard experiment was to take intellectually capable academic failures and to provide an entire twelfth-grade year, leading to a regular diploma, in which the former (or potential) dropouts finished their high school courses while helping in nearby elementary schools. The student-aides were aptly described as "the kids who are usually 'screened out' of special programs. We screened them in." (Bowman and Klopf, 1967)

Although this program is obviously unique in using adolescents and in not giving attention to establishing long-run careers, it is still exemplary of the attempt to involve residents or clients in solving their own problems, whether they be personal or institutional—in this case both. The following is a brief, abridged version of the Howard University-sponsored program as described by a Bank Street College (1967) review team

> Twenty-seven trainees were selected, of whom 17 were male. . . . Of those selected, approximately two-thirds were considered high risks by reason of academic record, attendance record, family background and a history of "acting out" their resentment at their life conditions in juvenile delinquency. . . . Of the 27 participants, eight were in training as health aides and the remainder as teacher aides. All were Negroes.
>
> In the initial stages, the general plan was to devote each morning to the work experience and afternoons to the academic curriculum. However, it became apparent that such a fragmented day was unproductive so that the trainees spent two almost full days on the job and one full day—Friday—in academic pursuits, with the other two days work experience breaking at 11 A.M., when the trainees left school to engage in their academic work. The core group work (group discussion sessions) took place on Monday and Wednesday afternoons. At this time the trainees were divided into two groups of 13 and 15 to facilitate discussion.
>
> In each of the three participating elementary schools, a few teachers who had volunteered to participate in the project were selected, and one aide was assigned to each cooperating teacher. Prior to the opening of the project, a meeting with the three principals was held to explain the nature of the program and determine how the aide trainees would be utilized in their schools. Subsequently, an orientation program was held for the cooperating teachers and for the supervisors of the health aides. . . .

The contribution of these formerly underachieving teenage aides was impressive. They were given a wide variety of classroom tasks to do, and the response was totally out of character with their previous pattern of behavior. They performed a variety of auxiliary functions including taking responsibility for the class when the teacher was called away, keeping records, such as attendance and health records, or playing educational games with the children. Teacher response was overwhelmingly favorable. But the Bank Street report does indicate considerable variety in the use of the young aides:

The degree of responsibility given to the aide and the extent of involvement with the pupils appeared to be a dynamic of each situation, varying in accordance with the personality of the teacher, the ability of the aide, and the particular need of the aide, and the particular need of the pupils. One teacher described her use of the aide assigned to her thus: "I tell the aide what needs to be done, and he then plans his own schedule to accomplish the assigned tasks. He works with one slow student who sits near him."

Another teacher said that she had to remind the aide every day of the routine tasks which were assigned to him. She expressed displeasure at such lack of initiative but countered this criticism by reporting that he had suggested a most interesting field trip for the pupils. She added that the little boys had so identified with this personable young man that she noticed an improvement in their personal appearance. This teacher evidenced no apparent jealousy over the fact that the pupils "really loved this aide." A Negro herself, she seemed sincerely pleased that they had this male role model with whom to identify. However, she said his emphasis upon being a "big brother" to the pupils seemed to weaken his control of the class: she could not assign monitorial duties to him when she was not present. Later the aide in a group interview said that he wanted to be a friend not an authority figure to the pupils.

Many teachers appeared to use the aides primarily for checking papers, preparing bulletin boards and running the duplicating machine rather than in direct contact with pupils. However, one teacher stated emphatically when her aide was withdrawn from class for a special assignment one day: "I find that I can't teach without him."

The Howard experiment obviously produced mixed results. This is to be expected. Although the youthful aides shared certain characteristics such as race, school failure, and youth (usually the features that preclude getting any kind of regular job), they were all different human beings, with considerable variety of personalities and attitudes. Still, the overall usefulness of these aides is consistent. They appear in nearly all cases to have been genuine assets to the classrooms in which they worked, thus justifying their employment without even looking at their own academic progress.[7]

The Howard University experiment, along with the Lincoln Hospital program, demonstrates the notion that new careers can be used to improve human service agencies by involving residents and/or clients served by the agencies. This is a distinctly radical notion and

[7] In fact, the program had a considerable payoff in terms of individual progress. All but one of these actual or potential school dropouts received their diploma within a year after the end of the program.

is the most controversial dimension of the new careers movement. The experimentation with this approach to new careers is still very limited. But at this stage of the game all signs indicate a "Go" condition. There is a vastly expanded role that the poor, welfare recipients, school dropouts, former mental patients and others can play in the delivery of the very services that they have received. In a very real sense the roles of the client and the professional may merge in the new careers concept. New careers brings potential recipients into the human service agencies and suggests a host of future innovations undreamed of until quite recently. In the schools the new careers idea can bring both pupil and parent into cooperative roles with the schools.

New Careers as an Escape Route   From the perspective of the nonprofessional himself, the most salient dimension of new careers is probably the personal opportunity provided to him. This has been relatively ignored by the major new careers ideologists like Pearl and Riessman. Most discussion of mobility through new careers has emphasized vertical mobility via the ladder of new careers to be established in an agency, that is, from teacher aide to assistant teacher to teacher. But others (including former Secretary of Labor Willard Wirtz) have spoken of both horizontal and diagonal mobility as important options open to a new careerist. Aronowitz (1968) talks of the greater control over personal affairs provided by new careers and new careers "unions."

In a recent study of dropouts from a new careers program, considerable change was found between early dropouts from the program and those occurring after nine months' experience or more.[8] Later dropouts were not giving up and going back to welfare or unemployment as had been true of numerous early dropouts; rather, they were leaving the program to take other, better jobs. Two were leaving to go into business for themselves, several were leaving for salaried positions in local poverty programs. In any case, there was clear indication that a sizable group of persons had used the new careers opportunity as an occupational springboard. One individual who had worked as a social work aide became a consultant on race relations to the assistant superintendent of schools.

The ability of persons to use the new careers type job for entry into other mobility channels is largely dependent (except in unusual cases, such as the person becoming consultant to the schools) on the

---

[8] This reference is to the author's own unfinished research in Minneapolis.

kind of training provided in conjunction with the new career. The job experience itself may be important, but in general *personal mobility will be linked to obtaining some recognizable education accompanied by marketable credentials.* Many, but not all, new careers programs are linked to junior college education. Others provide a mix of on-the-job training and collegiate work. There is no general national schema and no consistent thought on this point at present. Many points are unclear. The importance of an A.A. degree in doing social work and education, the willingness of the professions to accept people with new kinds of training, the need for remedial work with low-income adults, and their ability to respond to such remedial work are all subject to current controversy.

It is clear that people do change in the process of working as new careerists. Self-concept changes, motivation, and attitudes are characteristically affected, and literacy levels may rise dramatically. All this implies that the future of new careers will involve greater concern for the ways in which individuals use this opportunity to "crack the system" and turn experience to personal advantage in whatever way is open to them.[9]

Yankelovich (1966) in a study of new careers programs in nine cities uncovered considerable evidence testifying to the personal influence imparted by the new careers experience. He clearly distinguishes between what we have called the personal mobility and delivery of service dimensions of new careers.

> The worst part of urban poverty appears to be a byproduct of the lack of money. There is an assault on the very fundamentals of human life: on the person's hope, on his self-respect and on his feelings of being treated with justice. To be without hope and self-respect is to have one's sense of justice ravaged, and is the very definition of despair. For many people hired in the CAP's (Community Action Programs) the effect of being paid to help others like themselves is dramatic. To feel that you are able to help others to break out of a trap that you yourself have been caught in, boosts a person's self-respect and awakens new hope.
>
> Thus, the study seems to highlight the important finding that there are two very different effects achieved by various government programs. There is a recipient-of-service effect and self-help effect. The recipient-of-service effect ameliorates a difficult situa-

[9] For a strong attack on this point of view see A. Haber, 1968. Haber argues that some programs turn new careerists against their own community, whereas the object should be to change the delivery of service so that the aides are a permanent resource for the poverty-ridden communities.

tion, while the self-help effect does this and *also* bolsters the person's own sense of self-worth, thereby galvanizing his own resources.

New Careers Ladder The most important dimension of the new careers concept has been saved until last in order to emphasize the characteristic priority given it and to highlight its implications for the public schools. The primary thrust of new careers has to do with what Pearl (1966) refers to as "career ladders." Closely related to personal mobility, this notion emphasizes the way in which agencies following the new careers ideal must open up their own recruitment policies and restructure their entire delivery of service to provide a structure whereby a person can come into the agency generally untutored and unsophisticated and yet rise, usually in conjunction with formal education, to the level of a full-fledged professional. The difficulties of an astronomic rise (for example, from teacher aide to certified teacher) are not overlooked, but the emphasis is on building toward a system that can, at least potentially, provide this opportunity for a reasonable percentage of new careers recruits.

Pearl dramatizes this core aspect of the new careers concept when he talks about two professional systems that have some similarity to the new careers idea but that differ in critical points. These other two systems are the "plantation system" and "the medical system." [10] Both can be contrasted to a genuine new careers system. The plantation system is described by Pearl as a system in which the nonprofessionals compose a permanent proletariat lacking any possibility for advancement. Although recognizing that very few systems are explicitly organized with this kind of rigid stratification as a planned feature, he argues that many systems, especially school systems, actually operate in this fashion. In fact, very few teacher aide programs have given any thought whatsoever to providing opportunity for advancement to higher paraprofessional responsibilities. Only a handful of experimental programs have been aware of the possibility that aide work might be the first step on a path toward full-fledged professional status.

The medical system is similar to the plantation system in that neither provides any real opportunity for mobility, except that in the former the illusion of mobility opportunity is provided through the use of job titles and a complex chain of command. Using the Ameri-

[10] This typology appeared in an oral keynote presentation given at a Planning Conference on New Careers, sponsored by Kansas City Association of Trusts, Excelsior Springs, Missouri, 1967.

can medical system as a metaphor, Pearl notes that the complex division of labor between orderly, practical nurse, nurse, scrub nurse, and physician really constitutes an unbridgeable system for someone starting at the bottom. Mobility in the medical system is dependent on a nearly impossible feat of educational perseverance. An adult male starting as an auxiliary employee in an American hospital faces a conservative estimate of ten years of high-priced education if he wishes to reach the top rung. If he chooses to become a male nurse, the training does not plug into medical school but instead represents another dead-end track into what Pearl calls a "satellite profession." Pearl is convinced that many human services now entering into new careers programs are inadvertently adopting a "medical" type program with only the appearance of a career ladder.

Pearl argues that a genuine new careers system must be tied to relevant education. This education must be continuous in the sense of linking one professional level to another. An individual must have a reasonable chance to move from one level to another following a combination of education and experience as preparation. Pearl argues that educational requirements for professional status have typically been rigid and unnecessary. He argues that at least 80 percent of the premedical education of a future physician is irrelevant and represents nothing more than personal luxury. It also functions somewhat efficiently to cut down the access to medicine for poor youngsters unable to afford the requisite decade of education. Pearl extends this reasoning to other professions such as teaching, social work, and law. In all of them the long educational process is an effective barrier to recruiting low-income people. This is obviously detrimental to the individual unable to afford the education, but it also hurts society, which is losing many of the best potential doctors and teachers due to the inequities of recruiting.

Pearl would urge a heavy component of on-the-job training and cooperative work-study higher education [11] to overcome these rigidities of the nation's professional groups and of the professional schools. Going further than most of the new careers ideologists, he advocates putting low-income people into actual teaching situations early in their career as aides. These people would typically work under supervisory personnel, but for certain specialized teaching jobs they might be more effective than certified teachers.

Generally speaking, Pearl's ideas have had little experimental

[11] See also Riessman, 1967b.

testing. However, one recent experiment by Rademacher (1968) at the University of Oregon has used low-income college students (with a minimum experience as aides, but intensive in-service training) to give basic literacy and skill training to high school dropouts attempting to pass a high school equivalency examination. This was part of a nationwide High School Equivalency Program (HEP), funded by OEO.

> The aides were selected from students who had participated in the Upward Bound programs at the University during the previous two years. Three of the students had originally come to the University from the Job Corps programs. Most of them came from the population popularly known as "culturally disadvantaged." Four had completed one year of university work and had earned sophomore standing; two were freshman; one was a junior, and one student was taking courses in the Division of Continuing Education in order to attain a grade point average which would make her eligible for admission to the University.
>
> The program at the University of Oregon is one of eleven HEP units centered in colleges and universities throughout the country, but is unique in its emphasis on interesting and challenging students to prepare for entrance to the University. Although a short-range goal is enabling the student to pass the GED examination with a score high enough to qualify for admission to college, much emphasis is placed on the concurrent long-range goal of awakening interests of students and motivating them to continue an academic education. Central to the philosophy of the program is the importance of the peer group in providing support to the student as he learns to negotiate his way around the academic community. As a result the three groups into which the students were randomly assigned, each with a group leader and two or three aides, form the core of the program around which all activities—social, academic, and recreational—are organized.
>
> Each aide assumed responsibility for selecting the best references for his block of lessons, extracting the basic essentials and planning an orderly presentation. Continued emphasis was placed on identifying the prior information and concepts necessary for mastering new material and teaching these concepts or processes before new material was introduced. The process of starting from the very beginning in a subject was helpful to the aides.
>
> As they helped outline the material to be covered, developed lesson plans, and presented lessons to the group in role-playing sessions, they had an opportunity for a thorough review themselves, repairing gaps in their own mastery of these skills. In addi-

tion, they gained confidence as they worked up the easy first lessons for presentation to the group and gradually gained competence as they proceeded to the more difficult material. (Rademacher, 1968).

The young teacher aides met on an intensive basis for several weeks prior to the beginning of the five-week HEP program. They were drilled in a general model of learning experiences (Ausbel's hierarchically ordered sequential model) and entered into the actual selection of remedial materials to use with their future pupils. The student-aides were encouraged to relate the theory and planning to their own experience as disadvantaged youngsters in the Upward Bound program. It soon became apparent that the students were making an important contribution of their own, and in retrospect it becomes clear that it was their contribution that guaranteed the success of the program.

These low-income college students (*trained in four weeks*) bore the brunt of the teaching duties and all the face-to-face interaction with the pupils.

A tentative outline of a five weeks review in math and grammar which identified the skills and knowledge to be achieved was drawn up. Each of the aides assumed major responsibility in one subject—either math or grammar, and in that subject developed resources and lesson plans for certain blocks of work, e.g., addition and subtraction in math, or plurals and capitalization of nouns in grammar. During the first week one two-hour session was held in the curriculum library on campus, during which each of the aides reviewed the textbooks in his area and selected those that seemed most helpful. (These were not available in sufficient quantity for use as textbooks by the HEP students, but were useful as resources for the aides. The Continental and Hayes ditto-master series at the fifth, sixth, and junior high levels in grammar and math were selected for use as instructional materials because of their low initial cost and adaptability to flexible use. Since no prior information was available regarding the instructional levels of the incoming students, these were considered the most economical and best adapted to the particular needs of the program.) As they began to feel more competent in handling the subject matter and the role of teacher, they became more supportive of each other. The reality of the impending deadline when they would need to be ready for the incoming students was a unifying experience. They also shared a certain dedication (as they became more convinced of their own capability) which was generated by the type of program HEP is. The total program, and particularly the training in counseling which they were receiving concurrently with the training for teaching roles, contributed to this sense of the importance of their jobs in the lives of the incoming students. By the end of the four weeks the aides were working together as a group. They used the role-playing sessions to explore and discuss feelings of apprehension and anxiety, as well as to work out creative ways of presenting material and engaging the class in learning activities. Their interaction was frank, but helpful and constructive. They assumed the major responsibility for establishing norms for the group, such as being on time for class sessions, dressing appropriately, being sufficiently rested to be capable of doing an adequate job of teaching, using appropriate language, etc. (Rademacher, 1968).

Training became more problematic when the actual class sessions began with the dropouts.

The regular group training sessions of aides were discontinued when the students arrived and the actual implementation of the program began. The three sub-groups, each under the leadership of a group counselor with two or three aides doubling as counseling aides and teachers for that group, were the focal points of the program. Since it was essential for the success of the program that these groups be able to provide support in meeting the psychological and social needs, as well as the academic needs of the students, responsibility for both the teaching and counseling functions of the aides was placed with the respective group leaders. The expressed function of the remedial education consultant was to serve as a monitor of the group classes (and also to diagnose cases of extreme learning difficulty and provide remedial help where needed). No provision was made for continued in-service training of the aides other than that provided by the group counselors. Since their primary interest and emphasis was in the counseling area, this arrangement resulted in a virtual termination of academic preparation, with the loss of the opportunity to develop teaching skills and provide mutual support which the group sessions had furnished.

In addition to the lack of continued in-service training, there was no provision made for communication on a planned and regular basis between consultant and group leaders or between the consultant and the aides, either as a group or individually. Attempts to adapt the structure to include such contacts resulted in a haphazard, catch-as-catch-can, inefficient functioning.

In order to meet the needs of the aides in the teaching situation, the consultant interpreted the role of monitor rather liberally. She helped provide the necessary materials, suggested lesson plans and ways of presenting new material, sometimes taking over the class if an aide was absent or not feeling well or even just not confident enough of his knowledge of the material. The terminology of teacher's aide which has been used in this paper was obviously somewhat inappropriate, a fact that the aides mentioned more than once. In fact, they were teachers, for the most part taking total responsibility for the managing of the classroom. While their performance was exceptional, in view of the limited preparation they had had, the responsibility was a heavy one, particularly since counseling duties often kept them up late at night. They needed at least one master teacher as back-up, someone who could pinch-hit, help meet emergencies, and sometimes serve as a model for presentation of a particularly difficult lesson. (Rademacher, 1968)

The University of Oregon experiment is one of the most ambitious of all new careers or teacher aide programs with which we are familiar. Despite the audacity of the idea of training people for an important (and sensitive) teaching function (plus attendant counseling) in four weeks, the program is reported to have had a high degree of success in terms of the migrant children pupils. All pupils showed significant improvement on performance measures in math and grammar. Six pupils felt confident enough to take the GED (General Equivalence Diploma) examination immediately following the end of the summer program and five passed with scores (51 of 100 points) high enough to obtain consideration for admission to the University of Oregon.

But Rademacher and her colleagues considered the most important outcome of the work to be in the provision of a role model for the disadvantaged youngsters. They report:

It is interesting to compare the effectiveness of experienced teachers who have the advantage of superior preparation, knowledge of the subject matter and methods of presentation, with that of the HEP teachers in "getting through" to the pupils. On the basis of informal observations, which need to be followed up by more systematic study, the HEP teachers, perhaps because they were not experts and obviously not much ahead of the students, provided a model which gave the message, "If I can do it, you can too. It's not that hard." For some pupils this seemed to be the needed antidote for the years of failure in a school setting, and a beginning of a new image of themselves as people who could succeed at academic tasks. . . . If this appraisal is accurate, then there is a valuable resource for re-educating the "culturally disadvantaged" among the ranks of youth who have shared their experiences and when given the opportunity have been able to develop skills needed to share their knowledge while adding to it. (Rademacher, 1968)

Training: OJT versus the Junior College

The new careers concept as opposed to the medical model or plantation model has implications for training programs. There are quite obviously two models that can apply to the training of teacher aides. One of these would stress preparation of job related skills and the second would stress long-term training of people for new careers in the schools. The two approaches are not inherently inconsistent, but they tend to be alternative approaches fitting the type of aide program to which they are applied.

On-the-Job Training

On-the-job training for aides can also be divided into two types: preservice or in-service. Most programs in the country seem to have provided in-service training and only a few have had preservice. A few programs have had no training at all.

In general, on-the-job training is not as simple a concept as might at first appear. Aides typically do a wide range of tasks, and it is difficult for any training program to cover all the contingencies (National Education Association, 1967c). It has also been pointed out in a number of places that there is a lack of trained staff for these in-service programs (Riessman, 1967c). And trainees differ drastically in ability, sophistication, and experience. It is an educational truism that teaching increases in difficulty with the heterogeneity of the pupil population. In most aide programs the heterogeneity is very great and there is only the most limited experience with training. In the St. Paul program, for example, training sessions were planned for aides ranging in educational background from college graduate to ninth-grade dropout. All aides went through the *same* training.

As a consequence of these innate handicaps, in-service or preservice training has tended to remain rudimentary. It has emphasized basic skills of assured use to the teacher, such as, clerical abilities, record keeping, typing (for secondary aides, especially), and operation of audiovisual equipment. Training sessions have been put together on a makeshift basis, often on unpaid aide time, and have been taught by whatever personnel happened to be available. They have ignored any attempt at general education. General knowledge is either felt to be unnecessary for the high school graduate or too difficult for the present corps of trainers to cope with. There has been little provision for training in psychology, pedagogy, teaching methods, or school policy. These all demand sophistication in presentation and a certain amount of literacy for comprehension.

Nor is it clear what teachers want their aides to know. Teachers sometimes complain that aides have not had adequate preparation for their classroom roles. But they do not always specify the kinds of training desired. Very few studies are available on training programs for regular teacher aide programs.

Bank Street Training Studies

Bank Street College, however, completed a 1966 study of 15 in-service and preservice training programs for new careers aides. Nine of these were preservice programs, and six were in-service. Organized for new careerists, these sessions were associated with local CAP (Community Action Programs) poverty programs. They were not typical aide programs. They all involved low-income aides, including groups of migrant workers, high school dropouts functioning in elementary school classrooms, reservation Indians, and two groups of rural poverty residents. A large portion of the aides were nonwhite. Several groups had English language problems. Half the programs were residential in that the aides lived 24 hours a day on the training site.

All the in-service programs included a practicum with specially selected pupil populations. All the training programs were sponsored by institutions of higher education, including New York University, Ohio University, the University of Miami, and a series of junior colleges. All involved professional training staffs that were ideologically committed to the new careers idea. Nonetheless, the studies represent the best survey of attempts to train school auxiliary personnel and provide some introduction to this largely unexplored area.

The single most salient fact is that these OEO programs provided unusually comprehensive training for the aide recruits. What is especially unique about these training sessions when compared to the more common run of training is the systematic inclusion of material from education, child development, and psychology. It is widely assumed that this material is irrelevant for teacher aides. And this may be a correct assumption in the aide programs lacking any involvement of aides with pupils, but the movement would seem to be in the direction of greater teacher aide involvement.

Beyond Technical Training

If the aide role is designed as more than menial and includes more than "technical assistance" to the teacher, then something more than technical training is called for. At least one other in-service training program for aides (again associated with a new careers concept) has utilized a heavy component of these general education subjects. A course offered on an optional basis to aides in the Minneapolis teacher aide program dealt extensively with psychology and sociology. It covered such topics as the concept of intelligence, specific learning problems, behavior disorders (such as stuttering, enuresis, or nail biting) and neurotic complaints (like neurasthenia). It tried to provide both some relevant discussion of real job problems along with an introduction to conceptual tools. The instructor reasoned that to some extent knowledge is power in the schools and that aides were disadvantaged in the school setting without some elementary knowledge of behavioral science.

The Minneapolis course moved on to cover social problems in education, including an extensive discussion of *de facto* segregation, political pressures on the school, and educational reforms demanded by the black community (a hot topic in Minneapolis in the winter of 1968).[12] Only half the class were high school graduates, yet the instructor found the aides deeply interested in these topics and often quite knowledgeable in a practical way about the dimensions of these. community problems. As an example of level of work required of these aide trainees, one might look at the final "examination" given the trainees as a "take home" assignment. They were to write for two hours on the following subject.

Examination: School and Community

The problem of "de facto" segregation in American schools is being argued by many people, white and black. There have been many solutions suggested as to how this problem may be solved. Blacks disagree among themselves as to how the situation should be handled, with some black leaders, like Floyd McKissick of CORE, opposing putting very much effort into integration. The little book (*Ghetto Schools*) which we read for class also discussed the problem. One author argues against investing heavily in techniques to end segregation, the others favoring integration. Yet none of these writers are racists.

How do you feel about the problems? In your own words write what you think the best solution might be. You may use any of the arguments we have studied or you may take a position different from any of these. You may talk about such things as "bussing" or learning centers, or you may suggest some answers of your own. Use whatever facts or personal experiences are available to

[12] The Minneapolis program is discussed in greater detail in Chapters 6 and 7.

you. You may certainly call upon experiences gained as an aide in the Minneapolis schools if you feel that this experience has affected your opinion.

You have two days to do this examination. But you are on your honor *not* to spend more than two hours in the writing of it. I want this to be your own opinion, so there is no need to go to the library to look up additional facts. Just use those things that you have seen and heard and read in your life so far.

The Composite Career Ladder

There is, then, a decided movement toward providing a two-pronged training program for people to work in the schools. This would combine in-service training with a junior college program. However, several points are not clearly understood. First, there is little utility to establishing a two-year collegiate curriculum if there are not new kinds of positions in the schools. The graduates of an A.A. degree program cannot be used (or should not be used) as classroom menials, but they must be prepared for new kinds of educational functions, whether it be psychological trouble-shooter, bridge to the community, tutor, or whatever. There is no point in gearing junior colleges to prepare people for positions that exist only in fantasy. The educational development must go side by side with the development of new instructional roles.

A second major consideration, which is not essential but is, nonetheless, very important (and also not clearly grasped by educators), is the way in which two-year educational programs may be a stepping-stone to full teacher training. This is the extension of the new careers ideal to its logical conclusion. After becoming an assistant teacher or an advanced educational technician (titles are obviously plentiful), the person can easily be encouraged to go on to become a certified teacher. He could pursue this advanced training while working at this middle-level position. This fully implements the new careers emphasis on "careers" as opposed to "jobs." It would put the entry level aide in a career channel that theoretically can lead to the top of the ladder.

The most articulate advocate of this complete, untruncated career ladder is Frank Riessman. Riessman has, of course, designed this career ladder as a sophisticated antipoverty strategy. But there is actually no need to look at it solely within the poverty framework. What Riessman and other new careers ideologists propose could be applied across the board as a general means of recruiting more people to teaching. The shortages in certified school personnel are drastic and certain to become worse in the near future (Pearl, 1968). Riessman's model could lead to reducing this shortage by some significant amount by moving the goal of teacher training within the reach of many who are blocked from pursuing it under current recruitment policies.

Riessman's proposals are ambitious; some might say almost utopian. They project a distinctly new pattern for teacher training. It would be well to take a close look at these proposals and to try to separate the relevant from the irrelevant, to distinguish fantasy from reality.

> If the nonprofessional movement is to grow, if the opportunity structure is to be opened up so that jobs can become careers and aides can rise to become ultimately professionals, major institutional changes will have to be considered: Civil Service requirements will have to be altered, educational institutions will have to accredit on-the-job training and enormous new cadres will have to be developed from among both professionals and sub-professionals. The significance of training has not yet been fully grasped. No national training institute has been established, although it is needed. No national plan exists for training of trainers, nor for retraining of professionals to work effectively with nonprofessionals. The Job Corps has not been utilized for the development of training for nonprofessionals or their trainers. If the nonprofessional revolution is to create more jobs, if it is to develop genuine careers for the poor, moving them up the ladder, step by step, authentic training is the key. . . .
>
> The need for long periods of training before the individual can even apply for a position is not adapted to the needs of the poor [perhaps more than just the poor], the dropout, the delinquent functioning in a future world that has been unsure and in a school environment that has been unencouraging. The best way to educate many school dropouts is not to send them back to school immediately, but to provide them with nonprofessional human service jobs. This will provide them with the stimulus for obtaining the necessary education on the job and returning to the educational structures where appropriate and needed. (Riessman, 1967b)

A return to the "educational structures" is the heart of Riessman's model for promoting teacher aides to teaching positions. Although one might argue, and many do, that much of teacher training is irrelevant, it is dangerously impractical to hope that the credit and course requirements for a teaching certificate are going to be dropped or even seriously changed within the next generation. It is apparent that something like four years of college, including educational methods and other required courses, are going to continue to be part of the training process. Riessman recognizes this reality. He would argue more for a *cooperative* arrangement between the public schools and the training institutions whereby individuals could work in the schools over long periods of time and only periodically return, as income or interest allowed, to continue on the path toward a certificate.

Riessman has described (1967) the outline of a coordinated set of educational and job steps that would lead from an entry level teacher aide position to certification. It involves four basic steps: aide (technical assistance role), assistant (supportive and supplementary roles), associate (basic teacher role as it exists today), and credentialed teacher (consultant, trainer, or supervisor). The individual moves through these jobs steps in conjunction with education progress. The educational progress, especially, needs some explanation, which, unfortunately, Riessman has not yet provided in detail.

The most futuristic educational suggestion is that college work be undertaken at the aide level and largely completed by the time of entry into the associate position. The associate then works toward being a credentialed teacher mainly on the basis of classroom work experience. Classroom experience would begin early in the process, but the latter part of training would be made up almost exclusively of on-the-job teaching under a credentialed teacher. Most professional and pedagogical training would be imparted by people working *in the schools,* not by college staffs. The college staff would lay the groundwork and the latter part of teacher training will be completed by "indigenous" school personnel.

There is no doubt that the Riessman model is an ambitious one. It is, in fact, an attack on the entire teacher training system. It would be well to point out the core components of the suggestions for using aide service as a new route into teaching. The following is probably a decent summary of the main components of the idea.

1. Cooperative work-study pursuit of college credentials.
2. Immediate involvement of new recruits to education *in the teaching process* in a real classroom.
3. Use of an A.A. degree in education as a basic stepping-stone to the B.A. degree.
4. Continuous provision of economic maintenance to low-income people while they pursue a teaching certificate.

5. Recognized collegiate credit for the classroom experience; perhaps as much as one full year of credit for supervised experience.

Career Incentive Plans

The most radical, and the most intriguing, of these five basic suggestions are numbers four and five. These compose what Felton (1967) has called a career incentive plan. They are a response to the need to cut decisively into the total amount of time needed to obtain a professional credential—without watering down the nature of this education.

Many teacher aides, and a majority of those recruited to new careers programs, have less than a high school education. They have a very long way to go to obtain a degree and a certificate. Full-time schooling is out of the question for a family breadwinner whose only source of income is $4000 a year for a full-time job. If the aide follows the typical night school course of study, he can expect that it will take him eight years to obtain a B.A., and perhaps longer if he still has high school work or remedial training to clear away first.

The career incentive plan involves two major aspects: (1) paying the aide-trainee to go to school and (2) granting credit for the work experience. Neither of these have any major precedent in American education, and they are something beyond the general run of modest proposals for helping adults obtain higher education. The key is obviously to tie these opportunities to a new careers job ladder. Institutionalizing these points will mark a major change in schools and colleges alike.

Paying Aides To Go to School

Paying a teacher aide to go to school is certainly a novel suggestion. Felton (1967) has proposed what she calls the "one-fifth study plan."

> . . . the plan proposes that one-fifth or eight hours of an aide's working week be set aside so that he can attend college courses at the job site, if possible; or at special centers for such instruction, or at a nearby cooperating college.
>
> These courses would be structured so that the aide could clearly grasp the relationship between theory and his practical experience. Such an approach is particularly useful for persons who have had negative experiences with regard to education and re-

quire a transitional stage to assist them back to the academic mainstream.

Under the one-fifth study plan, an aide could complete 16 college credits yearly toward the 126 credits required for a B.A. degree: 12 credits in fall and spring, four in summer sessions, accumulating 80 credits in 5 years, exclusive of credit for work experience.

Provision of direct support for education is extremely important in a career incentive plan. Scholarships are generally limited to those of high previous achievement. They are specifically designed for young people, require that the recipient attend school full time, and frown on more than ten hours of work per week. The adult working as a teacher aide needs both full maintenance (a living weekly wage) and direct payment of tuition and books.

At present only a handful of new careers type programs scattered around the country are paying any of the direct costs of education or providing maintenance; and only a fraction of these (only four programs known to the authors) are paying for regular collegiate credit. Many aides are enrolled in irregular courses: institutes, workshops, or seminars not carrying college credit but dealing with college-level material.

A second important part of the career incentives plan is the granting of college credit for work experience. At present, only three institutions of higher education appear to be offering credit for intern or on-the-job training of paraprofessionals. San Francisco Community College in cooperation with Oakland and the California Board of Education offers a work-study program for teacher aides. This program includes two credits per semester for night courses at the college and three credits per semester for work experience. The program will soon be expanded to include aides employed under a combined United States Office of Education and Labor Department sponsored program at a local junior high school. The college is working with the Board of Education to develop a career line from teacher aide to assistant teacher. The latter will require the A.A. degree. Also, the college is discussing a program to enable teacher assistants to continue study toward the B.A. at a local four-year institution.

The University of Minnesota and Fairleigh Dickinson University (in New Jersey) are the only large universities to offer some credit for the on-the-job experience of teacher aides. The credit granted by the New Jersey institution is tied closely to classwork offered on the job site. It is not tied to work alone. The University of Minnesota, however, in conjunction with the Minneapolis new careers program and

Minneapolis public schools is offering two credits in its General College (two-year institution) for the work experience of aides assigned to the schools. This opportunity is open to about 105 low-income teacher aides or school social work aides. They can accumulate 15 to 18 "field work" credits during the two years in which the program will operate.[13]

The career incentive plan is an embryonic development in American education. It can be an essential part of any genuine career ladder in the schools, but it would be foolish not to recognize that few school systems and probably fewer junior colleges or universities are ready to move ahead with such a program. Generally speaking, these institutions are too insecure, especially the junior colleges, to allow rapid development of this idea. Too many will view the internship credits as cheap education. Many institutions will be unwilling to accept these credits on a transfer basis, and states will not consider them part of legitimate training (that is, for a teacher aide certificate) for work in the schools. Only more adventuresome institutions will make the first moves in this direction.

Summary

This chapter has been an extended discussion of the tricky questions of recruiting, training, and organizing teacher aide programs. It is quite clear that these issues must be discussed in relation to the new careers idea in the use of teacher aides. The issues of recruitment, training, job development, and the relationship of aides to other professional staff are all affected by the acceptance or rejection of the new careers idea.

The new careers idea as developed by Riessman, Pearl, and others sees the teacher aide position as a means of recruiting and utilizing low-income people in America's schools; the concept emphasizes the way in which school aides can be (1) a bridge between the middle-class institution and the community or minority group, (2) a new way of recruiting the poor, the Black, or the disadvantaged into teaching, and (3) a new form of personal opportunity for individual members of these groups.

Adherence to the new careers concept definitely affects recruitment to aide positions. It emphasizes an open entry approach in which there are no formal educational requirements and where those

[13] See chapter 7 for an expanded discussion.

usually discriminated against may have a special chance. It stresses the hiring of aides from the school neighborhood. It distinctly implies that even entry level aides will, if recruited from the school community, be able to play a supplementary role as a bridge between middle-class professional and the poor or ghetto residents.

The new careers concept also has profound implications for training. Without a concept of new careers, training concerns will focus on preservice or in-service work. The training will also tend to de-emphasize general education for aides, although it need not necessarily do so. Nonnew careers programs could include psychology, social and community problems, and some introduction to education methods in a sound in-service program, but practical considerations often militate against it.

The major difference in training under a new careers concept is represented by the concern for college courses and credentials. The new careers concept would see aides as potential future teachers. The A.A. degree is seen as an important way-station on the route to certification. Only by linking aide work closely to educational opportunities can the aide be expected to advance through the career ladder implied in the new careers concept. Education must be made both economically and psychologically possible for the teacher aides. This implies the development of alternative paths to teacher certification and totally new modes of teacher preparation. This development, however, is only in the early experimental stages; the major changes will probably occur in the next decade.

Likewise, it must be stressed that although the new careers concept represents the more dramatic side of aide use and holds very important implications for the future, the vast majority of teacher aide programs are not at the moment following the new careers concept. Nor is there any reason to believe that the new careers idea will ever have any broad applicability to suburban schools. Its importance is largely for the giant urban systems and the disadvantaged sectors of this community.

Most teacher aide recruitment today tends to be selective and centralized. It is at the same time somewhat "loose" in that there are no generally accepted standards for selection. Too much of it probably follows administrative whim, with the whim being that of central office administrators, not principals. Similarly, most aide training tends to be limited to preservice or in-service sessions. Training tends to be as haphazard as recruitment. Relatively little thought is given to such projects as building up a permanent corps of trained aides or using the aide jobs to help people get a start on higher education.

Thus, the present norm tends to be at odds with the new careers idea. Because the various aide programs have grown quite rapidly, most administrators are not clearly aware of the alternatives. Some have never even heard of new careers or open entry recruitment nor have they thought about the A.A. degree for aides. The trend, however, will be in the direction of new careers. It is too useful a concept to the society and too important to the poor and to American school systems to go unnoticed much longer. The following chapters will try to give a detailed description of one teacher aide program that has launched itself in this still only crudely charted direction. It is hoped that this will provide some concrete understanding of the dimensions and problems of this approach.

6 A New Careers Ladder in the Minneapolis Schools

The scope of new careers in the schools should be fully appreciated as a program for structural change. New careers is nothing less than a major strategy for change in our society and in the provision of human service. Education is at the heart of this strategy, and schools are the largest potential developers of new careers type programs. The new careers idea has profound implications for the nature of teaching and the organization of the instructional process. It is related to almost all current developments in education from the introduction of talking typewriters to the concept of "black power" over ghetto schools.

The next four chapters will try to explore some of the empirical aspects of the varied dimensions of new careers. One must ask the important sociological question: Just how do these things happen? We will begin this discussion by describing the efforts of one new careers program to institute a career ladder in a large urban school system. This will involve a detailed account of the new careers portion of the Minneapolis teacher aide program.

The Minneapolis program overlaps two other programs. The new careers teacher aides in the Minneapolis schools compose about one third of the total aides employed. Although all aides in the Minneapolis schools are recruited in a manner coincident with a new careers idea (see chapter 5), about 100 of them are involved in the Labor Department's New Careers Program, which explicitly aspires to provide a new careers ladder. The remainder of the aides are employed under Title I of the Elementary and Secondary Education Act, 1965.

New Careers in Minneapolis

The following description of this administratively complex program is based largely on personal observations and public records of the program. We were closely associated with the program, at least for a short while. However, neither of us can take any credit for the success of the Minneapolis program. We came to the program in the capacity of researchers from a background of teaching and research in sociology. Although pressed into administrative duties during 1967 and 1968, whatever expertise we have was gained from the program, not brought into it. In fact, the Minneapolis program, which is widely known as a successful new careers program, has moved forward mainly because of the efforts of Esther Wattenberg, the director of New Careers Training Component, of Frederik Hayen, full-time consultant to the Minneapolis Public Schools for Teacher Aides, and of Frederik Boeder the project director, Minneapolis New Careers. It is these three individuals who were responsible for the early successes of the Minneapolis program.

Scheuer Program Beginnings

In early 1966 the Scheuer Amendment to the Economic Opportunity Act was passed by a congress still earnestly waging war on poverty. The Vietnamese war had not yet begun to cut so deeply into OEO appropriations. At this point Congressman Scheuer of the Bronx, originally skeptical of the idea of new careers, wrote an ambitious piece of legislation embodying the concept in a far-ranging way. Highly influenced by the ideas of Riessman and Pearl (1965) and aided by insightful staff work on the part of Edward Cohen, a young former University of Wisconsin student body president, Scheuer fashioned a bill providing $50 million for new careers. This money was to be available for new careers in any field that could be construed as human services. The bill passed Congress with amazingly little difficulty. Under a general agreement governing authority over poverty programs, the Scheuer program is located in the Labor Department, Bureau of Work Programs.

Like all government programs, politics seems to have drastically affected the actual progress of the Scheuer program. In choosing between cities for the first set of programs, consideration of the troubles or potential troubles during the summer of 1966 seem to have played a major part. A number of major cities and metropolitan areas considered among the top 25 in terms of size and/or manpower problems were surprisingly passed up. Smaller cities, like Rochester or Oakland, that had real potential for urban violence were funded for Scheuer programs. Among those passed up in the first round of negotiations was Minneapolis–St. Paul.[1]

The New Careers Offensive

However, in the late summer of 1966, the Minneapolis Northside did explode in a brief but intense civil disturbance. This riot appears to have assured Minneapolis a place in the second round of program funding. In the spring of 1967, with several million dollars in funds still unexpended, the Bureau of Work Programs approached other cities about establishing new careers programs. Minneapolis was one of these, which, like the others, had indicated original and continuing interest in the new careers idea. It was suggested to the local Community Action Program (CAP) agency that Minneapolis (or, more accurately, Hennepin County) could receive about $600,000 for new careers. This information was extended about mid-May. Because the funds had to be distributed by June 30, Minneapolis had six weeks to design a program.

To most people this schedule would have seemed impossible. Indeed, it is a very poor approach to programming. But despite the crush of time, Minneapolis did have an operating program by August 1 and also had the financial scope of the program doubled to a little over $1.2 million. By mid-September (1967), when an informal national planning conference took place in Kansas City under the spon-

---

[1] The speculations in this paragraph are based entirely on our impressions and do not involve any access to "secret" government guidelines or communications.

sorship of the Institute of Community Studies, Minneapolis had acquired a reputation as one of the better (at least one of the more adventurous) programs in the country. At the beginning of this conference, Art Pearl stated categorically that "there are no new careers programs!" By the end of the conference he admitted publicly that "maybe" Minneapolis had something close to a new careers program. Specifically Pearl indicated that Minneapolis was making progress, or had immediate plans for progress, toward genuine new careers ladders especially in the field of education.

Institutional Readiness

What allowed Minneapolis to make such rapid progress, at least initially, toward operationalizing a new careers program in education? This is an important question because behind it lies another question. Why were about twenty programs at the same time making little progress toward the development of career ladders. At that point in 1967 (and it is, unfortunately, still true in 1970) numerous programs were floundering badly despite the fact that they had been operating for nearly a year and had received much more planning time than had Minneapolis.

The Need for Structural Changes

The remainder of this chapter, by taking a close look at the structure of the Minneapolis new careers program, especially with reference to the two thirds of the program involving new careers in education, will attempt to provide some specific suggestions for operationalizing new careers. But some general preliminary comments are in order.

It should be clear that Minneapolis has been a *relative* success. Many mistakes were made, and personnel in this program were just as naïve as those in other programs. The following is presented not as an adulation of one program but, rather, to see what structural factors existed that allowed this program to move ahead. If there is any key to the success of the Minneapolis program, it lies in two areas: institutional structure and personnel. Of the two areas, institutional structure is by far the most important, for the development of new careers in education demands two essential institutional adjustments: adjustments in the schools as well as adjustments in the colleges.

Educational Structures

First, the public school system must be willing to experiment with new uses of personnel. It must be willing to make a beginning in the development of new roles in the school system. And it must be willing to make this beginning or at least to continue the program on a permanent "hard money" basis from local sources. The entire educational structure from budget to recruitment and from personnel policies to curriculum must be involved in the development of new roles in the schools and in a new relationship between school and community.

Minneapolis perhaps as ambitiously as any city in the country had made a beginning in that direction. The use of neighborhood residents in the schools (as described in Chapter 5) and the recruitment features of this program were one indication of the beginning made in Minneapolis prior to Scheuer. The commitment of $500,000 of local money for extension of the teacher aide program over a three-year period (1968 to 1971) is an indication of a far more substantial movement. Other indications of relatively far-reaching changes in the Minneapolis system will appear later in this chapter. These include attempts at state certification for "career aides" and efforts to allow aides almost full responsibilities for teaching in certain ghetto classrooms.

But if development of new careers has to depend on changes in the school system alone it will probably not be effective. Equally important in structural change is that the local institutions of higher education respond to the training needs of new careers in education. Through some simple mathematical reasoning, one may say that new careers in education (nc) is equal to the changes in the public schools (ps) multiplied by changes in the colleges (c):

$$nc = f(ps \times c)$$

The moral of this mathematical model is that even if the development of a career ladder in the schools reaches great proportions while the change in the local colleges or universities is zero, the product in terms of genuine new careers will likewise be zero.

The Minneapolis new careers program was equally dependent on the existing structure of the University of Minnesota. (It could just as well have been the state junior college system; this is not an argument that only a university can sponsor new careers programs.) The University of Minnesota was able to respond rapidly to the demands of the new careers program. It did so through the unique presence of a training center for community programs (TCCP). The training center had been in the business of supplying various kinds of training, advice, research, and other kinds of educational service to the large Twin City metropolitan area for about six years. It may be stressed that this was not predominantly an organization of university academics whose major job was teaching and research and who helped out in a hit-or-miss fashion. It was not an urban studies center, as is so commonly found. Rather, this was an organization whose major job was community training and whose personnel were individuals with long practical experience with community programs. In some ways the training center was a collection of academic mavericks.

All this was absolutely essential to the university's response. In fact, the CAP leadership initiated the contact in that the Training Center was called in because of its reputation (and especially the reputation of its personnel) to be able to deal with community demands in a pragmatic way and to assure that research was secondary to service. We probably do not have to reiterate the trained incapacity of the many "community" experts whose specialization is research.[2]

The training center was able to act as a broker for the university. It could take the needs of the community (in this case the new careers program and the schools) to the university and arrange a variety of responses. It was able to line up several different branches of the university (as will be described in chapter 7) to service the program; it could bring together the professional schools to discuss the future of the new careers idea and to plant seeds of interest in hitherto fallow ground. It could obtain the collaboration of competent research assistance, and, most important, as part of the university it could itself initiate some of the training on an experimental basis. When this experimentation has been demonstrated to be in the proper direction it will be institutionalized into the regular university program. It was able to pull together a counseling unit from diverse sources and begin experimenting with special guidance and counseling programs for the low-income adults in the new careers program.

The training center was perhaps not an essential structure. Other

[2] This brief polemic against the university research establishment should not be interpreted as a criticism of research per se. Indeed, research is vital to good programming and planning for the long haul. It is only meant to point out as vividly as possible the importance of keeping research separate from the response of a college or university to immediate training needs of a community program. It is far more important that the university people have a sound understanding of the people, the institutions, and the needs of the specific community, *not* of communities in general. It is equally important that the community people (for example, school administrators) know and trust the university personnel. Research often gets in the way. For this and other reasons, it is best done by an *independent* group.

structures could have responded to the community need. The point is that the university and the college must be in some way able to move as fast or faster than the community agencies involved if a new careers program is to move ahead. Within a large and highly complex institution like the University of Minnesota, however, it is hard to see how anything other than an independent center like TCCP could have put together all the relevant pieces. The structural ability for rapid and flexible response must exist in the college or must be developed. A good many new careers type programs and the progress of many teacher aide programs in this direction are halted because of the built-in barriers in higher education. The attack must be two-pronged, involving both public schools and college.

Personnel: The School and the University

In addition to the institutional structures that have just been discussed and that are of critical importance in the development of a new careers program in education, the personnel making up these structures is of almost equal importance. Another way to put this would be to note that leadership is extremely critical in this process of change. People must be involved in both the schools and the college who understand the new careers concept and who are willing to push their own organizations from the inside. This would be a truism except for several deductions from it that seem equally obvious but that are not always recognized. At least they seem to have been missed by many otherwise well-designed programs.

That is, if a school or college is to become involved in a new careers program, the initiating agency should look hard to find someone with experience in new careers programming and with teacher aides (perhaps upgrading an experienced teacher to direct the program, or to teach in a junior college), rather than give the job to an already overburdened administrator or shift someone from a totally alien area. Another fairly obvious and really very minor tactic is to assist local people to tie into the national movement for new careers by allowing them to attend conferences, training programs, and the like, on a national level. In a new area like this, where very little is yet written, this may be the only way to get badly needed technical information; and it also serves the function of motivating local personnel by allowing them a good perspective on the broader importance of what they are doing. In Minneapolis, east St. Louis, or Pipestone, Minnesota, it is very easy for someone to feel that one is swimming upstream, and it seems a very long stream indeed. The tie-in with national activities can be of major importance.

Finally, the identification of the leadership personnel with the cause of the poor or the black is critical. The development of a new careers ladder involves negotiation with many other parts of the school and community. The person doing this negotiation must be an advocate for the kind of people new careers is to serve. If at all possible, there must be minority group representation on the staff, not just for its appearance value but for its ability to empathize with the needs of the target population and its ability to represent that population in the councils of the community or university. Although change is occurring in this area, many segments of our universities, for example, are hopelessly out of touch with the political realities of the ghetto or the inner city. Face-to-face encounters are often helpful.

The Minneapolis new careers program did benefit from the kind of commitment, identification, and empathy mentioned above. This empathy helped accomplish some things probably not otherwise within reach. But it also helped to soothe the hurt from some mistakes that were made, in the sense that a person will not mind a few bruises as much if his commitment to the game is high and if he feels that the overall direction is correct. Identification and empathy of staff was, of course, a variable within the Minneapolis program, and sometimes the insight or experience of one person acted as a corrective for the well-meant but naïve actions of others. Perhaps a story told *on* one of us illustrates this as well as anything can.

Early in the year, caught between his teaching, on the one hand, and the rush of demand of the program, on the other, the senior author had failed to take advantage of a chance to increase a book allowance for new careerists in the Minneapolis program, and in the same bad week he had overlooked the necessity of making provisions for meetings for preservice sessions for new careerists. Both errors created some considerable anxiety on the part of the new careerists, still largely uncertain of their ground. The problem was brought immediately home to the author by another member of the staff, a black teacher who was involved in these preservice sessions with the telling comment: "You damn people in these federal programs are all alike." The truth hurt and the author tried to take a closer look at his bureaucratic self in the mirror each morning. This ability to criticize is very essential to any program that seriously attempts to bring about change. People secure enough to offer this kind of criticism must be employed. People who know enough to offer criticisms from the standpoint of the aides must be found.

The Scheuer Amendment, New Careers, and the Minneapolis Schools

It is now appropriate to turn to the description of an operating new careers program with its combined occupational and educational opportunity.

Table 6-1

	Original Slots	Slots Filled by January 1968
Minneapolis Public Schools	115	78
Twin Cities Opportunity Industrialization Center (TCOIC)	53	39
Minneapolis Urban League	1	1
Minnesota Department of Employment Security	9	9
Family and Children's Service of Minneapolis	2	2
Minneapolis City Workhouse	6	4
Minneapolis Police Department	6	4
Agricultural Extension Division, University of Minnesota	9	9
Minnesota Department of Corrections	8	4
Total	209	150

Participating Agencies

New Careers is definitely not limited to the public schools. Nor does an operating new careers program necessarily observe the pre-established educational structures of a city school system. In Minneapolis, nine different agencies (in 1967) were involved in the new careers program, as funded under the Scheuer Amendment. In all, the Minneapolis program received about $1.2 million of Labor Department money to develop their program. Administered through the local CAP office, the program actually involved 209 job slots in nine different human service agencies. Table 6-1 is an original roster of the agencies and their job slots. It is obvious that there is quite a variety in the size and scope of the experiment.

The Minneapolis new careers program was heavily slanted toward education.[3] The two largest participating agencies were educa-

[3] Not all programs have this slant; the Kansas City Scheuer program involved only medical new careerists; several other programs feature new careers in social work.

tional institutions: the Minneapolis public schools and the Twin Cities Opportunity Industrialization Center (TCOIC). These educational institutions, one traditional and the other radical and controversial, employed 78 and 39 new careers–type teacher aides, respectively. We will devote most of the remainder of this chapter to the Minneapolis Public Schools, mainly because its experience is useful to a far larger group of school people, but a few words should be said about the program at TCOIC.

Twin Cities Opportunities Industrialization Center

In the Old First National Bank Building of Minneapolis a new and unconventional kind of educational experiment began to take form in 1968. Modeled after the first such center in Philadelphia (Opportunity Industrialization Center), the Twin City branch (TCOIC) is attempting to offer a wide variety of adult education courses to hardcore school dropouts and the adult unemployed. Their sources of students are the bars, pool halls, and street corners of Minneapolis. They are going after the clientele that does not reach the Office of Minnesota Employment Security. They are looking for the people to whom it has never even occurred to take up the adult basic education offered by the schools.

A few have wondered why a separate agency is needed. The city's offices are plastered with flyers from the Adult Basic Education Office of the public schools. Several government manpower programs are likewise going full blast in the Twin City area. Dunwoody Institute offers a high caliber post–high school vocational education at a very convenient location. TCOIC officials are merely amused by these public doubts. The young person whom they serve, whether· he be black, white, or Indian (there are 2000 Indians in the Twin City area) do not frequent the government offices, they do not read brochures, they do not watch the educational TV channel.

TCOIC has gone out and recruited students. Nearly 40 percent of the TCOIC staff is involved in recruiting. The general philosophy is that the first step is the hardest. Getting the unemployed adult into education and making him feel that somehow this institution is for him and involves, at all levels, people like him—Black, Indian, or, recently, poor—is one of TCOIC's major goals.

TCOIC has thrown its new careerists into the breach as aides to the recruiting staff and their small group of counselors. These aides are often very close to the clientele in background. They come from the same neighborhoods, and they have the same problems, mainly money. They provide a bridge into the training program that only a rare professional could provide. In a very real sense they provide a continuity with the community that is missing from practically every other American educational establishment that purports to serve a lower economic level constituency.

TCOIC offers a variety of adult education and basic literacy work ranging from fundamental (third grade) reading to calculus and from grooming and personal presentation to a required course on minority history (until recently, taught by a young black historian by the name of Milt Williams). The instructors for these courses represent a wide range of professional preparation. Many of the full-time teachers are not certified teachers; some, including one excellent instructor of business and secretarial work, do not have any college education. Actually, most of the instructors work part time, teaching at night after other jobs are over. An engineer, a doctor, and a biochemist are numbered among the part-time staff.

These instructors are liberally assisted by new careers teacher aides. Some actual teaching (for example, a drafting course) is done by a teacher aide. Many of the aides are used for individualized instruction or to expand drill and recitations that busy part-time instructors have no time for. Aides can work with students during the day when many instructors are not available.

TCOIC has great promise. It is certainly representative of one of the most important new frontiers in American education. But even this brief description should not ignore the problems involved; for, to a large extent, they are the problems of building a new careers ladder in this type of education institution. Most specifically, is TCOIC a new type of school, or is it merely a transitional institution filling in while the public schools catch up with the needs of the time? Similarly, are there careers here which would have a permanence that is not dependent on the shaky financial structure of these new privately controlled institutions? Are there long-run careers in an organization like TCOIC?

Financial difficulties are continually rumored for TCOIC; if TCOIC should fail or other institutions fill the gap, what happens to the "careers" of their teacher aides? These are tough and complicated questions. The answers are not clear to any of them. The key, however, seems to be to link the teacher or counselor aide jobs in a TCOIC-like institution to higher education so that these people, just as those working with the public schools, will have opportunities to move into the city school system as certified aides or certified teachers. Teaching experience in these institutions (in any situations where there is likely to be competent supervision) should be given credit in public school systems. But wishing is not having, and hurdling the many barriers to this kind of horizontal mobility from private education into the public schools has never been easy, even when private schools had high prestige. All of these factors should be taken into consideration when planning new careers in education on a city-wide basis. New careers can be an important link between the public schools and the rebellious community-based self-help educational efforts like TCOIC. But, this will only be true to the extent that both institutions can see their mutual goals in educating the poor and in recruiting teachers from these same disadvantaged populations.

The Minneapolis School System

There are four broad categories of new careers in the Minneapolis schools. These are elementary school aides, secondary school aides, counselor aides, and social work aides. These areas are functionally distinct in that aide work in one area is not immediately transferable to the other. Cutting across this functional distinction is an important differentiation between full-time new careers aides, on the one hand, and a larger group of half-time aides employed under Title I of the ESEA on the other. There are 115 new careers positions, and in 1967 to 1968 there were 130 Title I aides.

The difference between new careers aides and Title I aides is an important one for the development of new careers in Minnesota. It is also a tangle of problems for the Minneapolis programs. The existence of two types of aides means that nearly every administrative decision has to take into account the interests of both groups. More important for our discussion is the fact that one group, those under the new careers program, are involved in a genuine career ladder, whereas the other group (Title I) is employed in a basically dead-end job.

Salaries and Benefits

The entry level aides are employed full time, with a full (if not bountiful) income maintenance of $2.00 or $2.80 per hour. The Title I aides can work only half the time (by law) and are all paid only $2.00 per hour. It would, in fact, be virtually impossible for any Title I aide to support a family on this salary, thus eliminating heads of households from employment.

New careers aides also have their education paid for up to eight university credits per quarter. They receive a yearly book allowance and most important, they receive this education on paid time. This latter provision makes it possible for a head of household, say a young Black father who dropped out of school seven years ago, to work and to go to school at the same time. The income maintenance will not allow the person to become wealthy or even to save anything; but it will allow the person to work, support his family, and go to school on some sort of reasonable terms. This is of the utmost importance. Title I aides receive neither the time nor the money from the job to allow them to go to school.

Finally, the new careers aide is allowed a certain amount of university credit for his on-the-job work. He receives two credits per quarter (up to a maximum of ten credits) for his work in classrooms or with out-of-school youth on the streets. This is a boost to educational goals, but it is also beneficial in other ways. The new careers program has made a systematic effort to reach all supervisors of aides. Money is available for special supervisory training programs. The teacher or school social worker is sensitized to the role of the aide and to the new careers concept. The teacher is required to make certain commitments to training the aide in the classroom. None of these advantages apply to the Title I aides. The latter do not receive university credit for their work and their supervisors are not involved in any systematic training effort.

As must be clear, the difference between Title I and new careers aides approaches an invidious distinction. It has caused considerable competition for the new careers positions and has created growing friction between the two groups. There is no doubt that the existence of the Title I program acts as a drag on the development of new careers. Nearly all observers on the scene are in agreement that the new careers opportunity should be available to all aides who want to participate in such a program. But the funds are not available. This situation is very much an artifact of patchwork funding procedures. Two sources of funding are pending to develop two types of aide programs; one would suspect that six sources of funding would lead to six types of aide programs, at least in the absence of systematic local coordination (usually impossible under federal guidelines).

The Career Ladder

The most important aspect of new careers portion of the Minneapolis teacher aide program is the development of a genuine career ladder. At present this is still in an embryonic state, but progress is being made. For those full-time teacher aide employees, there is a real likelihood that they can be the first individuals to acquire teacher certification by upward mobility through two or more non-professional teaching jobs.

The Entry Level Position

The entry level teacher aide position has been alluded to frequently throughout this book. As presently viewed by the Minneapolis schools, this entry level job is open to nearly any one in good health and willing to work on a regular basis.[4] The entry level job is designed so that anyone can meet its requirements with a minimum of in-service or preservice training. The ability of the person to assist the teacher in this position is largely a function of the aides' personality and innate ability. The formal expectations here demand little other than menial assistance with domestic classroom chores. However, a person's unique abilities (for example, in music) may greatly expand the aide's utility to the teacher.

Among the variety of people filling entry level positions in the Minneapolis program, the widest latitude of performance is probably given to the school social work aides. A combination of the shortage of trained school social workers and the diffuse nature of the social work job in the schools allows for the aide to move in and, with a relatively short orientation period, function as a social worker. Many of the most satisfied aides in the program are in these positions. By and large, they function outside the immediate supervision of any professional. In several cases they have the responsibility of an entire elementary school to themselves. They check in with their professional perhaps only twice or three times a week.

Social work aides visit families, check on truancies, follow up school problems, and are consulted by school officials in deciding school expulsion cases. In a somewhat specialized use of their talents, several Black aides have recently acted as mediators between the

[4] In fact, even regular work commitment has been observed loosely in Minneapolis, especially where the small number of American Indians are concerned. It is recognized that many Indians are not regular residents of the city; they are in fact seminomadic, drifting back and forth between rural reservation and the "red ghetto." Alcoholism has also been a problem. Yet the American Indian aides have been important people in school crises and in handling Indian youngsters. Their importance has encouraged the school system to be a bit flexible on "sick leave" for these new careers employees. This is precisely the kind of institutional flexibility that is required if new careers is to be the community link it is expected to be.

school and groups of angry Black parents in several "incidents," including the slapping of a Black student by a white mathematics instructor. One new careers aide has already become a consultant to the assistant superintendent on race relations.

Classroom Aides

Admittedly, the entry level classroom aides have nowhere near the latitude and responsibility that the social work or counselor aides do. Their present scope is much narrower. They do, however, work in a number of different capacities. There is also a clear distinction between elementary aides and secondary aides.

Elementary aides typically perform their role in the classroom. In helping in the classroom they perform a vast variety of jobs. Several lists have been made (in Minneapolis and elsewhere), but none seems really comprehensive. At the entry level, however, the jobs are typically limited to things that can be done under the teacher's immediate and direct supervision. Entry level aides typically would not take a class alone for longer than twenty minutes, except in a rare emergency. Interviews with aides in the Minneapolis program indicate that in the initial months on the job the aides' utility is limited to housekeeping chores and nurturant tasks.

Under "housekeeping chores" are a range of useful tasks from cleaning up the paints and brushes to helping prepare a bulletin board or display. There is no doubt that these jobs are useful to the teacher. A fantastic amount of teacher energy (relatively high-paid energy) is expended each year in simply keeping house for poorly disciplined and careless youngsters. This is in the nature of things; but the aide can very nicely fill the gap.

The entry level classroom aide also usually fills a nurturant role. Along with housekeeping chores, the supplying of nurturance to children makes the entry level aide role nicely continuous with the housewife-like role that typically is the most recent role of the newly recruited classroom aide. Like the housekeeping chores, the provision of nurturing does not require much, if any, training. Interviews with 30 new teacher aides in the Minneapolis program seem to indicate that these women were overwhelmingly oriented toward a nurturant role in the classroom. This is where they saw their utility to lie, and this is where they most certainly got their rewards.

But what about the men? If a school system is to recruit men to teacher aide programs, can men be expected to fit this entry level position as easily as the ex-housewife and mother? It seems clear that they cannot, and this creates a serious dilemma. It is vitally important to recruit more men, especially more minority group men, to teaching. New careers is an excellent way to accomplish this. Yet, the entry level position is defined in distinctively female terms: housekeeping and nurturance. Is there any way around this impasse?

The Minneapolis program has provisionally solved this problem by assigning most of the male aides as social work aides or as aides to counselors. In one case a male aide has been assigned to the coaching staff of a high school. But there is a major problem with this approach, and that is that these aide jobs are somewhat divorced from classroom teaching and tend to lead the recruits into community organization work and not into interest in a teaching career.

We would like to propose one other alternative that, as far as we can determine, has not been proposed elsewhere. This is to hire men into the schools as *administrative aides,* attached to the principal or assistant principal. The school officials are nearly as beleaguered by busy work as are classroom teachers. There are a vast range of jobs that could be filled by these male aides. Hallway monitoring, talking to parents about more-or-less minor problems, filling in for the teacher in the classroom when he is ill and no substitute can be found, looking after organizational arrangements for school events, or working on community relations are all jobs with which a weary administrative staff could use day-in and day-out help. In this way the male interested in new careers in the school could enter into such a program without having to serve an apprenticeship as a resident nursemaid in a first-grade classroom. In any case, it is vitally important that administrators of new careers programs think of imaginative entry level jobs that will attract males to careers in the schools. There is a real challenge in this area to which the previous ideas are no more than a partial response.

Steps on the Career Ladder

A genuine career ladder for teacher aides will develop a series of positions beyond the entry level job. Earlier we discussed various dimensions of the teacher aide role. This included distinguishing among technical assistance, supportive, and supplementary roles. Technical role performances are generally associated with the entry level position. Beyond the entry level the career ladder should, in general, attempt to develop two or more positions that would be defined as supportive roles with increasing emphasis on supplementary performances. Accompanying a change in function from technical to supplementary roles there should be an appropriate increase in salary and a change in status within the system.

At present Minneapolis has an embryonic career ladder. Beginning in the spring of 1968 Minneapolis had two career levels for its teacher aides. The beginning position is referred to as school aide I and has a salary range of from $2.00 to $2.80 per hour. All aides begin at $2.00 per hour and may work up to the higher salary through several different pay levels. An aide may stay at the school aide I level indefinitely, but after a year's experience and a certain amount of training an aide may move up to the position of school aide II. Promotion to this position indicates that the aide is ready to assume various types of direct teaching chores, although always under the immediate supervision of a certified teacher. Similar kinds of responsibility are given to social work aides promoted to the aide II level. The salary level for the aide II position begins at $2.30 per hour and runs up to $3.05 through six steps. In the first year of the program 40 aides were assigned to the aide II level, with 60 more scheduled for promotion during the past year (1969 to 1970).

Finally a third step on the career ladder has been developed in 1969–1970. This is the position of school assistant [5] which represents a further increase in job responsibilities. The salary schedule for school assistant runs from $3.20 to $4.40 and ten aides were promoted to this level in the fall of 1969. In general, this promotion is based on three factors: experience, capability, and the attainment of an A.A. degree or the equivalent. It is also worth noting that the money to pay these school assistants has come from local sources and is *not* dependent on federal programs, although all ten of the School Assistants were associated with the New Careers Program beginning in 1967–1968.

School Assistant

The specific assignments for the school assistant are still under development. Most of the ten new appointees to this position are or will be assigned to various emergency situations for the present year. But extensive discussions have been carried out about the long-term development of the role or roles to be associated with this job category. Most of these, however, are in the suggestion or discussion stage at the present.

One suggested job function for the school assistant is as a social

[5] The title School Assistant was chosen over the title Assistant Teacher in order to include a variety of nonclassroom positions under the general heading.

studies instructor in sections of inner city junior high classes. The middle years in school have been firmly pinpointed by numerous people as a watershed of academic achievement. This appears to be an even more decisive period of adjustment for poor or minority group youngsters in these urban schools. It has been argued that it is in the critical years of junior high school, so often ignored by education theorists, when many kids develop a decided alienation from the schools. Many do not regain an appreciation of education until a decade later.

It has also been argued that much of the substantive materials (novels, poetry, social studies, civics, and so on) seems totally foreign to the black or poor middle school youngster. This is partly due to the weak curriculum, and efforts are under way in nearly all sections of the nation to change this situation. But it is also partially due to the type of personnel teaching these courses. It is becoming more and more apparent that when studying man and his society one cannot separate the subject from the instructor, especially in the impressionable preteen period. Miss Jones, a white girl from a suburban home, will have trouble teaching poetry to a group of Negro inner city children. Even if she has heard of Langston Hughes, she may have difficulty teaching his songs of the ghetto or rural poverty to twelve-year-olds. She will probably have even greater difficulty singing Negro religious music or freedom songs with spontaneity. A rare middle-class teacher may be able to do so, but one should not expect such adaptability on a regular basis. These talents cannot be learned in an NDEA summer workshop.

Foreseeing these difficulties, Minneapolis has begun planning to use new careerists, promoted to the position of school assistant to teach social studies and literature to inner city youngsters. The structure of this program is extremely simple. The career aides will offer an hour of social studies three or four times a day. They will receive the children from regular social studies sections. They will continue to work under the general supervision of a certified teacher. But they will have wide latitude in the selection and interpretation of story or song or history lesson used with the children. The regular social studies teacher will continue to teach the more factual material of history, geography, and grammar. Ideally, the aide will work closely with the regular teacher. The aide can learn a great deal about teaching in general and about the substantive side of the subject from the teacher; at the same time the teacher may be able to learn a considerable amount from the aide about the local *society* in which he is trying to teach *social* studies.

Another new role that can be filled by certain school assistants would be that of tutor in the Adult Basic Education Division or in the Minneapolis Work Opportunity Center (WOC). These are both learning centers that share similar problems of curriculum and staff utilization. In both the night adult basic education program and in the work opportunity program the Minneapolis schools are trying to accommodate a range of adult, or near adult, pupils of widely varying ability. The "adult basic" program, like that of most cities, focuses on basic literacy training, plus general preparation for the high school equivalency examination. Minneapolis has made a special effort to individualize this instruction so that each student starting from a different base also proceeds at a unique pace. This effort puts severe strain on the instructional staff of the adult basic unit.

WOC shares some of these functions and faces some of the same problems. It is a unique educational center for high school dropouts (although pupils may go into the center directly out of high school classes) that allows boys and girls to take vocational training, to work part time, and to pursue basic educational subjects simultaneously. The basic educational subjects are taken at a pace amenable to the student. Minneapolis feels that this is perhaps their most innovative program and the one that comes closest to meeting the varied needs of low-income youngsters in one package. The center has an informal, almost homey atmosphere. Kids can smoke, bowl, or play pool during breaks from shop or classroom. Their movements are unrestricted between classes or training sessions.

The use of the school assistants, or some similar type of personnel, can be critical to the future success of both the new adult basic program and the new WOC. Pupils in both institutions have considerable need for personalized instruction. The design attempts to maximize the opportunity for the pupil to take basic educational work at his own pace. Pupils in both settings read at age levels varying from near total illiteracy up to tenth-grade levels. Instructional personnel can do only so much face-to-face instruction at the level of each pupil. Therefore, there is a concerted effort under way to find ways in which well-prepared aides can function as tutors in an individualized program of instruction. Aides in the new careers program are already helping out in the adult basic program by holding special study sessions and offering personal support and assistance to individual adult pupils. The aides also handle some of the grading and explaining of papers that the work of the center involves. It seems certain that some of the future work allotted to the school assistants will be group work in which small groups of pupils will help each other with study problems, all under the general help of a career aide.[6]

A third potential use of school assistants is as special instructors in physical education and athletic programs. The assistants could function as assistant coaches, especially at the junior high school level where there is some considerable shortage of personnel. They could take direct responsibility for certain athletic groups, such as the gymnastics or swimming teams, in which they have a personal skill. Very few junior high school physical education instructors have any experience (or interest) in all sports in the curriculum. Often they teach academic subjects on top of physical education duties. They are harried and badly pushed for time. Funds are limited for after-school work, and coaches are not able to provide much guidance or coaching in the time available.

The school assistant can fill an important gap here. Furthermore, these are the types of positions that may be able to attract and hold men to the field of education via the helping hand of a career ladder. The physical education field is the one thoroughly masculinized part of the educational area. It is also often the one area, as vast personal experience tells us, where the troubled youngster from a disadvantaged background can get a foothold into the education system. And beyond this, is the growing anger and alienation of a large group of black athletes in this country. It is basically true, even if a slight overgeneralization, that the world of top scholastic athletics in this country is to an alarming degree a world of black performers and white coaches. More black coaches must be found; and they can only be found via a new careers program and the imaginative use of career aides in high school sports. Thus, the use of school assistants in physical education has several things going for it, at several different levels.

There are many potential uses for the career aide or the school assistant (whatever title one prefers). Only three have been described

[6] We might note at this point that if things go as expected with the Minneapolis new careers program, some of the future career aides will be successful new careers recruits who have completed two years of college. Given the fact that about 25 percent of the current group of new careerists have started their education with some remedial work in the adult basic unit, it seems likely that some of these career aides will be actual graduates of adult basic education. This will certainly provide an empathy with the situation of the adult illiterate or poor reader not now found with today's adult basic staff. It has probably been several decades since anyone teaching adult illiterates has himself had the experience of being in this embarrassing position.

here. All three have been suggested as possible components of a career ladder in the Minneapolis teacher aide program. However, it should be made clear that the authors are reporting only discussions about future plans (for fall 1969 and beyond) that have taken place within the administration of the Minneapolis aide program. None of these are operational as yet, nor have any been fully cleared with interested parties in the school system. The previous comments are also somewhat infused with our own suggestions, because we worked closely with the Minneapolis program in 1967 to 1968. The preceding comments should be construed only as signposts to the future of the Minneapolis program.

Certification of Career Aides

On one aspect of the development of the second rung of the ladder, the Minneapolis program has received direct action. This is to advocate state certification for two levels of aides: *certified aides* and *career aides*. These obviously parallel the aide position at the aide II level and at the higher level school assistant position. An aide might be certified at either level, or might be certified first at one level and then, later, at the second. This system would provide official recognition of a change in status.

Thus far, no official action has been taken on these proposals to certify nonprofessionals. However, in September 1967, an *ad hoc* advisory committee was established by the Minnesota State Department of Education. This committee was charged with developing a plan for certification. After nearly nine months of meetings the committee came out strongly for certifying two levels of teacher aides, referred to as "certified aide" and "certified career aide." At first it was believed that the committee recommendations could be implemented directly by the state board of education. However, further inquiry has indicated that the committee proposals will have to go before the state legislature. This was something of a disappointment to "activists" on the Minnesota teacher aide scene. The activists wished the immediate development of new careers programs. But, in general, it is significant that a statewide group of educators were able to agree on the utility and the mechanism of certification procedures.

The certification procedure recommended by the Minnesota committee includes both work and educational prerequisites. Under the suggested plan an aide would be eligible for a certified aide status after one year of experience and the completion of at least 45 quarter credits of education. The person is to be recommended for the certificate directly by the supervising teacher and/or principal. In other words, a strong component of local control was assured in the certification of aides. It was not thought wise for the state department apparatus to become heavily involved in the mechanics of this process. By and large, the state department will rubber-stamp local decisions on aide certificates and maintain a general surveillance over the entire process.

Following similar procedures the state would also certify career aides. A career aide certificate would require 90 quarter credits and three years of on-the-job experience. The state will probably take more direct responsibility for certifying career aides, but a general policy of local autonomy will still prevail. For example, the structure of in-service training programs will be left up to local authority, and the definition of legitimate work experience will also remain local. As a general policy, the committee held that communities should have considerable latitude in hiring, training, certifying, and using aides. This goes along with a policy of decentralization in using teacher aides as an important component of the new careers idea. The teacher aide, certified or otherwise, should have an organic relationship to the community in which he works. Certification procedures should accommodate to this idea.

One other novel feature of the Minnesota certification plan should be mentioned. This is the provision permitting local school systems to provide some portion of the collegiate credit on their own school premises. This credit would be called Local College Level Equivalent (LCLE) and would issue directly from the local schools, independent of the colleges. This provision was added to meet two general problems. First, many aides will find commuting to junior colleges difficult and expensive, especially in the rural parts of the state. In a few remote districts commuting is simply impossible. Second, even where regular junior college attendance is feasible, the junior colleges are often not prepared to offer any specialist training for aides seeking a certificate. Although the general certification plan did not try to stipulate curriculum, the general feeling of the committee seems to have been that (at local discretion) certain kinds of specialist courses would be desirable. Most members of the committee felt strongly about a core sequence of courses dealing with educational methods and child psychology. This core sequence would be taken by any person trying to obtain a career aide certificate.

Why Certification?

Many people have asked the question, Is certification necessary or appropriate for nonprofessionals? Although the Minnesota planning committee ended in general consensus concerning the desirability of certification, this unanimity of opinion appeared only toward the end of the series of meetings. Many committee members questioned the entire proposition at the beginning, and some harbored reservations even at the end. Despite general support for certification by the NEA, the local representative of the Minnesota Educational Association had many misgivings about certification. For a short while the representative of the "union" (Minnesota Federation of Teachers—MFT) was actively opposed. The president of the MFT even addressed a letter to proponents of certification in which he raised many questions about the aide program becoming a back door to teaching and as a way of weakening professional standards. The several school principals on the committee all had many questions. One representative of the state department of education (which was sponsoring the hearings) had questions about the practical feasibility and costs of certification balanced against what he saw as marginal advantages to be gained from such a program.

Against these arguments a steady elaboration of the reasons for certification took place. These reasons tended to focus on three goals: (1) providing job security for aides, (2) systematizing the training of aides to provide for a growing pool of trained aides ready for the potentially large demand in the next decade, and (3) providing a financial and status incentive for low-income persons to follow a new career ladder into the educational professions. It was pointed out repeatedly that large federal appropriations for aides already exist and that still larger programs are intimated for the future. It was pointed out that future programs will dwarf current programs. The appeal of the teacher aide jobs to low-income adults interested in teaching careers was stressed at many points. Numerous witnesses before the committee argued the case from their position in the field. Several black teacher aides gave emotional appeals for recognition of the potential value of certified aides in ghetto schools. These presentations, it seems, had a distinct impact on the committee.

But midway through the year, word reached the committee of certain events outside the state. These outside events probably had as much direct impact as anything in changing the minds of the minority opposed to certification. Toward the end of its 1967 session, the state legislature of Iowa passed a state certification bill authorizing

the certification of teacher aides who met certain statewide requirements. These requirements included experience and education. Three
years of experience and two years of collegiate work were required
for certification. Although more severe in its requirements, these provisions were similar to those being discussed for Minnesota. However,
several features of the Iowa teacher aide bill were not to the liking of
the committee members. First and foremost, the bill implied that all
aides (who were involved in the classrooms) would have to meet
these requirements within a prescribed time. Second, these requirements were being imposed at the state level and would allow no local
variation or adaptation. The requirements seemed like a blatant attempt to insure that only middle-class housewives with some college
already to their credit could work as certified aides. It seemed to
work strongly against the local flexibility required by a new careers
program. It would be very difficult under the Iowa legislation for a
school district to use poorly educated, low-income, or minority group
persons in any kind of creative fashion.

Looking more closely at the events in Iowa it appeared to the
committee that what had happened should not be allowed to take
place in Minnesota. It seemed that at the urging of a small number of
conservative educators, opposed to the new careers idea, the legislature had imposed a certification law on a state educational system
still only marginally aware of the potential uses of teacher aides.
Local autonomy was ignored, and the possibility of local adaptations
to the education requirements was removed. Even if this was not a
conscious plan on the part of individual interests, it certainly had the
effect of "outlawing" the new careers concept.

The Minnesota committee was especially concerned that this sort
of thing not happen, either by chance or direction, in their home
state. They did not want a solution to the problem imposed by the
legislature that would set up a system applying a single standard to
the extensive variety of teacher aide programs. No member of the
committee felt that he could live with such a system. If certification
was to come it must represent as closely as possible the real needs of
the various school districts. The Iowa legislation was then the final
spur to obtaining a recommendation for a flexible aide certification
program.[7]

---

[7] A summary of both chapters 6 and 7 will be found at the end of chapter 7.

7 The New Careers Ladder: Educational Component[1]

The preceding chapter discussed at some length the problems of job development in the Minneapolis schools. It emphasized that the efforts to build a career ladder for aides in the schools is closely tied in with the development of local training facilities. It implied that the relative success of the Minneapolis program was due to the fact that both the Minneapolis public school system and the University of Minnesota were able to respond in a coordinated effort. It implied that similar coordination between schools and colleges will be a prerequisite of any successful new careers type aide program. This chapter will look at the specific changes made by the University of Minnesota

[1] This chapter was written with the close collaboration of Esther Wattenberg, Director of the Educational Component, Minneapolis New Careers Program. Mrs. Wattenberg is, in most cases, the architect of the ideas embodied here. Any error in these chapters is, of course, the fault of the authors.

that provided the educational component for the Minneapolis new careers program.

It was likewise noted in Chapter 6 that the educational component of the new careers program served a larger audience than the school system. Although about 75 percent of the aides were in one way or another involved in education, the educational component had to serve 9 different agencies in the first year and an expanded list of 11 agency programs in the second year. Although it will continually keep the problem of training teacher aides in the forefront, this chapter will broaden the discussion to include a description of the education offered to all the new careerists, including many in the public schools and some working in other kinds of new careers.

The inclusiveness is justified partly because any new careers educational venture will probably be aimed at a population broader than just school personnel. It was also true that in the Minneapolis program individuals shifted between school and social work agency with some considerable frequency. It is hard to pin down the new careerist in any specific human service area.

Profile of the Minneapolis New Careerist

The Scheuer program (new careers) in Minneapolis was a poverty program. It was originally part of legislation under the Economic Opportunity Act and, as such, was legally limited to low-income individuals. Recruitment to the program was based on a "screening in" process, in which qualifications were intentionally very broad, loosely defined, and geared toward an inclusive outreach.

The applicant simply had to be over twenty-two years of age, unemployed or underemployed, and the head of a household. Educational qualifications and previous job experiences were not considered relevant for recruitment. In terms of the career ladder, this had the effect of bringing aides in at several different job levels. Educationally, it produced a population of greatly varying ability. The latter was a major problem for the educational component to contend with.

In general, the recruitment program was designed to avoid what critics of new careers have called the "creaming process." This refers to a selective recruitment process in which only the poor are chosen who have special natural ability and/or past experience in human services. The use of highly selective techniques in recruitment typically results in hiring as aides only those who have middle-class values and life styles. This style appeals to the professionals, and at the same time the aides tend to identify very closely with the professional rather than the community or client population. A program that creams will encounter very little conflict between professional and nonprofessional, and it will find the nonprofessionals taking naturally to the idea of training for professional roles. A creamed population will likely value education much more than a noncreamed population. On the other hand, a noncreamed group is likely to have many individuals with serious deficiencies in basic literacy skills (for example, reading at the fifth-grade level). As a program that studiously avoided creaming, the Minneapolis new careers program was heir to all these difficulties. Many of them fell directly on the educational component.

The Statistical New Careerist

Some understanding of this heterogeneity of subject population can be gained from the socioeconomic data collected from the new careerists. This picture is by no means comprehensive, but it does give some idea of the background of a typical group of new careerists.

Table 7–1

Sex	Number	Percent	Dropouts	Percent
Males	49	32	20	43
Females	93	68	27	57
Total	142		47	

People were recruited to the program beginning in July 1967. The total recruit population was phased in by November 1. The totals in Table 7–1 then refer to all those who actually were members of the program. The second column indicates the similar percentages for those who dropped out of the program. Comparison of the 47 dropouts (those resigning from the program before June 1, 1968) with the total of 142 recruits gives some indication of the kind of person who will stick with the new careers program as organized in Minneapolis. There will be some delayed comments on the dropout population.

As of November 1, the program was about 70 percent female. Since that time, however, there has been a greater dropout rate on the part of women, thus bringing the percentages slightly closer together.

Teacher aides and new careerists also have children. When we are talking about new careerists, as opposed to teacher aides, as an isolated group, we are talking about people who are entering teacher aide work in order to have a regular job at which they can support a family. In the Minneapolis program all careerists are heads of households. Many are women who were on AFDC before entry into the program. Including men and women alike, the median number of children was three. The proportion with large families is obvious (see Table 7–2).

Table 7–2

Number of Children	Number of Careerists with Given Number of Children	Percentage of Careerists	Percentage of Dropouts
0	13	10	22
1	21	16	15
2	13	10	22
3	25	19	13
4	28	22	9
5	11	8	4
6	10	7	2
7	3	2	6
8	3	2	2
9 or more	2	1	0
Total	129		

The median age for the Minneapolis careerists was 34 with a rage of 22 to 50 years of age (see Table 7–3). This alone accounts for one major form of diversity with which the educational component had to deal. Many of the people in the program had been out of school from 10 to 15 years. And much of their early schooling had been of poor quality. The age range of the group gave rise to some considerable counseling problems as well. There was a cultural gap (probably greater than that much heralded gulf between middle and lower class) between young males in the program and the contingent of fortyish AFDC mothers. Many of the young men had criminal records, most of the women from AFDC had simply had a run of bad luck (usually bad husbands). These pose vastly different problems for the would-be advisor or counselor.

Table 7–3

Age Groupings	Number of Careerists	Percentage of Careerists	Percentage of Dropouts
22–29	38	28	47
30–39	55	41	26
40–49	31	23	23
50–55	9	6	2
Total	133		

The data on the marital status of the careerists indicates that there is a significant proportion of separated and divorced people in the group (see Table 7–4). Fifty-two percent of the group is in one of these two categories. This could have been easily predicted, as national data clearly indicate that family instability is a chronic concomitant of underemployment. This will be a factor with any group of low-income nonprofessionals.

Table 7–4

Marital Status	Number of Careerists	Percentage of Careerists	Percentage of Dropouts
Single	22	16	21
Married	39	28	28
Separated	25	18	13
Divorced	44	32	26
Widowed	6	4	10
Other	0	0	0
Total	136		

With a low-income recruitment requirement there were naturally many careerists with a history of having been on welfare. From the distribution of means of support in Table 7–5 it can be seen that the largest category was that of welfare recipient. Most of the others were self-supporting, although an informal check indicated that *virtually 100 percent of this population had received welfare*, either as an adult or as a child. This is probably the best indication of the social status of the group being served here.

From the standpoint of their educational needs, a most important statistic is their past years of schooling (see Table 7–6). In fact, the group had a slightly higher average educational attainment than expected. The median years of schooling was 12, with a significant minority of the group having had some college. However, the bare figures do not accurately reflect the quality of educational experience. Much of the education was some years in the individual's past. Some of the higher education appearing in Table 7–6 is credit received at segregated Southern colleges. A table can give only a very sketchy picture of the combination of educational limitation and personal worldliness found with this group. Many of these people had received a pretty good education, at least in the social sciences, from their experiences on the street.

Table 7–5

Previous Means of Support	Number of New Careerists	Percentage of Careerists	Percentage of Dropouts
Self-supporting	61	45	53
Spouse	14	10	8
Parents	1	.7	0
Welfare	50	37	34
Pension	6	4	4
Other	1	.7	0
Total	133		

Furthermore, although these people seem to have considerable education, they were in fact underemployed. This is another fact typical of those recruited to new careers program. For example, one man with three years of college was employed as a bus boy in a restaurant. Another man with one year of college worked part time as help for the park board picking up brush.

Table 7–6

Years of Schooling	Number of New Careerists	Percentage of Careerists	Percentage of Dropouts
8 or less	2	1	4
9	6	4	2
10	24	17	6
11	17	12	17
12	59	43	42
13	14	10	12
14	11	8	8
15	2	2	2
16	1	1	1
Total	136		

This is probably a good place to emphasize that satisfying and useful job opportunities are not automatically available for individuals just because they have some college to their credit. A Negro high school graduate can still (statistically) expect to make less than the typical white high school dropout. In any case, it seems clear to the authors that the new careers concept is especially suited to the underemployed, but relatively well-educated, low-income person—male or female.

The racial or ethnic identity of the enrollees is also an important factor (see Table 7–7). The new careers concept is closely related to the aspirations of the minority communities in this nation. The entrance to teaching for a large number of young Black adults (for example, 20–35 age range) could at this stage of their lives come only through a new careers type program. It is also through a program like this that many of these people can get a crack at the college education for which they had no chance as teenagers.

Table 7–7

Ethnic Background	Number of New Careerists	Percentage of New Careerists	Percentage of Dropouts
American Indian	11	8	19
Negro	33	41	45
Latin American	0	0	0
European Origin	55	40	34
Asian	0	0	0
Mixed (part Negro)	8	6	0
Other (mixed)	4	3	0
Total	133		

The Minneapolis program was very nearly half (49 percent) nonwhite. This seemed to be an appropriate figure for a metropolitan area that is only about 4 percent nonwhite. Perhaps the really important group was the 8 percent Indian representation. Minneapolis is one of the urban areas with a large Indian population. The income level of this group is significantly below even that of Negroes and their poverty of a near desperate variety in some sectors. Yet, it has been terribly difficult to recruit Indians to any antipoverty program. They are the most isolated social group in the Twin City area.

Although initial recruitment to the new careers program was promising, the sizable dropout figure (9 of 11 recruits) dashed these hopes. The Indian recruits were badly needed as new careerists in the schools. Two Indian men in their twenties who dropped out were both doing excellent jobs as social work aides. They were able to bridge a gulf between the Indian community and the schools, at least to some limited extent, in a fashion that was far beyond the reach of a white worker.

The enrollees in the program were also asked to indicate if they had ever been members of other antipoverty programs. The results indicated that most of the people had not been in any other program (see Table 7–8). This alleviated some concern that the new careers program was simply picking up the "program migrant" hopping from one OEO program to another.

Table 7–8

Response	Number of New Careerists	Percentage of New Careerists	Percentage of Dropouts
Yes	42	29	30
No	100	70	70
Total	142		

Summary Portrait

In general this picture of the new careerist reveals the enrollee to be a thirty-year-old individual, with children, probably divorced, and with some history of being on welfare. The statistical careerist is likely to have finished high school, but has been effectively blocked from meaningful employment in later years. In Minneapolis, the chances were about 50–50 that the person would be nonwhite. (In other sections of the country the proportions would probably reflect a large minority representation.)

But this sort of caricature does not tell us very much. In more human terms, the new careerist coming into the school system as an aide and into an educational program designed to make him a senior aide or teacher is an adult coming from a background reflecting some more-or-less arbitrary handicap (color, poverty). He is a member of that large one fifth to one fourth of American society that does not really have an equal opportunity in the educational system and that does not have any real economic chance to become a "professional." [2]

[2] To take the extreme example, ask yourself how many kids from families of incomes under $4000 could contemplate becoming a psychiatrist with its 11 to 15 years of higher education.

The new careerist is very likely someone who added to the disadvantages of poverty the additional handicap of early marriage and an unstable family situation. Some of the careerists were early college dropouts (due to early marriage) in a situation where there was no mother or father or aunt Maude to provide funds to support a small family and education at the same time. These were generally people who had done fairly well in school, yet whose education had never really had a chance to pay off. These were poor people whose talents and inclinations tended toward human service rather than construction work in a world where it is easier for a poor boy to get a job on a work crew than to become a teacher. They were, by and large, people who for good reason were not happy with their occupational situations and were looking for a way to break through the formidable barrier of middle-class educational institutions. In new careers many of the enrollees felt that they had found such a way.

The Educational Component

The training Center for Community Programs acted as broker for the new careers program. Working closely with participating agencies and the University of Minnesota it organized an educational program that would support the job ladders developed in the agencies. Specifically, in the case of the public schools, this meant a program that would provide the education for movement into several aide positions of increasing responsibility and also provide a possible springboard into the teacher training program itself. This curriculum also had to be designed with the special needs of this low-income adult population in mind.

Operational Goals

The philosophy of the Minnesota new careers educational component embraced several operational goals. All these were commensurate with the notion of a new careers ladder in education and/or in social work. The goals included (1) the provision of basic education for all new careerists at whatever level was appropriate, (2) the Arts Associate degree for all those capable of working to that level, (3) the provision of special courses relevant to the new career lines being pursued, (4) assistance to participating agencies in designing and staffing in-service training, and (5) undertaking counseling and guidance for this unique group of college students.

The primary concern was to shape a curriculum that provided

for the thoughtful development of the new careers concept but at the same time provided a maximum opportunity for the individual enrollee. To coordinate efforts in an assault on these objectives, it was felt necessary to keep the administrative control of the program somewhat independent of either agency or university. Under the stress of change either institution may try to impose its own interests on the program to the disadvantage of the enrollees. These institutional pressures may often operate in very quiet ways and seem perfectly reasonable from the limited perspective of agency or college.

Sources of Instruction

In reaching the program goals two major sources of education were utilized. The primary source of education was the General College (two-year institution) at the University of Minnesota with close assistance from the General Extension Division of the University. In the first year of the program both these parts of the University played vital roles. It was helpful to have a well-established junior college as the main support of the program while the General Extension program was available for experimentation with courses. This quite obviously made it possible to institute courses on a highly tentative basis (through General Extension) and to learn something about the feasibility of these courses before asking the junior college faculty to make adjustments in their program. The program was able to draw instructors from any source (liberal arts colleges, community, or professional schools) to teach these courses, thus assuring as broad a basis for experimentation as possible. The program was not locked into the relatively narrow framework of the existing junior college program or faculty.

The secondary source of education was the Adult Basic Education (ABE) program in the Minneapolis public schools. Most of the new careerists took regular collegiate courses in the General College (or General Extension), with course loads varying from 3 to 15 hours. However, a minority began their education in adult basic, with a third small group splitting their work between the university and ABE. The numbers involved in these three options during the first year are as follows (by quarter):

Adult Basic Education	16
Adult Basic Education plus One university course	23
University courses	145

Within the university program most of the students are enrolled in General College as registered students. This is true even though some of the students are taking most of their course work in General Extension. Nearly all of this General Extension work will transfer to the two-year degree. On the other hand, no restrictions were placed on the enrollees, who may in fact enter any college of the university for which they are qualified. A small number registered in the College of Liberal Arts (four-year program) and one was in the College of Education.

General College   The flexibility of the General College was an essential ingredient in the successful progress of the program. Without the cooperation and support of the administration and key faculty in the college, no breakthrough could have been made in the formidable barriers of higher education. Definite accommodations had to be made for the new careerists and full cooperation of a well-established college was important.

A number of factors helped to make GC receptive to the new careers idea. Even as two-year institutions go, GC, University of Minnesota, is exceptional. Once referred to as the nation's first junior college, GC is an experimental two-year program fully integrated into the University of Minnesota. This gives to GC the advantage of being a separate two-year college, yet allows it to operate in close conjunction with the resources (personnel and physical) of a major university.[3]

GC had its beginnings in the 1930s as an experimental institution widely heralded by progressive educators. The brainchild of Lotus D. Coffman, GC from the beginning tried to provide a quality two-year "general education" to students unable to attend a four-year school (Cremin, 1961). It was also seen as a place where students whose high school record was too poor to allow them admission to the Liberal Arts College might get a second chance. It has always had a general mandate for experimentation. This was renewed in recent years by explicit directions from the Minnesota legislature to begin to experiment with vocational programs that would be exportable to the growing number of state junior colleges.

[3] This is obviously not an advantage that many other junior colleges will share. The value of drawing on the resources of a university, especially its professional schools, seems so great that we would recommend that junior colleges involved in new careers programs have some sort of formal tie (where possible) with a larger institution. Ties with a teacher training institution are especially important for the teacher aide training program.

Perhaps more important than the general experimental direction to GC, however, was its admission policy. The college has long had a policy under which any student may be admitted on the signature of the dean. There are no rigidly held, formal prerequisites for entrance. College folklore tells of several successful students who had no more than a primary education (as did two new careerists). One 1948 admission with a sixth-grade education is now a prominent physician in Minneapolis. This philosophy fits beautifully with the new careers ideal. It was a very practical aid in getting admission to GC for the nearly 35 percent of the enrollees who did not have a high school diploma. About half these high school dropouts were admitted directly into collegiate work.

Another advantage provided by centering the educational component in GC was that the A.A. degree offered by the college has widespread currency throughout the upper Midwest. This is of a distinct advantage to the new careerist wishing to work in another part of the country or wishing to transfer his credits to another school. The credential offered by GC was considered an important part of the program. However, this might be a good place to note that disagreement over the importance of a "credential" plagued the staff of the Minneapolis program all year. This was simply a reflection of a national debate over whether new careers should play the credential game or should fight it. In other words, is a new careers program to try to help people get a meaningful credential or should it be a force to weaken the influence of the credentialing system?[4]

The argument reflects a deeper schism within the new careers movement, and one that has not yet been resolved, over whether the new careerist should be an aspiring professional or be in conflict with professional rigidities in the human services. This complicated issue will be avoided except to point out that the philosophy of the Minneapolis program was that an attack on the credential system should not use the new careerists as shock troops. Despite inequities and inanities in the entire system of professional education, it is felt that the more important short-run goal is to organize an education component that moves people along toward a credential as rapidly as possible. The new careerists seem to be the individuals who can at this stage of the game least afford to do without a credential. In Minneapolis, most careerists had no credentials at all. It was generally felt that if there was to be a campaign against credentials, it could better be led

[4] For an excellent presentation of the "antiprofessional" position on new careers, see Alan Haber's paper *The Political Content of New Careers* (1968) available through the Center for the Study of New Careers, New York University.

by individuals who had one or two degrees (for example, B.A. or M.A.) already.

In any case, GC found itself at a point in its own history when there was a considerable interest in mixing vocational programs with liberal arts work. Having a strong staff in various behavioral science areas, GC felt especially well equipped to innovate in the training of nonprofessionals. The General College has large departments of psychology and social studies, both of which stood ready to respond. Furthermore, GC had long had a series of practical courses of general interest, covering such subjects as "the law of everyday business transactions," "popular culture," and "home budgeting." These courses were often of direct interest to the new careerists. Almost all courses in the college were interdisciplinary in nature. All these things contributed to a relevance and lack of abstruseness that was appropriate to training adult students to work in the human services.

A final word should probably be said about a seemingly trivial point. This is the location of the college. The logistics of the day of a new careerist can be a difficult thing. Going to school half time put the Minneapolis new careerists under quite a strain in terms of time. Their schedule was very tight in time allowed to commute between agency and campus. The central location of the Minnesota campus helped a little on this point. Even so, some real inconveniences were encountered by the new careerist-student. As the year went on, it became apparent that the scheduling of classes needed serious study. Mothers with small children wanted early afternoon classes, men working with agencies where work tended to begin about 10 or 11 A.M. wanted late afternoon classes. Others needed evening classes. Others found it impossible to travel to the university other than early in the morning. This collection of personal schedule problems turned a trivial matter into a near crisis.

Many people, especially in agencies, urged that courses be offered in agency facilities, that the university travel out to the community. This was an attractive idea that could be justified on several bases: the needs of the students, the value of "springing" the university from its ivory tower, and so on. There is strong ideological support for this idea. And in many cases it may be highly desirable to break the university loose from traditional moorings. But the Minneapolis program decided against this policy for what it thought were several hidden defects in the idea, especially as it might apply to new careers.

First, research indicated that the new careerists, despite travel difficulties, took considerable pride in being on campus. The very fact of being in the regular university environment seemed to have a distinct effect on role definition. The whole idea of college work and a professional career seemed more real in this setting. Second, and more easily demonstrated, the quality of instruction was generally higher on campus. It was far easier to recruit teaching personnel for one on-campus class than it would have been to fill four teaching spots in remote parts of the city. It was felt that the educational experience of the new careerists and the experimental goals of the program were both served by keeping the great majority of the course work centralized on campus.

A final, more pragmatic, concern was that, unless each agency using a new careerist (about 30 different offices or school buildings) had its own class in each subject, there would be considerable rivalry and jealousy over where a particular class was located and when it was offered.

The Work-Study Program A grievous shortcoming of many new careers programs, in the public schools and elsewhere, has been the failure to allow sufficient time for education. Nearly all programs have perceived the need for an educational ladder to accompany the job ladder, but many have not been willing to recognize the severe costs of higher education—costs in both money and time. Time has been overlooked more often than money.

Early in the game, the Minneapolis program saw the possibility of severe educational pressures on the enrollees. Not only were these people taking on new and novel work roles but they were becoming part-time college students at the same time. This was seen as a major undertaking for anyone, let alone a low-income individual with no resources to fall back on for family care, baby-sitting, and so on. Many of the new careerists had three demanding roles: single parent, teacher aide, and college student. Solutions needed to be found to ease the pressure to some extent.

The major solution devised by the Minneapolis program was to assure that the half-time educational load be a full 50 percent of the person's paid time. It was equally important that within this paid educational time sufficient room be allotted for study. It was reasoned that the typical college course requires two hours of study outside class for every hour spent in class. It was further reasoned that most people who have gotten college degrees in this country have considered a full course load a full-time job. Middle-class kids have had their college time fully paid for by their father, or scholarship sources, for generations. These middle-class adolescents typically have much less outside responsibility. It seemed only fair, therefore, that these hard-pressed low-income adults have their study time (two hours per credit hour) fully subsidized by the program.

The final structure of the work-study arrangement was that the enrollee would typically take 6 to 8 hours of collegiate credit. He would then receive about 12 to 14 paid study hours that he could spend at home or in the library or wherever he chose. He would then work a variable 20 to 22 hours in the agency, depending on the exact nature of his university schedule. This would give him the total of 40 paid hours that the program called for.

It should be noted, however, that even these arrangements gave rise to severe pressures on the enrollees. There is something about having two masters (agency and university) at one time that seems to provide added headaches, even when the logic of the hourly schedule is worked out. An ordinary job in the human services will characteristically have very busy periods followed by periods of lull. In the busy periods the stress of the job tends to absorb large amounts of daily time (sometimes evenings, too) and will steal time away from education. Anyone who has ever finished a professional degree while working in the field can probably attest to this difficulty. It was especially rough on the new careerists who, by and large, had never had any great experience in budgeting their own time.

An Alternative Work-Study Arrangement Another solution to this problem that might have worked better would have been to stagger periods of work and periods of schooling on a quarter or semester basis. This is the kind of schedule that Antioch College has followed for several decades now and that has been instituted by several engineering schools, including the University of Cincinnati, which pioneered the idea. In this "cooperative" system the student goes to school full time for some period (one university quarter at the University of Cincinnati) and then works full-time for a similar period.

The original motivation behind this kind of program is to allow students to pay for their college education as they go. This would, of course, apply directly to the new careers idea. But far more important, at least as it was seen in Minneapolis, this arrangement would allow the new careerist to turn full attention to a new occupational role for a set period of time and then turn full attention to his new role of college student for a fair amount of time. The role strain is great for the new careerist, and it is this kind of flexibility that can make the difference between a successful educational experience and another major failure for an already troubled group of people.

The Counseling Program

A major component of any new careers educational program must be the supportive services. The idea of low-income adults breaking out of a cycle of poverty and entering higher education also implies a wide range of personal, social, and even psychiatric problems. Ordinary college populations are generally a "mixed-up bunch" (usually by their own admission), and there is no reason to believe the relatively unsophisticated new careerists will be any different. At the very least some of their problems will be novel ones (to college counselors) and will call for new strategies.

Personal Problems Chief among the problems unique to the low-income adult college student are marital and family problems. There are many married college students, and they do have problems. But all the new careerists had families, and nearly all had problems different in kind from the ordinary young marrieds. Only two examples should indicate the extent of these differences.

A large number of the participants in the program were "single" women with families, some quite large. The families in nearly all cases were a problem for effective reading and study. The growing children around the house made demands that greatly cut into study time. The homes were often crowded and noisy, with little peace and quiet until late at night. To a lesser extent this was true of the married men in the program. Seven had more than five children. This is, of course, the student's problem; the parallel counseling problem was to know how to help the person to deal effectively with the situation. There was quite a variance among the careerists as to their tolerance for this type of stress. Some seemed able to bear up under it and move ahead despite the rugged schedule. Others came near to giving up, and a few did in fact quit.

Counselors, most of them somewhat naïve to this problem in the beginning, had to learn when and how to guide these students in reducing course load or taking drastic steps to find study time. The first response was one of across-the-board concern. All the women should reduce their work! But it soon became apparent that only some of the students needed this kind of solution; others were (to some extent) actually drawing strength from their difficulties. In short, an entire range of counseling decisions appeared that were quite beyond the typical purview of college guidance personnel.

Another new problem in this tangle of family difficulties had to do with the fact that several people in the program lived in some real fear of violence from spouses, estranged or otherwise. The absolute quality of the fear and anxiety over physical threat had a way of reducing the student's ability to function in any capacity and forced this reduction without the usual neurotic symptoms. It was the latter that was quite new to the counselors. The problem was more difficult to perceive, not tied directly to personal psychopathology, and often a source of considerable embarrassment for the individual involved. This made it a difficult thing for the counselor to pick up and to deal with it in traditional ways. Several people dropped out of the program in circumstances that in retrospect indicate that violent family situations played a significant part. In at least one case the counselor was never aware of this problem until afterward.

The HELP Center   These are only two of the problems that made counseling this group a unique venture. Given these difficulties, the program was fortunate to be able to call on the already existing (one-year-old) HELP (Higher Education for Low-Income People) center in the Training Center for Community Programs. But one year of experience is not very much, and the staff felt that a great deal was learned during the second year. Early counseling and guidance had frequently been naïve and at points badly misdirected. The entire HELP staff was agreed that counseling low-income adult college students involved major adjustments in counseling tactics and a large body of new special skills. This was true without even touching the additional major question of how to use and interpret tests with low-income students.

Any program hoping to deal effectively with the new careerist as college student must make these adjustments. In most cases it would be well to give the counseling program some administrative autonomy from the main counseling program of the college or university. At Minnesota this autonomy was found in the HELP center. As noted above, HELP was developed to provide financial aid and counseling to low-income students at the University of Minnesota. It was co-opted into the new careers program and with additions of staff (two counselors, two guidance people, and one social worker) took over the major share of supportive services for new careers.

Academic Assistance   In addition to the numerous adaptations in counseling strategy just referred to, the HELP center made some structural innovations designed to assist the new careerists in entering higher education. These included a special university orientation program for all careerists and a separate registration process as a windup for this orientation. The new careerists were generally as naïve about the university as the typical freshman (or any outsider), but were further handicapped by time pressures and lack of access to the inside information about the undergraduate culture, as typically passed on by upperclassmen. The first registration session bordered on utter chaos. The new careerists had neither the time nor the conditioned indifference to tolerate the usual bureaucratic entanglements. The usual problems were complicated by the lack of planning time of a federal program; and some of the chaos was endemic to the special position of the new careerist student group. Without a special orientation and registration, 50 percent of the enrollees would probably have dropped out on first contact with the university. Things were bad enough as they were.

A second structural innovation of HELP was the development of special study or discussion groups for the careerists. The students met once a week in these voluntary meetings. The time was typically utilized according to the needs of the group or individuals in the group. Attendance was good and most of the time was spent on study problems, projects required in particular courses, and general discussions of the stresses and strains of new careers. During the middle of the year an abortive attempt was made to switch the sessions to nonvoluntary "ego-strengthening" sessions. This new tack included making the sessions required for all careerists. The attempt failed badly, in general running into massive covert opposition from the new careerists.

In retrospect it seems that while some careerists did need deeper ego-strengthening sessions, many did not. This was simply one example of the natural tendency of the middle-class staff to see the problems (which by this time nearly all students seemed to have) in subjective or psychiatric terms, rather than as a result of real environmental presses, like the threat of violence, chronic family illness, and so on. Careerists were perhaps only partly aware of this conceptual confusion on the part of the staff, but they nonetheless resented the psychological force feeding, and the ego development program was dropped at the end of winter quarter, 1968.

A third structural innovation was the systematic use of other (upper-class) students of low-income background as tutorial aides to assist the new careerists in their studies. Many of the careerists had been out of school for many years, and many found the large university a much more impersonal institution than anything in their past experience. The tie with an individual tutor, even if only for a short time each week, helped to bridge the considerable gap between the adult careerist and the rest of the students. It also provided some much needed help in studies from a person not totally different in status from the careerist. It was an opportunity for individualized complaining that even the study sessions could not provide. Although something of a hit-or-miss affair because of the great variability in skills represented by the student tutors, the weekly meetings often led to recognition of severe study difficulties that might have been ignored or rationalized until it was too late if the tutor had not been there and been oriented toward the study problems of the careerists. Severe problems were then sometimes taken to professors when under ordinary circumstances the careerists would have stumbled along on their own, perhaps even unaware that a difficulty existed. This again is a typical freshman difficulty, exacerbated by the role pressures suddenly placed on the careerists.

Curriculum Development

Of more central importance, but even less firmly developed than the supportive services of HELP, was the special curriculum designed for the New Careers Program. This received the major share of staff time during the year and is, of course, the critical factor in the educational component. No program will be worth more than its curriculum. It is extremely important in this early stage of development of new careers that systematic consideration be given to the appropriate kinds of courses for paraprofessionals in the human services.

For reasons that should be clear from the extensive discussion of the new careers concept and the commitment of the Minnesota program to it, the local program avoided the temporary institute or workshop concept of training. The goal of useful general education, combined with a moderate amount of specialist courses, was adhered to throughout. This education was offered at whatever level was appropriate for the enrollee. The specialist courses were the constant part of the curriculum. The enrollees tended to take the same special courses in education or social work without regard to general education level; in terms of enrollment in the educational methods course, for example, it did not matter whether the person was working for a high school equivalency certificate or was half way through a B.A. degree. Differential grading was provided by instructors keyed to the difference in background of his students. These special courses will be dealt with more extensively in the next section.

The basic sources of the Minnesota curriculum were

1. Adult Basic Education (Minneapolis Public Schools)
2. General College (University of Minnesota)
3. Special Courses offered through the General Extension Division, University of Minnesota

Adult Basic Education

These components were synchronized (via guidance from HELP) in trying to provide as individualized an educational experience as possible for the enrollee. On the judgment of the HELP center counselors, a few new careerists were referred to Adult Basic Education (ABE). Apart from the intrinsic value of the ABE center sequence, the staff had two specific goals in mind here. First, the ABE center could test and analyze the academic potential of those who were obviously [5] functioning well below college levels. Second, the enrollee could then work toward the level of basic literacy (and information) needed to pass the General Equivalency Diploma (GED) assumed to represent the high school degree in Minnesota. Although neither a requirement for the program nor a requirement for admission to the General College (care was taken not to hold back people already capable of college work), the GED does provide a meaningful goal and a meaningful credential for that 10 percent or so, for whom completion of even one year of college work seems unrealistic. It is quite common for employers (especially in service occupations) to require high school graduation even of the lowest level of employees. Whether this requirement is reasonable or not may be questioned, but solid manpower data on the upper Midwest indicated it to be true in the urban sections of the region.

Finally, the ABE program was seen as a possible preparation for later college work. Although the time limitations of the program (two years) oblige one to point out that not much time was left for college education after, say nine months in ABE, it was still felt that some ABE people could get a start on college credit under the program. It

[5] The *obviously* here refers to a literacy level decision made on the basis of a local comprehensive examination given by General College for which they have norms going back 30 years. The "comprehensive," as it is referred to in GC, gave good evidence as to a person's likelihood of success in GC (although a few chances were taken even against local norms); but the use of this local examination indicates one weakness of the Minnesota educational component, and this was the failure to attack the tough problem of devising (or interpreting) tests for low-income adults. More work should have been done in this area. Findings could then have been generalized to other programs. With this in mind, testing became a somewhat belated goal for the second year of the program.

should also be noted at this point that time was precious for all careerists. Only a continuous pursuit of college credits (without break) could produce an A.A. degree for someone who started the program with no college credit to his account. The staff was well aware of this limitation, and they pushed hard to encourage agencies to continue to subsidize the education of enrollees who continued in their employment after the first two years. The staff also lobbied hard, with less optimism, for the general extension of the program by the Department of Labor. In any case, no breakthrough has yet been reached, and it is obvious that the time handicap is greatest for those referred "back" to Adult Basic at the outset of the educational component.

Despite the reliance on ABE when appropriate, the program was conceived as basically a junior college program. Nearly all enrollees were urged to take at least one university or special extension course as soon as they could possibly handle it. The special courses, as just indicated, made an attempt to accommodate students with different levels of general ability.

Three Types of Collegiate Courses

Within the university program a major distinction was made among three types of courses. First, there were the regular General College or university courses that were open to new careerists on the same basis as to the other 36,000 university students. In the case of the GC courses, these were the richly interdisciplinary courses in accord with long-standing GC policy.

Second, there were a number of courses (increased in both winter and spring quarters) that were "sheltered" in the sense that all, or nearly all, the spots in the class were reserved for new careerists. In these courses, then, the careerist found himself completely surrounded by other careerists. In some cases these were regular GC courses in which special sections were set aside for new careerists; for example, a section of Oral Communication, a basic speech course, was reserved for careerists in each quarter.[6] The use of this kind of course was a subject of some debate and some very rudimentary research. At the time of writing, the general indication is that the differences among students is so great and the effect of sheltered courses is so dependent on the ability and personality of the student that no general conclu-

[6] It is an ironic afternote that subsequent investigation shows clearly that it is Oral Communication in which the new careerists by and large do their best in competition with regular undergraduates. Speech is the forte of the low-income adult student.

sions can be drawn without a more thorough research effort. Preliminary empirical findings do not, however, indicate any great performance advantage accruing to students in sheltered classes.

Finally, the overall curriculum contained as a third component the specialist courses organized as the backbone of the new careers preprofessional program. These courses, five at first, and later seven, were taught in the General Extension Division on a special contract arrangement with that branch of the university. These will now be discussed as the "core curriculum."

The Core Curriculum   In the Minneapolis new careers program there were three broad functional divisions among the aides. These divisions cut across agency lines and involved three major types of new careers. The three divisions are (1) classroom-instructional aides, (2) social service–counselor aides, and (3) corrections work aide. There was a core curriculum for each of these aide groups. Although this book is predominantly concerned with classroom aides (and other new careers in the schools) this section will look at the curriculum for all three groups. This is not just a pursuit of a tangential interest: school people were in both the classroom aide and the social service aide group, and several people doing correctional work were actually used in classrooms within state correction facilities. Therefore, a look at all three core curricula is quite appropriate. Teacher aides took courses in all three sequences, and all three are potentially relevant to the schools.

Each of the core programs has several things in common. We can break down the common components into four parts:

1. A social problem course adapted to needs and interests of new careerists and open to all enrollees
2. Two core courses especially designed for the career needs of the enrollee
3. Two credit hours per university quarter for the field experience gained on the job
4. A one-credit course designed as in-service training and to be developed in conjunction with the participating agencies

This gave each new careerist a basic core of nine required credit hours for course work, two credits per quarter for the on-the-job experience, and the possibility of two additional credits for special job-related seminars. The seminars could be taken no more than twice.

All the rest of their educational work, up to the A.A. degree that at least formally was the goal of all enrollees, was elective work. The

leeway granted to the student was in accord with the ideal of liberally educating people for the human services, with providing
flexibility for individual enrollee needs, and with the policy of General College.

The only course taken in common by all new careerists was the
course entitled Social Problems. This course was seen as a keystone
in the entire educational framework. The course was broadly designed to introduce people to the social sciences and to higher education at the same time. The course was taught by Caroline Rose, a nationally known sociologist and co-author (with her late husband,
Arnold Rose) of a number of sociology texts, including a general introduction to sociology for high school students. The choice of Mrs.
Rose to teach the course is an excellent example of the philosophy of
instruction followed by the Minnesota program. It was felt that in the
key core courses, obtaining solid, knowledgeable, and creative personnel was more important than a formal syllabus. The new careerist,
perhaps more than the typical college freshman, needed the stimulus
and guidance of a first-rate instructor.

Mrs. Rose adapted the social problems course from an already
existing sociology course at the university with several program-re-
lated goals in mind. These included (1) introducing the new careerist
to relevant social problems (not a very difficult task for people with
the background of the new careerist), (2) helping them to understand
and use social research and statistics (very broadly conceived), and
(3) helping them to develop skills of library use and composition by
writing a paper on a topic of direct relevance to their job experience.
The following is a brief catalogue description of the course:

> Social Problems. (Sociology 3) A survey of contemporary so-
> cial problems, including methods of social analysis. A major
> portion of this course is devoted to teaching the new careerists to
> research and to write up a problem relevant to their work. This
> course is designed to be of general interest to all new careerists.

Special Courses The programmatic development of the special
course involved the construction of two courses in each of the three
areas: classroom aide careers, social service counseling, and corrections. At the time this chapter is being written, these courses are only
experimental efforts. They have been taught for only two or three
quarters apiece. They are still largely on paper or in the proposed
innovations of the individual instructors.

The following brief synopsis can give some idea of the direction
of the special courses. An asterisk following the description indicates

that the course was actually taught during 1967 to 1968. The 1968 to 1969 program included all six courses, as well as a seventh, entitled Dynamics of Community Organization. The following are the actual course descriptions as presented to the new careerists:

Instructional Aide Courses

School and Community.° Intended for people working as educational aides, this course covers (1) the school as socialization process, (2) some limited introduction to modern educational methods and techniques, (3) the educational problems of special social groups, for example, lower class, middle class, Negro, white, and so on, (4) the role of the school in community change; and other selected topics.

Introduction to Educational Methods.° A general introduction to educational methods plus a selection background in (1) educational developmental sequences, (2) learning problems, (3) introduction to testing, especially the concept of IQ, (4) methods of teaching reading, (5) teaching number concepts, (6) introduction to social studies, (7) discussion of creativity, (8) new equipment (hardware) in education, (9) educational philosophy (nontechnical).

Social Service Counseling Aide Courses

The Helping Process and the Social Services.° This course includes material on (1) "the helping process," (2) problems encountered in relating to other people, (3) interviewing, (4) community resources for people in trouble, (5) record keeping.

An Understanding of Welfare and Social Policy.° This course has no formal description as yet, but it will probably include a brief *modern* history of public health and welfare problems, a description of past and present legislation, and a discussion of the social, political, and legal implications of this policy. Above all this discussion will try to make this history and legislation relevant to the work of the new careerists.

Corrections Aide Courses

Delinquency and Adult Crime.° This course will be an adaptation of traditional criminology offerings. It will include discussions of (1) concepts of "law and crime," (2) crimes of violence, (3) crimes against property, (4) "social" crimes, e.g., drug addiction or homosexuality, (5) juvenile delinquency, (6) organized crime and the rackets.

Courts and Corrections. Adaptation of traditional work in penology; but no formal definition of course yet available. (This was the only course not taught in 1967–68.)

Career Incentive Credit An earlier chapter discussed the possibility of using credit for the on-the-job experience as an incentive to help the person progress toward a degree or credential. The Minneapolis program tried to follow this philosophy by granting, as part of the core curriculum, two units of college credit for each quarter in which the student was a bona fide registered college student. This arrangement amounts to a kind of internship at the nonprofessional level in which the experience on the job, in the agency, or on the street is considered a relevant learning experience and is, therefore, worthy of collegiate credit.

The staff of the Minneapolis educational component was thoroughly convinced of the correctness of the career incentive philosophy. It was, however, perplexed as to how to implement the philosophy in an equitable and honest way. In short, how could it operate such a program so as to assure that agencies provided a meaningful work experience at the same time that the university staff refrained from doing what it could not do, intrude directly into agency operations? It was unclear how to supervise the program so that some persons did not receive credit despite little work or poor performance, while at the same time the staff not interfere with professional judgments of agency supervisors.[7]

The temporary solution to this dilemma took the form of five guidelines to the agencies. The agency was asked to agree in principle with the guidelines and to follow through on the various requirements embodied in them. It then became the function of the university staff to supervise the agency's implementation of the guidelines without becoming involved in any direct supervision. If the guidelines were met and certain reporting procedures were followed, the enrollees from that agency automatically received the extra credit (up to an individual limit of 11 credits toward the A.A. degree).

The first year guidelines were formally stated as follows: [8]

[7] It should be noted that agency personnel were quite sensitive to this situation and in many cases were opposed or ambivalent to the idea of university people being involved in their decisions. School teachers, perhaps because of the experience of student teaching, were more amenable than were social workers.

[8] These guidelines were not considered a final solution. Even as this chapter is being written, serious problems are arising that seem to demand an extension of the guidelines—or elimination of the "incentive program." First among the problems is the great variation in directed instruction given to the aides in the agencies. Some supervisors are very attentive; some are not. Sometimes the failings have to do with agency policy; other times they reflect the personality of the supervisor. In any case, a change of the guidelines was made. This change re-

1. Each enrollee must be assigned to a supervisor (teacher, social worker, recruiter, and so on) who has direct and face-to-face responsibility for the work of this aide. This supervisor must be aware of the nature of the New Careers Program and of the concepts involved. [Note: A general meeting of all supervisors for a workshop or a seminar would take care of this requirement.]

2. Each enrollee must be given a balanced exposure to all the aspects of the type of aide work to which he has been assigned (for example, classroom aide). He must be given a chance to perform a variety of jobs in the relevant subprofessional area. He must not be assigned to a single task and kept at it alone for a long uninterrupted period of time.

3. Every enrollee should participate in some kind of study group or reading program to be organized and supervised by university personnel. This will not be heavy work but consist mainly of discussion groups or a reading assignment closely focused on the enrollee's job experiences. A typical program might include two meetings during a month. [At present, work on such a program might be considered experimental.]

4. Every supervisor should set aside some short period of time (15 minutes) each week for regular conferences with the enrollee(s) assigned to him. This should be a time for taking up specific problems encountered during the work week. These problems might be technical problems, but might also involve problems of human relations, including the relation between enrollee and supervisor.

5. Finally, each supervisor must make a brief but specific monthly report on each enrollee to the university personnel. This report will be used in the decision as to whether the enrollee should be allowed credit for his work experience in that grade period. (It should be clear though that no gestapo system is intended; it is expected that, if the program is organized properly that every aide will be able to receive credit for his work in each quarter. These reports will provide a means of monitoring this system so as to assure that each aide

---

quires some type of regular individual meetings between the aide and the university staff to allow the university personnel to assume more of a direct teaching role. But it has not been possible to gain the cooperation of all agencies in this extension of supervision and the area remains filled with unresolved problems.

has carried through his part of the bargain and deserves
credit for his work. All grades will be on a pass-fail basis.)

As has already been indicated, implementation of this program
has had its difficulties. Chief among them has been the problem of
linking university supervision with agency supervision. The university
staff includes three part-time "field work instructors" who are the link
between the two institutions. Each enrollee is assigned (usually on
the basis of the type of aide work) to one of the university staffers;
and the latter has final responsibility for granting the credit. As the
guidelines indicate, this has been on an agency basis during the first
year, but plans for the second year call for the instructors (possibly
increased in number, or in time) to play more of a direct role in assessing enrollee performance. If this risks friction with the agency,
this friction seems like the necessary cost of a career incentive program that in the long run is highly desirable for aide and agency
alike. At present, however, the new plan does not seem likely- to
cause more friction than that already created by the university supervising the overall agency aide program. Some amount of friction will
be generated by any type of career incentive plan. Any program that
attempts to offer this kind of direct link between professional "shop"
and college class had best be ready for a certain amount of conflict.
The career incentive plan breaks sharply with established procedures
and role relations. Its implementation is a very sensitive task.

Building Institutional Relations

It should be obvious from the preceding pages that the idea of
education for new careers is a complex idea hitting deeply at certain
built-in rigidities of American higher education. It asks for changes
in the counseling of freshmen, for suspension of certain admission requirements, for a new approach to course offerings at the lower-divi-
sion level, and it suggests changes giving lower-level college credit
for field work in the human services. Indeed, this is only a partial
summary of changes. At Minnesota, as elsewhere, there were, and
will be further, resistance to all these changes. In some ways, new careers is an administrative nightmare. From the point of view of the
colleges it asks that they actually do something to help cure the dis-
ease of poverty, not just provide consultants for large fees or offer a
few new courses on the culture of the disadvantaged.

Given the fact that new careers is a proposal to actually change the structure of higher education, the problem of building institutional relationships and, most important, of building support within the institution becomes a major focus of attention. It deserves at least a few words here.

In attempting to build an educational component it is very important that critical sectors of the college structure be involved. One must go to the faculty very early. Substantial faculty support must be lined up, and promises of faculty participation should be obtained. However, it may not be necessary, or desirable, to stir up the entire faculty at once. It is probably sufficient to line up key personnel, especially department chairmen, who will teach or provide teachers for experimental courses. These people can be gathered together informally during early stages of planning.

Beyond the faculty (presumably, junior college faculty) it is important to seek ties with the relevant professional schools, for example a college of education. This is a more drawn-out process. Although the professional schools need not play any direct role in the training of nonprofessionals, they are important for a number of critical extensions of the job-educational ladder. First of all, professional schools must move to make their professional curriculum available to someone who successfully completes the two-year program. If the professional schools will not cooperate on this point, the two-year program may proceed in defiance of the situation, but it must recognize the development of a genuine job ladder reaching to the highest levels is now a lost possibility.

Another important role for the professional school is the systematic preparation of professionals to use aides. The professional school must make the presence of aides a fact of life in professional training and can even offer special courses in the various working relationships between nonprofessional and professional. It can also act as an important point of information dissemination concerning aides, new careers, and the many related problems. No institution is in a better position than the locally rooted professional school to help in the implementation of an operational job ladder for nonprofessionals in its area of service. However, in most cases it is the local two-year program that must make the professional school personnel aware of the need and cognizant of their responsibility. Thus, another round of meetings—but in most cases, very important meetings—between professional school staff and the architects of new careers programs is in order.

Summary of Chapters 6 and 7

Despite some ignorance on the matter, it seems clear that the development of an education component is every bit as important as the development of a formal job ladder in implementing the new careers concept. The two are logically and practically inseparable.

The Minneapolis new careers program took this proposition quite seriously. *Minneapolis tried to give equal attention to both job development and educational opportunity.* It had successes and failures in both areas, but in the last analysis there has been distinct progress in each area. The Minneapolis Public Schools developed the beginnings of a three- or four-step job ladder for new careerists. It was able to build on an already existing open entry and decentralized recruitment policy. The schools initiated consideration of certification of teacher aides at the state level. Finally, the schools made considerable progress on in-service training for its aides and participated wholeheartedly in the new careers program that now includes about 110 school aide personnel.

The University of Minnesota in a directly parallel set of actions began the development of a two-year training program for nonprofessionals, with special emphasis on the preparation of instructional aides. The university program involved altering existing admission requirements, adapting the basic two-year curriculum of the General College, experimenting with seven new special courses, instituting new counseling procedures (and a special counseling component) for low-income adults, and offering college credit for work on the job in human service agencies. Paired with changes made in the Minneapolis schools (and one independent private educational venture, Twin Cities Opportunities Industrialization Center), this marked the beginnings of a new career ladder in education for the Minneapolis area.

As any number of comments from the preceding pages indicate, the going was often rough during the first two years. Things may get even rougher in the future. Questions of supervisory responsibility between university and schools remain to be resolved. The need for and appropriate content of remedial education were not given the attention they merited during the first year and changes during the second year have not been fully analyzed. Ignorance of testing and evaluation (due to some unique local factors) was also a serious blind spot in the program to date, and has led to serious individual crises for a few new careerists who have tried to complete education beyond the grasp of their limited literacy skills. There were personal failures and administrative oversights. The potential for legal and even criminal involvements on the part of the new careerists was badly underestimated due to middle-class naïveté. The dropout rate was somewhat higher than expected (although significantly lower than the national rate for Scheuer Amendment programs).

Nonetheless, at the end of the second year (1968–1969) the staff of the Minneapolis program had a general sense that something important had been started. As one neutral reader of these chapters observed, the new careers idea seems both very radical and very practical. It is indeed, both. The new careers idea, especially as it was embodied in the elaboration of the educational component, is nothing less than an attempt (radical, if you wish) to overcome an age-old process of discrimination in recruitment to college, graduate school, and the world of the professions. It is an attempt, despite seemingly outrageous aspects like paying people to go to school (!), to give to poor or minority group individuals the full middle-class chance in education and the work world. It offers nothing more to these people than is regularly offered to intellectually able middle-class kids. It seemed to the Minneapolis staff and to us that no further argument is necessary at this point in history. All that is needed is to find a way. To find this way was the primary purpose of the Minneapolis program locally and the new careers movement nationally.

8 New Careers and Personal Change

Introduction

Of the three dimensions defining new careers, priority has usually been given to the problem of building a job ladder. In this book, two full chapters have been devoted to the general concept of career development. But this primary focus should not blind one to the existence of other goals, namely, the encouragement of personal mobility and the improvement of human services.

There is at present a serious shortage of empirical data concerning these latter goals. There are not even very much observational or impressionistic data available. There is nothing approximating thorough research on, for example, the gains in human service brought about by the use of nonprofessionals. At this point, it is simply assumed that there is considerable improvement in delivery of service, although some commentators, like social work teacher Sherman Barr (1966), have raised questions about the efficacy of new careerists in the human services.

In light of the general ignorance on the matter, the next two chapters will present some tentative data that bear on both questions. These are data gathered either on personnel in the Minneapolis new careers program or the broader teacher aide program in the Minneapolis public schools. In addition to presenting these data, attention will be given to the theoretical and methodological problems encountered. Chapter 8 will look at the question of personal change among new careerists, and chapter 9 will turn to an examination of the boost to teacher effectiveness provided by the use of teacher aides.

Personal Change among New Careerists

Individuals working as teacher aides, especially those in new careers programs, move into new worlds. In all cases they enter a new occupational sphere, and in many cases they are thrust into college or university settings. This typically represents a dramatic change of environment for the aide. Even middle-class housewives working in the schools encounter a new role and a new set of self-other relations in their work. The low-income person, with a varied background of AFDC mother, waitress, or perhaps even prostitute, may move through social light years upon entering a new careers program. A close working relationship with a teacher in an elementary school classroom, a college lecture hall, or a social work agency are usually quite foreign experiences for the new careers enrollee. His contact with these settings has often been a "from the back of bus" type.

It seems a common-sense observation that these environmental changes lead to new types of personal response and real durable changes in the person himself. It seems equally obvious that these changes will be in the direction of middle-class (and/or professional) behavior and will be advantageous to the person, in terms of social and economic stability. Yet, on a second examination of the situation, one is left with some very large questions. Just what is it about an individual that does change? Are these changes in basic personality and attitudinal characteristics? How can one describe these changes? And how might one plan for them in order to guide teacher aide programs in the right direction or to help an individual who may be left struggling between two worlds? What follows is an account of an attempt to deal with these questions within the context of one program.

Resocialization after Childhood

Sociologists have always placed great importance on socialization. In the past, however, this has usually meant primary socialization, that is, the process by which an individual is inducted into society during the prolonged childhood and adolescence common to modern society. There is often an assumption that this process is largely completed by early adulthood (Brim, 1968). Most socialization studies deal with people's experiences before they are 21 years old.

Recently a small group of sociologists have pointed out two things about this emphasis on primary socialization.[1] First, the position has general theoretical limitations in that important socialization experiences happen to almost everyone after childhood. Common sense indicates that some people change dramatically in personality, attitudes, or opinions after childhood, especially as they come in contact with new groups. Second, it has been pointed out that there is another factor that would encourage looking beyond childhood for socialization. In traditional society, whether it be tribal or urban, agricultural or pastoral, the amount of change after childhood may be minimal or may occur only in the few individuals who have experiences with foreign lands or exotic groups. However, in modern society many more people are affected by dramatic changes in their social milieu. Scholarships, travel, military experience have shifted many adults into strange new environments on a relatively permanent basis. There has been little counterpart of this in any traditional society.

Perhaps most important in adult socialization are what we have called "radical resocialization settings." This somewhat awkward phrase is used to refer to a large number of formally organized efforts by government and other institutions (for example, the church) to alter the behavior of identifiable groups in our society. Job Corps camps, Project Upward Bound, modern mental hospitals, rehabilitation projects like Synanon, despite gross differences, all have a common concern. They all intend to remake some aspect of primary socialization and to create a "new" individual in some significant way. They all share the intent to do this in part through the impact of a drastically new social environment, a sort of a controlled cultural shock. To these dramatic examples can be added a host of less powerful government training programs, community renewal projects, and community centers that possess aspects of resocialization settings without making this their primary goal.

[1] For further discussion, see especially Brim and Wheeler, 1966; and Clausen, et al., 1968.

New careers programs and teacher aide efforts generally fit this latter description. New careers programs like the Minneapolis programs (as described in chapters 6 and 7) have many qualities that allow them to be described as resocialization settings. Certainly there are strong implicit assumptions that the new careerist will adopt new behavior patterns and perhaps new attitudes as a result of working in a professional agency.

Yet—and here is the question posed by the present chapter— sociologists or social psychologists do not have much empirical evidence of the ability of adults to change in any capacity. Studies of conversion and other supposedly dramatic changes in adults have sometimes revealed that these changes are largely superficial and that the personal genotype of the convert does not change as much as it might seem. For example, a criminal converted to the church may continue his predatory patterns by conning the church; still later converted to a civil rights group, he may con the leaders of this group. Therefore, the notion of adult resocialization is largely a question at this juncture.

One must ask just how extreme the resocialization setting must be to bring about permanent change. Was the Minneapolis new careers program able to change anything fundamental in its enrollees? If so, what are these changes and how are these effects fed back into the program?

Major Dimensions of Change

There are, in fact, a wide range of important variables that one might want to look at for evidence of change as a result of participating in new careers. Much sociological literature has been devoted to the importance of values, motivation, self-concept, attitudes, opinions and beliefs, occupational aspiration, and other variables. In doing a small study on changes in new careerists it was impossible to deal with all these variables.

The selection of variables for study was made around one major theoretical orientation to the socialization problem, that usually referred to as symbolic interactionist, or Meadian (after its major proponent, the social philosopher and early social psychologist G. H. Mead.) The symbolic interactionist orientation places major importance on the *responses of others* (especially important, or prestigious, others) that an individual encounters. It stresses *contemporary* social influences (for example, an approving audience or an angry wife) as far more important, especially when cumulative (for example one's wife is *always* angry), than biological factors or early childhood experience (see Strauss, 1964).

Symbolic interactionist theory has had many advocates and has taken many different directions in recent years (Meltzer, 1968; Rose, 1962). There has been an ambitious attempt to formalize parts of the theory and to apply empirical tests to deductions from it. We rely heavily on one such model that stresses the importance of self-concept for changes in behavior and, in turn, emphasizes the responses of others as having major influences on the self-concept. The most succinct work in this area is that provided by Kinch (1963) in a tight set of four interlocking propositions. These propositions are as follows:

> 1. The individual's self-concept is based on his perceptions of the way others are responding to him.
> 2. The individual's self-concept functions to direct his behavior.
> 3. The individual's perception of the responses of others toward him reflects the actual responses of others toward him.
> 4. The behavior that the individual manifests influences the actual responses of others toward that individual.

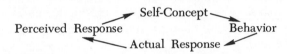

Our research focused especially on the first two propositions: (1) that greatly changed responses of others can change self-concept, and (2) that changed self-concept can change the person's behavior. In particular, the research attempted to see if experience in working as a teacher aide in a new careers program would influence the self-concept of the aide, and whether this change in self-concept would be related to changes in behavior or intended behavior. Two particular behavior patterns were singled out as important for new careers—occupational mobility and role orientation.

The new careers program provided an excellent opportunity to test both the theoretical problems associated with adult resocialization and the particular impact of the new careers program on its Minneapolis enrollees. We were on the scene at the very beginning of the program (August 1967) so that each new careerist could be given a questionnaire before entering the program and then could be tested at several later points in time. Changes in self-concept were assessed along with similar changes in behavior. Some of the findings will be reported in the concluding section of this chapter. Findings in regard to changes will refer to changes over approximately nine months from August 1967 to June 1968.

The Case of Myrtle

The stimulation to do more thorough research into the changes wrought by new careers programs derives in part from the nearly universal perception that teacher aides and other recruits to progressive new careers programs do undergo all sorts of changes. Changes in dress are common observations, as are changes in mannerisms and everyday speech habits. Among male new careerists, ties and suits appear with great flourish after several months of the program. Women teacher aides from low-income situations are usually quite easily distinguishable from teachers in the first week of the program. The aides wear flashier dresses, heavier lipstick, and flat shoes in contrast to the more conservative attire of the teacher. Few female aides have (or wear) suits at the beginning of the program. After a few months the distinctions between aide and teacher are much more difficult to see, and aides are often seen in suits and heels.

These stylistic changes may be partly a function of the increased income for the aide (although the basic increase, over, say, AFDC payments, is not that great), but it does not seem reasonable to attribute all the changes to increased affluence. The changes in language and mannerisms are not attributable to a slightly increased weekly income. They are more likely the result of aides imitating the role model provided by the teacher and other school personnel. Very likely this type of role modeling precedes any deeper change in attitude or behavior.

In addition to general impressions, the existence of a few dramatic and singular cases affirms the probability of radical change, at least for some new careerists. One such example, by no means unusual, from the Minneapolis program is the case of Myrtle. By any standards, Myrtle is a somewhat ordinary person whose main importance is, however, that her life changed direction abruptly in apparent response to her experience in the Minneapolis new careers program.

Myrtle entered the teacher aide program at the age of 34. Her father was a factory worker who had had a steady income sufficient to send Myrtle to a private parochial school. But Myrtle dropped out of school while still in her junior year in order to marry a man nine years older than herself. By the time she was 21 she had 3 children. She was divorced (after being deserted) 2 years later when only 23. Despite an adequate basic education and a family of at least lower-middle-class standing, Myrtle was at this point directly behind the economic eight ball. Myrtle had an IQ of over 120, but the idea of going to college could only be a bad joke. She had 4 kids to support and had very little training that would allow her to support them. College could not be a viable goal or source of motivation for her.

At this point she began working at a series of low-paying and uninspiring jobs. Only one job had any particular appeal to her. This was clerking in a pet store. She was especially fond of animals, and while working in the store (a job she eventually gave up when she could not make ends meet and had to go back on welfare) took the opportunity to become familiar with many different types of animals and their care.

By the time Myrtle entered the teacher aide program some three years later, she had most of the characteristics of the welfare mother. Alternating back and forth between welfare and a series of dull unstable jobs she had little faith in herself and little hope for the future. She was not destitute but she could see little possibility of getting out from beneath the burden of small debts and financial pressures. There was not the slightest possibility that she would be able to finance her four children to a college education; she could not even provide them the private school education she had dropped out of. Like many AFDC mothers she generally thought of herself as below average in intelligence (definitely not true in her case), lacking in self-confidence (very true), and ineffective in most of the things that mattered to her.

Myrtle took the teacher aide job partly because it payed a steady dependable wage (only slightly above welfare rates, however) and provided the astonishing possibility of going to college. A year of education was undoubtedly important for Myrtle, but as an example of resocialization the effects of certain experiences in the classroom seem more dramatic. In the classroom she had, at first, been given a variety of housekeeping chores and some personal responsibility for individual tutoring with reading problems. Her teacher noted that Myrtle's capability increased over the first few months, but it was not until a field trip to a farm that the teacher recognized anything special about Myrtle. On the farm Myrtle was able to provide a great deal of information for the students about the various animals. She clearly was better informed than the teacher and assumed the instructor's role.

After this the teacher noticed a marked increase in Myrtle's self-confidence. This had the reciprocal effect of getting the teacher to allow Myrtle considerable responsibility for teaching the children about animals and other science topics. The teacher was somewhat uninterested in science, and Myrtle nicely complemented the teacher. Myrtle participated more and more in classroom activities.

At the end of the year Myrtle did something that she had toyed with for the past five years. With a friend of similar interests she applied for a Small Business Administration Loan to open a pet farm. With the help of references from school personnel, plus about 12 hours of college credit with passing grades, Myrtle was able to acquire the loan and embark on another new career.

The added work experience, the references, and the college credit were obviously of some importance here. But they were certainly secondary to basic changes in Myrtle herself. She seemed to think of herself in a much different light and had a considerably improved attitude toward her own competence. These changes seem unambiguously related to her experiences as a teacher aide. She could probably have obtained her business loan any time during the past five years, but she had thought the business responsibilities beyond her. Indeed, without the changes of the past year the job might have been too much for her and might have ended in another failure.

Methods of Data Collection

How typical is Myrtle's case? A look at some of the project's research can provide some idea. The following is a brief, nontechnical discussion of the research methods used in assessing personal change in the new careers recruits.[2]

Self-Concept

The theoretical discussion of change in recruits has focused on self-concept as a key variable. *Self-concept* can be defined as the *verbal description a person attributes to himself as a person in a particular role*. This definition focuses attention on the way in which a person perceives himself or describes himself. Now, this is a somewhat complex concept that cannot be exhausted here, but at least it can be noted that the English language provides two ways for a person to conceptualize himself. The first is through the use of nouns. The second is through the use of adjectives. A person thinks of himself as a father, but he may also think of himself as intelligent, sophisticated, and so on. Formally, of course, an adjective modifies a noun by adding certain qualifications; therefore, the two verbal references are quite often tied together (Falk, 1966).

---

[2] More comprehensive reports of this study, including data on long-term (two-year) changes, will be reported in later publications.

A thorough study of changing self-concept will look at both nouns and adjectives used in self-descriptions. However, the present study has for a number of reasons supplied the noun by way of a role designation ("teacher aide") and then asked the person to describe his performance while in that role (see Table 8–1). All subjects were in fact teacher aides, and we were especially interested in the way in which self-concept might change in relation to the occupational context.

Table 8–1 Self-concept Inventory

On this page we are interested in knowing how you would evaluate *yourself* on the following descriptive adjectives. Remember this is how *you* see yourself. If you find it difficult to rate yourself on an adjective because you do not ordinarily think of yourself in these terms, circle the "x" at the far right of that adjective. Regard the middle of the scale as average for teacher aides. Circle the appropriate number.

Adjectives	Most			Aver-age		Least		I Do Not Think of Myself in Terms of This Adjective
1. Intelligent	7	6	5	4	3	2	1	x
2. Self-confident	7	6	5	4	3	2	1	x
3. Selfish	7	6	5	4	3	2	1	x
4. Mature	7	6	5	4	3	2	1	x
5. Physically attractive	7	6	5	4	3	2	1	x
6. Leadership	7	6	5	4	3	2	1	x
7. Friendly	7	6	5	4	3	2	1	x
8. Aggressive	7	6	5	4	3	2	1	x
9. Honest	7	6	5	4	3	2	1	x
10. Cooperative	7	6	5	4	3	2	1	x
11. Talkative	7	6	5	4	3	2	1	x
12. Foolish	7	6	5	4	3	2	1	x

Focusing, then, on a person's description of himself when compared to others of his occupational group, self-concept was measured by use of the Self-concept Inventory. The inventory (see Table 8–1) consists of a list of 12 adjectives, which the individual is to apply to himself using a 7-point rating scale following each adjective. The subject rates himself on each adjective in comparison with others of his occupational group, in this case teacher aides.

The technical details of the inventory are reported elsewhere (Falk, 1966). It is sufficient to point out here that the inventory compares favorably with all other similar instruments, including the well-known semantic differential technique. It has a very high reliability. It is also clear that all 12 adjectives are *independent* of each other, something that has not been demonstrated for several other self-concept scales. Each adjective has some importance of its own, and rating on one cannot validly be combined with the rating on another.

Another major characteristic of the scale is that it is thought to be exhaustive of the kinds of adjectives used in self-concepts. The adjectives were selected on the basis of those volunteered by a wide sample of respondents. Preliminary tests gave subjects the chance to add adjectives that they considered personally relevant but that did not appear in the scale. In all cases, added adjectives were found to correlate highly with those already in the scale and, therefore, did not need to be included because they provided no new information.

Behavioral Measures

In the just mentioned theory, self-concept is directly related to behavior. Many significant changes in behavior are said to be related to changes in self-concept. Two behavioral areas of great interest to new careers programs are occupational mobility and role performance. It must be immediately recognized that any measures of these behaviors will be according to *reported* behaviors given on questionnaires. This is less than perfect as a measurement technique, and its limitations should be recognized; however, it really is nothing to apologize for. Nearly all sociological studies deal with reported behaviors rather than with actual behaviors (for example, one's *intended* vote rather than one's *actual* vote,) (Biddle and Thomas, 1966).

Mobility orientation was the most salient behavioral variable. As noted in several earlier chapters, individual mobility on the part of enrollees is a major goal of new careers. Basic changes in self-concept (or other personal characteristics) are only important to new careers if they produce social mobility.[3]

Mobility is defined as the future educational and occupational aims of the respondent. A number of questions were asked each new careerist concerning his future hopes and aspirations. A more com-

---

[3] The necessary relation between mobility and self-concept can probably be put quite definitively, despite the fact that a few radical advocates of new careers have attacked the middle-class bias that says the individual is to pursue middle-class goals. Middle-class goals do not have to be embraced in total commitment for one to hope that occupational mobility will come from new careers. The recent status of many new careerists is that of welfare recipient, and only a few would advocate that they remain in this status.

plex form of analysis may eventually come out of this collection of data, but for preliminary purposes the responses to several questions were summarized to yield a simple two-point scale for each item: upwardly mobile or nonmobile. Any new careerist would fit into one of these categories. Beginning with the consensual validity (as established by a group of judges) of these items, the relevant mobility items were found to yield high reliability scores in a pretest conducted on nonnew careers aides. Despite the simplicity of the procedures, we felt that the scores gave a good indication of the future occupational intentions of the respondents.

The second major behavioral measure is that of *role performance*. It has already been noted that there have been strong criticisms of new careers on the basis that teacher aides, welfare aides, and so on overidentify with the professional and forget the client.

This proposition holds that the new careerist at first sees his role as different from the professional in that he is a bridge to the community and can expand the effectiveness of professional services by changing their (middle-class) nature. The critics, however, claim that within six months the new careerist wishes to perform the same role as the professional and rejects his unique role in relating to the community (Barr, 1966). In fact, it is implied by one critic that new careerists may soon reject the community more than does the professional. Aides, the argument goes, are on the move and have more to lose by their identification with the old neighborhood and groups than does the professional.

We made a preliminary attempt to research this question. But a basic dilemma must be pointed out. The new careers goals generally push the recruit toward middle-class behaviors and attitudes and at the same time the goals demand that the new careerist should remain sufficiently "lower class" to act as a bridge between agency and community. Perhaps, this asks the new careerist to make a subtle distinction between right and wrong middle-classicisms that would be beyond his ability.

There is no simple answer to this question. We are convinced that the general answer is for new careerists to use their knowledge and empathy for the community at the same time that their own educational and economic goals become higher. In fact, it seems clear that some new careerists will move far in the direction of adopting the professional role, and others, perhaps equally interested in personal advancement, will choose to remain close to the community.

Similar to the scheme used with mobility aspiration, a set of diverse items was developed that seemed to cover a number of different perspectives on role orientation in a new careers position. The items attempted to pose a variety of questions that allowed respondents to choose between a professional and a community orientation. Although these two orientations may not always be mutually exclusive, it was thought that a number of diverse items might pick up any underlying tendency for the careerists to move in one direction or the other over time. All items were set up in such a way as to allow responses to be coded into two categories, *professional role orientation* or *community role orientation* (see Table 8–2). Each respondent was classified as *professional* or *community* oriented on each item. The questions, as well as original classifications, were developed on the basis of limited pilot work with regular teacher aides.

Table 8–2 Role Orientation Items: Professional versus Community Role Orientation

Item	Percent Professional Orientation before	Percent Professional Orientation after	p = Value of Change
7. What is the most important characteristic for a new careerist?[a]	55	56	not significant
8. A new careerist should be a semiprofessional?	62	70	$p < .20$
9. The new careerists are usually the most concerned persons in their neighborhood?	30	47	$p < .025$
10. New careerists are usually different from other poverty residents?	20	21	not significant
11. New careerists have more understanding of poverty than do professionals?	49	25	$p < .001$
12. I consider myself a professional worker.	21	35	$p < .01$
13. I would not like to be a supervisor.	69	58	$p < .05$

[a] The categorization of responses to this question took the form of coding answers to an open-ended question.

Findings

As in many preliminary studies, the results of the research on personal change in new careers recruits yielded fruitful, but at points inconsistent, findings. Some of the hypotheses were borne out, some were not; and some of the findings seem contradictory. However, at the very least they are instructive for future work in this area.

Self-concept

Changes in self-concept were studied for two independent groups, new careerists and regular teacher aides. In that the new careers program embodied more distinct changes for its recruits, as well as being more inclusive of their time, our original hypothesis was that although both groups would change in self-concept, the new careers recruits would show greater and more consistent change.

In fact, just the opposite occurred. Both groups did change in self-concept (see Table 8–3). But the regular teacher aides showed the far greater change and were likewise more consistent in the pattern of change. As the summary table (Table 8–3) indicates, the regular teacher aides changed dramatically on all 12 adjectives in the Self-concept Inventory. The changes were statistically significant in all cases. The new careers recruits, despite the radical changes in their environment, did not show this degree of change.

The new careers recruits changed markedly on only three adjectives, with marginal group change on four others.[4] The distinct change occurred on *mature, aggressive* (the people saw themselves as more aggressive), and *talkative,* not perhaps the most obvious dimensions for self-concept change. If there is a pattern in these findings on self-concept, it is that the new careerists seem to have changed in the direction of higher self-concept ratings on dimensions that are not typically approved or encouraged (for example, talkative) by supervisors. We speculate that this change was because of the frequent encounters with professionals and agency personnel who were less talkative than the aides. Comparison with the new reference group led the aides to see themselves as more socially aggressive at the later date. It was also true that one of the negative stereotypes of the aides, as seen by professionals, was that they were overly aggressive. The new careerists may have caught a good bit of feedback to this effect.

---

[4] A p-value of $p > .10$ was taken as a cut off point. For those unfamiliar with statistics, this roughly means that if one asserts that there has been a real change in self-concept, he will be wrong only about one in ten times. Three cases met this criteria; the four marginal cases had p value of $p > .20$.

The contrast of the regular teacher aides to the new careerists was startling. The former group showed marked overall change in self-concept. The group change was significant on every one of the 12 items. Of the half dozen or so studies done using the inventory, this is the most striking group change recorded to date.

Table 8–3 Mean Change Scores on Self-concept Inventory for Teacher Aide Recruits and New Careers Recruits

Adjective	Mean Change	Value
Teacher Aides (N = 31)		
Intelligent	1.19	$p < .001$
Self-confident	1.19	$p < .001$
Selfish	1.09	$p < .01$
Mature	.78	$p < .001$
Physically attractive	1.35	$p < .001$
Leadership	1.09	$p < .001$
Friendly	.93	$p < .001$
Aggressive	1.51	$p < .001$
Honest	1.05	$p < .001$
Cooperative	.96	$p < .001$
Talkative	1.16	$p < .001$
Foolish	1.29	$p < .001$
New Careers (N =)		
Intelligent	.02	not significent
Self-confident	.08	not significant
Selfish	−.19	$p < .20$
Mature	.26	$p < .025$
Physically Attractive	−.05	not significant
Leadership	.18	$p < .20$
Friendly	−.08	not significant
Aggressive	.17	$p < .10$
Honest	.04	not significant
Cooperative	−.12	$p < .20$
Talkative	.25	$p < .01$
Foolish	−.11	$p < .20$

Why is it that the regular aides changed, whereas the new careerists did not change so dramatically? Looking at the findings in light of the theoretical model just presented provides a reasonable but *post hoc* explanation. It is true that the new careerists were entering a more changed environment. But what is not clear is just what the quality of the responses of others was in this environment. It had been assumed that the important people in the world of the new careerists would respond positively to the professional efforts and the educational struggles of the careerists. Even before these data were in, it became clear that the reception of the new careerists was, in fact, spotty and inconsistent. Not all supervisors or college instructors were reinforcing the recruits: some opposed the new careers idea, and a few were openly hostile to new careerists.

On the other hand, many new careerists were making great changes in their own work patterns, achievement levels were consciously being lifted, and a few recruits floundered beyond their depths before getting readjusted. The new careerists were under a time pressure and a work schedule totally foreign to most of them. Their own expectations, built up by the program staff, were frequently beyond reach, especially within the first months of the program. An example of this was the widespread but unanticipated educational aspiration that was generated by the program. Almost uniformly the new careerists evidenced expectations of completing a college program in less time than could reasonably be expected. This somewhat surprised the program staff, which was geared for resistance to college courses on the grounds of irrelevancy and inconvenience but which instead found overexpectation a more serious problem.

All these factors are probably reflected in the failure of the new careers recruits to show a major change in self-concept. It appears that although there were many favorable responses to the new careerists during the first year, there were repeated and systematic negative and deprecatory encounters (some "deserved" by the new careerists; others, more arbitrary) during the year. These negative encounters undoubtedly did much to balance the positive and self-enhancing encounters.

Role Orientation

The seven role items yielded inconsistent but interesting findings. As just indicated, pilot work seemed to indicate that all the items were related to role orientation. One would, therefore, expect some low degree of correlation among them. In fact, however, changes took place on nearly all items, but these changes were alternately in the professional or community directions (see Table 8–2). At first glance the results seem blatantly contradictory.

But the contradiction is probably more in the a priori interpretation of items by the investigator than in the actual pattern of response. As Table 8–2 indicates, the respondents show a strong tendency to change their attitude in the direction of greater professional orientation on the items that call directly for an espousal of a professional or semiprofessional title. At the later date (June 1968), they are more likely to use these occupational terms to describe themselves or their aspirations than in August (1967). For example, there is an increase from 21 percent to 35 percent in the number who are willing to call themselves a "professional worker."[5]

At the same time, two items (11) and (13) that relate more closely to the workaday world of the new careerists seem to reflect increased community orientation over time. There is a gain of 24 percent in the proportion of aides who feel that "new careerists have a greater understanding of poverty than professionals," and there is an increase in the number of aides who would not like to be a supervisor, thus seeming to indicate a desire to stay on the firing line.

These items probably do reflect a growing commitment to community affairs, but a type of commitment not inconsistent with the symbolic acceptance of professional status. In summary, the findings seem to reflect a growing awareness of the difficulty of the professional's job, accompanied by a parallel increase in the confidence that the recruit can aspire to the professional's job.

Item 9 becomes something of a "swing" item in this picture. This item asked whether the respondent thought that the "new careerists were the most concerned people in their neighborhoods." In the original coding procedure an "agree" on this item was scored as professional orientation, with the rationale that agreement indicated a differentiation of the person from the rest of the community (related to the special skills and technique rationale of social workers); but this classification is certainly open to question. It appears that there was significant increase in the number of new careerists who felt they were the most concerned persons in their neighborhood. In retrospect, this does not seem truly incompatible with orientation to the community. In fact, it seems to reflect the evolving identity of the new careerist as a newly trained person working in his own neighborhood, with special concern for, and special knowledge of, this neighborhood.[6] Accepting this interpretation, the data on role orientation

[5] Item 8 in Table 8–2, which asks about "semiprofessional" workers, is a difficult one to interpret. Results show a weak, insignificant increase in the percentage accepting this label. The weakness of response and the lack of change probably have to do with the general vagueness of the term. It was not a term that was used in the formal structure of the program, and many careerists seem not to have known what it meant.

[6] One should perhaps also not overlook the risk of self-satisfaction and condescension similar to that often criticized in professionals.

seem to reflect acceptance by the new careerists of the ideal role model. In their perceived role, the careerists neither reject the community nor do they fail to recognize the value of the professional world toward which a new careers job ladder is supposed to propel them.

Dichotomizing the role of the new careerist into community or professional orientation does not do justice to the problem. In fact, what the new careers model would seem to favor is a person who is both professional and identified with the local community. A subsequent study of a similar new careers population attempted to look at a number of dimensions of professionalization (see Thompson, 1969). These dimensions are professional solidarity, technical competence, specificity of function, "the professional mandate," affective neutrality, and universalism in judgment.

Thompson assumed that these dimensions are fundamentally independent of one another, and she measured each dimension with the following questionnaire items (Thompson, 1969):

> 1. I feel that my supervisor thinks of me as a professional and expects me to act like one. (professional solidarity)
> 2. Because of his training, I feel that my supervisor understands poverty better than I do. (technical competence)
> 3. The range of abilities and talents I have been able to use at the agency has become narrower during the time I have been a New Careerist. (specificity of function)
> 4. I feel that there are jobs at the agency that I can do better than the professionals can. (the professional mandate)
> 5. I feel that the professionals in the agency deal with problems of the clients too routinely, and often don't understand what the client is going through. (affective neutrality)
> 6. The problems of the low-income community cannot be fully understood except by the people who live there. (universalism)

To go into the theoretical and methodological details of this study is beyond the scope or interest of this book, but it is worth noting that the nature of the change in new careerists' responses varies considerably from item to item. Specifically, the new careerists increased (over a 12-month period) on Items 2, 3, 4, and 6. These somewhat limited data indicate that new careerists (at least in this program) became more professional when it came to technical competence, specificity of function, and use of universal criteria in judgment. Likewise, they showed no increase in professionalism in regard to professional solidarity and effective neutrality. There was an increased tendency for the new careerists to disagree on whether there were jobs in the agency that they could do better than professionals; and Thompson interpreted this as an indication of increased adherence to a "professional mandate." But it also seems plausible that this response could be an artifact of an increased respect for *individuals* with whom the new careerists had to work.

Thompson's findings generally reinforce our view that (1) there are numerous dimensions of professionalism, (2) new careerists may show an increase on some and not on others, and (3) they are most likely to show an increase in the aspects relating to technical skill and training prerequisites for professional work and least likely to change in areas relating to direct treatment of clients (especially poor or minority group clients).

Mobility

Contrary to the hypothesis, the mobility aspiration items did not produce any substantial evidence of personal change, except possibly in regard to education (see Table 8–4). Of six recognizable mobility items, only two yielded significant group change. Both of these productive items dealt with education (Items 2 and 6).

Table 8–4   Mobility Aspiration Items

Item	Percent Mobility Orientation before	Percent Mobility Orientation after	p-Value of Change
1. Do you see the new careerist position as leading to another job?	92	95	not significant
2. How much education must a person have to be a new careerist?	50	65	$p < .001$
3. Do you plan to get a college degree?	89	93	not significant
4. Would you like more responsibility on your job?	81	80	not significant
5. A new careerist could easily learn the skills of the professional.	58	58	not significant
6. Are you satisfied with on-the-job training only?	80	91	$p < .20$

Much of this failure to uncover change was due to the overwhelmingly high mobility aspiration expressed by the recruits in the first place. Table 8–4 indicates that an extremely high percentage (92 percent) of the enrollees viewed the new careers position as a stepping-stone to another job even before they officially began the program. Needless to say, there was only negligible increase on this mobility item after six months. Even more surprising was the initial finding that 89 percent of the enrollees aspired to a college degree before entering the program. (Recall that only 64 percent of the respondents had finished high school at this point.) Similarly, over 80 percent of the enrollees wanted more responsibility on their job before they had spent a regular day on that job. This was especially perplexing to the investigators.[7]

Another mobility item yielding a surprisingly high percentage of affirmative responses was the item (5) asking whether the new careerist felt competent to handle the job of the professional. Fifty-eight percent of the respondents agreed with this item on the first administration, and 58 percent agreed on the second administration, indicating no group change whatsoever. Although it cannot be finally determined from the questionnaire data whether all who agreed with the item in the first place also agreed in the follow-up, informal investigation among new careerists indicated that there was substantial consistency on this item. Those who responded in the affirmative on the first occasion also did so on the second.

The follow-up also indicated that this is an important 58 percent whose consistent response to Item 5 significantly marks them off from the other enrollees. This group represents a majority of new careerists who feel that although the professional deserves his status and is a well-trained person, he (the new careerist) could become a professional with the proper training. They see no intrinsic barriers to their becoming professional and are in no particular awe of the professional. They feel that they could easily learn the skills needed to do the job.

The sentiment of the 58 percent majority seemed in somewhat sharp contrast to the minority, who felt that they would not easily be

---

[7] At first it was suspected that the enrollees had misinterpreted the questionnaire item as asking if they wanted more responsibility on their *current* job [that is, the job (if they had one) they had before entering the new careers program]. But verbal query among the enrollees as well as the continuity of this response on the second administration of the questionnaire indicated that, indeed, a large number of careerists wanted more responsibility than they *anticipated* from the new careers job. They were quite eager to get on with the job!

able to learn the professional's job. The reason for this disavowal seems a combination of respect toward the professional and a lack of confidence in their own abilities. This breakdown, interestingly enough, did not change over the first six months of the program. The two groups were well formed at the outset and maintained their attitude toward their capacity for professional training *without any program impact*.

The only mobility items that did show change over the initial months of the program concerned education. The greatest degree of change occurred on the item asking about the amount of education needed to be a new careerist. Table 8–4 has summarized the data, making it difficult to tell exactly how much education was thought to be needed for a new careerist. "Mobility orientation" on this item indicates that the respondent felt some college necessary for the job. There was, in fact, an increase of 15 percent in those seeing college as desirable. In the beginning only 50 percent thought college necessary; after six months this figure had shifted to 65 percent.[8] On a similar item (6), there was a distinct upward shift in the percent not satisfied with on-the-job training (OJT). At the time of the follow-up, over 90 percent of the new careerists were not satisfied with OJT.

Together, these items, plus a multitude of conversations with new careerists about their education, support the clear induction that the major change in the careerists in regard to mobility had to do with their increased sensitivity to the importance of education. There was general dissatisfaction with OJT work, and there was a growing sentiment that college was desirable.[9] The perceived importance of the educational component was a continual surprise to administrators of the program, who from time to time had second thoughts about pushing the new careerists into education.

It might be said that the emphasis on education by the program staff created these expectations in the careerists, and to the extent that change took place (for example, 15 percent on Item 2) this is true. But the unmistakable fact is that much of this concern for education was present before the program got under way. Eighty percent of the recruits rejected OJT in the initial response.

[8] This is undoubtedly partly because of the fact that the Minneapolis careerists were going to college on a fairly intensive basis. No claim is made here for the collegiate aspirations of nonprofessionals not directly exposed to the college setting.

[9] We make the assumption that these are dependent relations, but it is possible that OJT was being rejected because of some intrinsic lack of merit in the OJT component of the Minneapolis program.

This finding fits in with our broad observations that the desire for education was the real sleeper of this particular program. Although the recruits were a relatively unselected group of marginally employed low-income adults who were not screened for any educational aptitude, the program tapped a deep vein of interest in higher education. These people were not unaware of the gate-keeping function of education, and they were convinced, even without direct exposure to the program, that they wanted the gate opened for themselves.

Rightly or wrongly, the new careerists perceived education as the way out of their situation. They perceived higher education as possible for them, perhaps even leading to a professional career despite their late start and handicapped position. For this group of new careerists, in any case, mobility was definitely seen in terms of educational progress. This was true at the beginning and appears to have been emphasized by their experiences in the Minneapolis program.

9 New Careers and the Improvement of Human Services

We have stressed new careers programs in education and have focused on the pattern of change in the educational current with the greatest implications for broad changes in school-community relations. This emphasis may surprise some educators, and justifiably so. As indicated by figures in earlier chapters, the vast majority of teacher aide programs are viewed strictly in terms of direct assistance to the education process. They are not seen as a new type of manpower program. We have emphasized the new careers concept precisely to bring a broader perspective on teacher aides to the attention of educators.

However, in the last analysis, anything that happens in the schools should be analyzed in terms of its payoff in improving education. We have not tried to avoid this concern. Even within the new careers idea the goal of improving human service is given equal priority with the development of new career opportunity and the fostering of personal mobility. For any ongoing teacher aide program, the improvement in the classroom and the tangible achievements in pupil performance will probably be uppermost in the mind of the administrator.

This chapter will, therefore, provide a sample of what is known about the impact of using teacher aides on educational quality. This will involve a brief look at some data collected on the teacher aide program in Minneapolis (both new careers and nonnew careers portions) and will conclude with a discussion of the kind of thorough research that should be done on the contribution of teacher aides to the education process.

The discussion of research in this critical area will be brief, in comparison to the space given to other issues in this book, mainly because there are no reliable empirical data. What is available is a patchwork of crudely conducted evaluational research carried out by local programs. We are not aware of any methodologically sophisticated study done on the utility of teacher aides. In addition to being empirically crude, the handful of research projects of this nature have been published in the context of a general defense of the local program. They are written by federal project officers justifying their own programs.

This situation must be remedied in the near future. New careers programs can have short-lived support as poverty programs providing jobs to ghetto residents; they will receive long-run financial support only if their real contribution to education is shown. Facts and figures will have to be brought before congressional committees and state legislatures. Government bureaus will have to justify their support of these programs. At this point there is an almost total lack of anything that a well-trained social scientist would accept as evidence for the substantial expansion of any kind of teacher aide programs in any branch of education. Beyond this, we do not even have any well-formulated hypotheses about where in a school system aides might be of the greatest use. Are aides of more use in mathematics classes or in language work; could they be used with greater payoff in social work roles or in the classroom? The authors are not aware that anyone has even raised any of the large series of questions relevant to the proper tactical development of aide programs. Considering the vast ignorance, this chapter is designed to raise questions and to *stimulate* research in this area rather than to provide answers.

Potential Teacher Aide Contribution

An earlier chapter discussed some of the various role orientations for a teacher aide. These included technical, supportive, and supplementary types of performances, as we have defined them. In fact any of these types of performance may assist in the instruction of a class, and any one may allow the quality of education in that class to improve. The technical type of role will at least allow the teacher an increase in preparation time.[1] Supportive tasks will give the teacher an instructional "third arm." Supplementary tasks will clearly add to the total educational experience of the class. The hypothesis would be that there will be an increase in contribution as the aide moves from the menial (technical) role to a totally supplementary role. Again, there is little empirical data showing that the increment to class achievement is contingent upon the type of aide role developed. It is sheer guesswork at this point to assert that the same aide employed (with proper training) in a supportive-type role will make a greater contribution than if he were limited to a menial role. This is one major task for future research.

There are, however, two radically different types of additions to the classroom that might stem from the use of aides. These will be reviewed here.

Psychological Support

The presence of a teacher aide in a classroom, especially an elementary school classroom, can allow for greater psychological support for children. This can take place in two quite different ways. Perhaps the most primitive supplementary role that an aide might perform is to provide an additional shoulder for a child to weep on. As discussed in an earlier chapter, it is clear that the nurturing relationship is one of the most natural for female teacher aides to assume. It is the form of relationship most compatible with their previous roles as wife and mother. On still another level, a male from a ghetto neighborhood may be more successful at providing support for a boy

---

[1] An interesting recent study indicates that the addition of a teacher aide to a class not only leads to the teacher taking more preparation time during class hours but also apparently leads to more time spent in preparation at home. This is an added factor not really accounted for by our model. It may have something to do with a change in the audience for whom the teacher is preparing (Erickson, 1968).

from this neighborhood than the most motherly white woman. Nurturance, it seems, is not just a matter of putting an arm around someone's shoulders; it can be very much a matter of providing a role model. The opportunity to say, "Here is someone whom I can realistically model myself after" can be a major form of security. This is the kind of support or nurturance (involving, please note, *no* training in psychology for its primitive provision) that the teacher aide can provide. It exists by the mere fact of his being there and being concerned with a child's education. This is not to say that this is the be-all and the end-all of psychological services. That would be absurd. But such basic support or role modeling is a starting point that may be forever out of the reach of the middle-class teacher or counselor no matter how good his intentions.

It is also true that the presence of an aide in a classroom will give the teacher more time to deal with each individual child. Theoretically, at least, this should give the teacher more of an opportunity to deal with the unique problems of the particular child. It may be that the teacher will use his time in other ways, but it seems that some small increment of attention will be granted to the children typically less demanding of attention. Smith and Geoffrey (1968) have nicely documented what every teacher knows; in any classroom, especially an inner city classroom, the energy used up dealing with the "squeaky wheels" leaves a dozen or more somewhat troubled kids without any real attention. These pupils can spend large segments of the day in dreamy inattention or frustration while the teacher deals with the crises of a noisy minority.

At a still more advanced level, it is conceivable that use of auxiliary personnel in an advanced program may make possible the development of entirely new roles for teachers, similar to the home teacher role in Stoddard's dual program, which involves full-time focus on learning and pedagogical problems. It seems likely that with a supportive staff the schools can look forward to some sort of specialization in this direction in the future (completely distinct from counseling and guidance roles, which serve a quite different function).

Student Achievement

The great $64,000 question of the teacher aide concept is: Just how much can the use of aides improve the academic achievement of students? If quality of education can be equated with student achievement, then the yardstick of teacher aide programs must be the degree of resulting achievement. But here one runs into a host of old questions. Just what is achievement? How can it be measured? What of long-run influences? What of creativity or social skills as forms of achievement? This chapter obviously cannot cover all of these questions. It will be sufficient if research on teacher aides can demonstrate a few clear-cut results using conventional achievement measures (for example, grade levels in reading skill). At this point there is virtually no research even at this simple level.

The contribution of teacher aides to student achievement can be studied from two different approaches. These approaches are different methodologies, but they also reflect different views of the political support for teacher aide programs. One can study the use of teacher aides, first, from the standpoint of a simple addition to the classroom scene. The teacher aide comes into the situation as a new instructional tool ready for use. The question then is whether or not the use of this tool is helpful, much as someone might ask if a new reading game does anything or if its presence is simply a fad or the result of some persuasive salesman.

This approach makes some important assumptions about the financial and political support for aide programs. It assumes that funding of teacher aide programs is unrelated to other sources of funding or parts of a school system's budget. It assumes that aide funding will be external, probably federal, and so will not involve local support. The school board and administration can go ahead and plan in whatever way they want, and the teacher aides will be there, their salaries paid by the federal government or the Ford Foundation. This is overstating the case, but perhaps it makes the point. The question of allocating money received for aide use has generally been within relatively narrow boundaries for application of federal funds. In most programs there has been no local decision about the value of aides relative to other possible expenditures. The question has been whether to accept or to reject federal money. The decision has usually been easy to make.

On the other hand, one can approach the question of aide use within the much broader context of a total educational budget. The question can be asked and research can be designed to test the relative value of teacher aides over other badly needed budget items (for example, books, science materials, salaries for school psychologists, and so on). Needless to say, this is a complex question in many ways, including the very problem of research design. We can state categorically that no research has been done within this framework.[2]

[2] There is one exception. In the later stages of preparing this book we learned that some work of this sort is being done at the University of Oregon.

School systems faced with allotting local money, coming out of the same proverbial pie as the money for books, physical education equipment, and teacher salaries, are eventually going to raise the question: Are teacher aides really worth it? Big school systems will soon have to face the question of whether or not programs begun with federal money will be expanded (as certain community pressures will demand) with local tax money. They may even have to face the question of whether local money should simply maintain a program that has been begun with federal money and then been abandoned or reduced following the whims of national politics. These will be hard decisions to make. And they will be especially hard lacking any empirical data or experimentation.

One could, indeed, raise these questions of the U.S. Office of Education (USOE) itself, except that so few locally based educators ever raise any questions of policy with USOE for fear of losing their spot at the feeding trough.[3] Federal programs are spending huge amounts of money that will shape the face of American education for decades to come. They are even doing considerable research on these programs. But they are not, with rare exception (not in the teacher aide area), sponsoring research on the cost and benefits of one kind of program compared with the same amount of money spent in other ways. It can be argued that some of this research would be of no practical value because the USOE is quite circumscribed in what it can and cannot finance. But who is to say what will be enacted in legislation in the 1970s? In addition to practical considerations, the educational scientists of the national establishment should appreciate the value of pure research. It is important to know how the costs and benefits of teacher aide programs compare with other educational expenses, and by and large educators are not finding out.

[3] We are perhaps wrong to make light of the silence among local schoolmen in the face of national education policy. The federal dollars are badly needed, and almost any allocation will be of some benefit. Likewise, the local administrators and teachers are completely enmeshed in the problems of local school politics. They are not supermen. Still it seems that *someone* must ask the question about the relative value of various national programs. There are some who will reply, "But look at the vast research apparatus of the USOE." In fact, the USOE research budget is a paltry 1.5 percent of the total budget, a situation that would be intolerable in a modern corporation. Furthermore, one need only note that despite large amounts spent for teacher aides there is not one single piece of funded research to compare whether the money is better spent for teacher aides or for more teachers. The total empirical data is a flat zero. Local administrators will be right to raise serious questions about this.

Research Findings in Minneapolis

Several pieces of research have been completed on the teacher aide program in Minneapolis.[4] This section will report what seems to be the most salient of these results. The reporting can roughly be divided into three sections: (1) definition of the aide role, (2) satisfaction of the teachers with the aide program, and (3) impact of aide use on student achievement.

All data in this section are taken from the teacher aide program in Minneapolis during 1966 to 1967 or 1967 to 1968. The aide population varied during this time from 225 to 300. Questionnaires were completed by 231 aides in the spring of 1967. Of these, 125 were assigned to elementary schools, 61 to junior high schools, and 45 to senior high schools. Twelve aides were male and the remainder female. Their ages ranged from 19 to 71, with a mean age of 39.5. They were predominantly high school graduates (little college experience) and of lower- or lower-middle-class socioeconomic status.

Because discussion in earlier chapters focused around the Minneapolis new careers program, it should be pointed out that the data reported here are taken from a combination of new careers teacher aides *and* regular teacher aides. The split is about 50–50, but because of an error in data collection it is impossible to give the precise figure. In any case, as was indicated in chapter 5, the Minneapolis program had many features of a new careers program even before the Labor Department support began in 1967.

Role Definition

In somewhat varying ways, Minneapolis principals, teachers, and aides were asked to define the teacher aide role. Agreement on most points seemed to be high, so only the major points of role definition will be noted.

Principals in the Minneapolis program did not feel that aide supervision was entirely their responsibility, nor was it totally the job of the teacher. The overwhelming majority of principals agreed that teachers and administrators should work together to define the teacher aide role. Seventy-four percent of all respondents agreed with a statement to this effect.

[4] All data reported in the remainder of this chapter appear in two research reports on the Minneapolis teacher aide program (Goralski, Hayen, and Fellows, 1967; and Goralski and Hayen, 1968).

There was also singular agreement on the content of the aide role as it presently existed (1966 to 1967) in Minneapolis. Each principal, teacher, and aide were asked to note the amount of time that the aide (himself in the case of the aide) spent at each of six categories of tasks:

1. *Routine duties*
   Clerical in the classroom
   Clerical outside the classroom
   Classroom housekeeping
   Operating equipment
   Maintenance of equipment and materials
   Grading papers
2. *Supervision of pupils*
   Taking charge of class in teacher's absence
   Taking charge of class while teacher works with smaller groups, planning, etc.
   Supervising a study hall (or helping to do so)
   Supervising halls, lavatories, lunchrooms, etc.
   Supervising recreation periods, field trips, etc.
   Bus supervision
3. *Giving personal attention to pupils*
   Listening to children's ideas and problems
   Sharing ideas and interests with children
   Praising children
   Giving encouragement to children
   Giving reassurance to children
   Helping children with reading
   Helping children with arithmetic
   Helping children with spelling and word recognition
   Helping individuals or small groups in any area
4. *Talking with parents about school values and rules*
5. *Helping the teacher to understand parents' beliefs, hopes, and fears for themselves and their children*
6. *Other duties?*

Each respondent was asked to indicate how he thought aide time could best be utilized. In the parlance of role theorists this covered both behavioral anticipations and norms (see Biddle and Thomas, 1966) governing the teacher aide role in Minneapolis in this second year of the program.

There was remarkable consensus among the three groups as to how the teacher aides' time had been spent and how it could best be spent in the future. When the mean was calculated for all responses it appeared that the anticipations and the norms for all three groups were quite similar (see Table 9–1). At this stage in Minneapolis it was recommended that aides spend just under 50 percent of their time at routine tasks. It was then thought appropriate for the aides to spend half of the remaining time supervising groups of pupils and the rest in giving personal attention to individual pupils.

Table 9–1 Norms and Anticipations for Teacher Aide Role, Minneapolis Public Schools, 1966–1967

		Principals ($n = 26$)	Teachers ($n = 332$)	Teacher Aide ($n = 231$)
Percent[a] time on routine duties (Category I)	Anticipate	47	51	50
	Recommend (Norm)	48	46	42
Percent time on supervision with groups (Category II)	Anticipate	26	24	23
	Recommend (Norm)	28	23	19
Percent time giving per- sonal attention (Category III)	Anticipate	20	21	23
	Recommend (Norm)	22	28	30

[a] There is a residual group, 3 to 5 percent, which opted for Categories IV, V, and VI, as described in the text.

In the language of our earlier analysis of teacher aide role (technical, supportive, and supplementary), it should be noted that a rough extrapolation would seem to indicate that the Minneapolis sample was indicating with remarkable consensus that the aides should spend about half their time in the technical role tasks and half in supportive tasks. The supportive role could be subdivided still further into one quarter of their time spent on routine instructional jobs under the teacher's supervision and another quarter on psychological support to pupils. It is possible that portions of this psychological support should be viewed as supplementary to the teacher role, but there is no clear-cut evidence in the available data that this is true.

The questionnaire also brought up the question of social status involved in the definition of the aide role. Principals were asked whether aides seemed to attach more status to some kinds of duties than to others. Most principals claimed not to have noticed this. They did indicate, however, that aides expressed a special satisfaction in cases where they were dealing with teachers and pupils. One principal stated that aides seemed to regard themselves as professionals and preferred to work with people. Another noted that aides appeared to enjoy feeling that they were making a contribution to the lives of others. Still other aides seemed to prefer clerical work.

Elementary and Secondary School Aide Roles

There were some differences in aide role between elementary and secondary settings. Secondary school principals and teachers indicated a strong preference that clerical tasks be assigned to teacher aides. They also stated that aides were and should be used to supervise halls, lavatories, lunchrooms, and so on. Fewer secondary teachers or administrators believed aides had been helpful in classrooms. They did not see the value of teacher aides offering psychological support to students. This latter opinion is interesting in that it is in the early years of secondary school that many target area youngsters could most use a role model or something of the sort and are at the same time least likely to find this model in the school. The role model would be especially appropriate for the male teacher aides, but at this point (prior to Scheuer) Minneapolis had only 12 male aides, 11 of them working, for some reason, at the junior high school level (here classified with elementary).

In the elementary schools, most principals felt that the aides were well suited to give personal attention to the pupils, to play a supportive role with them, and to perform limited instructional tasks. Most elementary school people felt the aide should be allowed responsibility for groups of students on his own. There was a vigorous minority dissent on this point, and a few teachers believed that an aide should not assume control of any group, large or small, in any instance.

Teacher Satisfaction

More easily researched than the tricky question of role definition is the question of teacher satisfaction with the aide performance. Although not an ironclad demonstration, the measurement of teacher satisfaction can be one index of the usefulness of the aides.

In the Minneapolis study the attitudes of both principals and teachers were assessed. The overall perceived utility of teacher aides was confirmed beyond dispute. Principals and teachers were asked, "Do you think that the teacher aide program is worth continuing?" The response was a strong affirmative:

	Principals	Teachers
Definitely yes	80.8%	80.0%
Not sure	11.5	12.9
Definitely no	0.0	1.3
Yes with qualifications	3.8	5.7
No response	3.9	.1

The qualification came from several principals who felt that they should be able to hire aides according to ability, not neighborhood residence. In other words, they did not buy the concept of open entry, which gives preference to local residents.

The school people were equally in agreement on the degree of usefulness of the aides: A majority of both teachers (51.5 percent) and principals (62 percent) rated the aides as "very valuable." It might be noted that although both evaluations were positive, principals were a little more positive in their evaluations than teachers. It is hypothesized that one not too effective aide could affect the view of the entire program for teachers to whom he was assigned. Such an aide would not have this negative effect on the administrators.

The study also attempted to assess teacher satisfaction in more concrete terms, by seeing just how closely they thought the proposed objectives of the program had been achieved. An attempt was made to determine (1) how much increased planning time was available to the teacher, (2) how much assistance was provided on clerical and housekeeping chores, (3) if the aide did function as a bridge to the community, and (4) if he did provide additional adult support for children with personal problems.

Free Time for Teachers Teachers were asked, "How much time did the aide free for you to do planning and preparation?" *Responses ranged from 0 to 30 hours per week.* Teachers stated that children's learning benefited because they (the teachers) were able to plan more carefully and prepare materials for activities that otherwise would not have been possible. Teachers claimed that they had more time to read and to inform themselves in greater depth about subjects they were teaching. The median free time noted was 14 hours per week, a considerable increase in time for preparation.

Teachers were also asked, "How much time did the aide's work free you to work directly with pupils?" Responses here ranged from 0 to 20 hours per week with an average of 2 to 3 hours. More project work was undertaken and a considerable gain was made in time free for working with remedial problems. An interesting side light to this finding is that it appears that teachers tend to fall into two groups, those who will utilize the free time for preparation and those who will use it for individual work. The correlation between the responses to the two questions just noted is a significant negative value ($-.43$).[5] It would make an important future piece of research to determine which teachers choose to spend their time in preparation and which in individualized work, and, further, to try to assess which has the greatest payoff in terms of pupil achievement.

Dirty Work Contribution As has already been reported, all three respondent groups indicated that aides spent about 50 percent of their time on menial chores, a rate slightly higher than desirable by the teachers' own standards. To indicate the extent of this contribution, it might be well to point out that if 244 aides (the total aide allotment at the beginning of 1966 to 1967) spent half their time (7½ hours per week) performing routine and clerical tasks, then collectively they spent 1830 hours per week on these jobs. If we assume also that nearly all of these jobs would have to have been done by the teacher if no aide had been available and that the aide was just about as efficient as the teacher, we can assert that the aide program saved a conservative estimate of 1500 teacher hours per week during that school year.

The Aide as Neighborhood Liaison

All respondent groups were asked to indicate (with some detail) the percent of time that aides spent in liaison work. The responses indicated a somewhat retarded development in this area:

Types of Contact	*Principals*	*Teachers*	*Aides*
Aide helped to interpret school values and expectations to parents	3.4%	1.8%	0.8%
Aide helped teacher to understand parents' values for themselves and their children	4.0%	2.2%	1.0%

[5] This correlation is for elementary school teachers only. It is a rank order correlation.

Many aides indicated that they were frequently asked for information about the school programs, but that they were usually questioned away from school—at the market or at home in the evening. Because this was not part of their 15 hours of work, it was not usually included in the questionnaire, nor would the teacher be aware of this time. Therefore, the percentage figures are probably systematically understated.

It should also be noted that the handful of social work aides are excluded from these figures. These aides spent virtually all of their time in some kind of contact with the community. The advent of the Scheuer new careers program in the year following this study greatly increased the number of social work aides to 27 full-time and 9 part-time persons. This provided a major force for community contact. Likewise, the Scheuer program made all people connected with the teacher aide program much more cognizant of the liaison role for the classroom aides. There is strong informal evidence that the aides did provide more community contact in 1967 to 1968.

Psychological Support to Pupils

Unfortunately, the formal questionnaire from which the previous data have been taken did not include any clear-cut measure of aide-pupil involvement. In order to get some indication of the contribution along these lines, a special set of interviews and pilot work was done at only one school in the system. This school employed 28 aides and was the largest employer. It was a ghetto school with about 500 students, 80 percent of whom were nonwhite.

During the interviews it became apparent that aides perceived themselves as very involved with pupils and felt they played a supportive role with them. Aides were enthusiastic about their work with the children and sincerely wished to communicate their feelings about it. The investigators made an attempt to construct an objective checklist of types of involvement of aides with students (see Table 9–2). This checklist was then presented to a larger group of (elementary) aides at other schools. The results are presented in Table 9–2, which ranks the items by percent of response to the "occurred often" categories. Table 9–2 gives all types of contact that were indicated as happening often or at least "once in a while" by more than 30 percent of the aides.

From the checklist, two things are quite clear. First, there are many types of involvement with pupils, ranging from the casual to the psychologically profound (for example, "a child hugged me"). Second, future research will have quite a job to do just to compare programs on the types and degree of involvement perceived by aides and to try to interpret the meaningfulness and educational importance of these myriad involvements.

Table 9–2 A Percentage Tabulation of Responses to an Assessment of Pupil Involvement by Elementary School Teacher Aides ($n = 138$)

	Often (%)	Once in a While (%)
A child waved or called to me when he/she saw me outside of school, for example, at the store.	85.6	10.8
A child stopped to talk when he/she saw me someplace other than at school.	75.5	19.4
A child just wanted to sit or stand near me.	73.7	21.9
A child showed me his/her art work (paintings, drawings, pictures).	71.8	21.0
A child held my hand.	71.2	23.0
A child showed me a possession—perhaps because he/she especially valued it, or it was new.	66.9	28.8
A child showed me a new article of clothing.	64.0	27.4
A child showed me his/her papers, for example, arithmetic or spelling.	52.9	25.0
A child hugged me.	51.8	32.4
I helped a child to recognize words.	47.8	25.4
I stopped children from fighting.	47.0	46.2
I tied a child's shoe.	47.0	26.9
I helped a child with a coat.	46.9	33.1
I listened to a child read.	45.3	23.7
A child wanted me to listen to his/her story.	45.0	32.6
I tied a child's scarf or bonnet.	43.6	31.8
I helped a child to pronounce words.	43.5	27.5
I wiped away a child's tears—with a few kind words.	41.2	47.3
I listened while a child told of a problem that was disturbing him/her.	39.4	41.6

Table 9–2 (continued)

	Often (%)	Once in a While (%)
A child introduced his parent or friend when he/she saw me someplace other than at school.	38.7	37.2
I helped a child with overshoes.	38.7	27.7
A child asked me to hold valuables while he/she played.	38.3	44.7
I used flash cards to help a child.	33.6	19.0
I helped a child with arithmetic.	33.2	35.7
A child wanted to walk home with me.	32.1	31.4
I helped a child with writing or printing.	30.5	31.9
I helped a child who had been in a fight.	28.8	47.0
I helped a child to find a lost article.	28.3	46.4
I read to children.	27.6	39.9
A child kissed my hand or cheek.	27.0	30.7
I helped a child with a special project, for example, paper dolls and clothes.	27.0	32.8
I listened to a secret that a child wanted to share.	25.7	41.9
I helped a child who had an accident.	21.8	49.2
A child sent me a card or note.	21.2	33.6
A child shared a treat with me.	20.1	44.6
I gave a child advice on a problem.	18.3	57.7
A child (or a group of children) brought me a gift.	18.0	40.3
A child visited at my home.	16.4	33.6
I took a child to the lavatory.	14.2	35.8
I helped a child who came to school with frostbite—or who was very chilled.	11.9	34.8
I helped a child who had a nosebleed.	11.1	37.0
I helped a child who was ill.	9.6	53.4
I helped a child to find his/her room.	8.2	41.8
I dried a child's clothing.	4.4	32.8
I found clothing for a child in an emergency.	3.8	31.6

In general, the aides were satisfied that they could communicate the quantity of their involvements, but they still felt that they would like to communicate (and they did communicate) the quality of their experiences. The anecdotes from the depth interviews conducted at the first school were very appealing. In one incident, a little boy had been taken to a pancake house, along with others in his class, in order to have the experience of eating out. As he left, the aide noted that he turned in the doorway, looked back, and softly said, "Thank you, *place*." This was only one among many indications of the important nurturant role played by aides.

An Experiment on Classroom Achievement

As already indicated at several points, very little is known about the actual contribution of aides to pupil achievement. As far as we know, the Minneapolis research team is the only one to have completed any sort of controlled experiment in this area. The data from the questionnaire of 1966 to 1967 did not provide this kind of evidence on the usefulness of teacher aides; therefore, during the spring of 1968 an experiment was set up to attempt to answer this question: Can teacher aides be used effectively to help develop reading and number readiness in kindergarten children? This is obviously a very limited kind of experiment, but it was felt that the preschool area would be as good a place as any to begin this work. Individualized teaching is especially important in reading readiness, and if there is no success here, one might not expect much anywhere else.

Nine kindergarten classes were selected, and six teachers were assigned. Each class consisted of approximately 30 children. Of the 30 children, one third had participated in Head Start during the previous summer. Approximately half the classes met in the afternoon and half in the morning. The schools were all target-area schools and the pupil population was about 50 percent Negro. Five of the aides, but none of the teachers, were Negro (a significant fact in itself).

Within the experiment, two variables were systematically manipulated: (1) the presence of an aide and (2) the number of aides. Three classes had no aides whatsoever, three classes had *one* aide, and the final three classes had five aides. Aides came to work in these classrooms on February 6, 1968, and remained for the entire spring term, in which reading readiness training was undertaken. The readiness of the pupils was assessed by the Metropolitan Readiness Test, Form R (1949). Pretests were administered to 254 children in 9 classes during January. Posttests were given to 248 children during the last week in May. Testing yielded 234 pairs of test scores.

The teachers were allowed to use the aides as they saw fit. Three in-service meetings were devoted entirely to a very general review of all the possible things aides could do; the aides were told that this was an experiment.[6] Generally speaking, there was no assessable difference in the way in which aides were used. Roughly 40 percent of the time was given to menial chores; the remainder of the time seems to have been given to some sort of work (by aides) with the children. All classes seemed consistent in these percentages.

The results of the experiment are slightly perplexing. If one examines the unweighted means for the pretest, posttest, and the gain scores, it does appear that the presence of an aide makes a considerable difference in both reading readiness and number readiness (see Table 9–3). But it also appears that the presence of one aide has a greater impact than the presence of five aides! Gain scores actually *decline* when five aides were placed in the classroom. It was also found through more complicated statistical analyses that there was a considerable connection between sex (of pupil) and treatment. Girls tended to have much higher readiness scores that did boys, and were less affected by the treatment. Statistical analysis did demonstrate, however, that there were significant treatment effects (in aide–no aide comparison) beyond the effects of sex or the interaction.[7]

The lack of any additional effect from the five aides was somewhat surprising. It was inferred by the investigators, however, that when five aides were present in the classroom, the teacher spent a great deal of time training and supervising the aides and less time working directly with the children. Because teachers are professionally trained to work with children, it was believed that directing the teacher's efforts elsewhere might not result in optimum pupil gain. The researchers did note that if the aides had been given more training before being sent into the classroom this might not have been a factor. But the final report does not go into detail about the kind of training that should have been given. It is also unclear why such a large extra contingent of aides was added. A more useful comparison would have been to match one aide against two aides. It is impossi-

[6] Despite some fear of a Hawthorne effect, the teachers were told that they were in an experiment. This was done both for ethical reasons and to explain the presence of five adults in one classroom.

[7] The details of the statistical analysis can be found in the official report (Goralski and Hayen, 1968).

ble to conceive of a situation in which five aides could be used in one kindergarten classroom. From an economic standpoint it would be totally unfeasible.

Table 9–3 Unweighted Group Means, Pretest, Posttest, and Gain, Metropolitan Readiness Test form R ($N = 234$) Influenced by Presence of Teacher Aides[a]

Test	Group A ($N = 75$)	Group B ($N = 79$)	Group C ($N = 80$)
Tests 1–4, Reading readiness			
Pretest	41.813	38.215	40.725
Posttest	47.400	47.785	48.788
Gains	5.587	9.570	8.063
Test 5, Number readiness			
Pretest	8.213	8.089	8.425
Posttest	11.613	12.114	12.665
Gains	3.400	4.025	4.350
Tests 1–6, Total readiness			
Pretest	53.453	49.684	52.775
Posttest	63.867	64.835	66.563
Gains	10.414	15.151	13.588

[a] An inspection of Table 9–3 revealed that Group B, classes with a teacher and one teacher aide, experienced the greatest mean gains on tests of reading readiness and total readiness. Group A, the classes with a teacher and no aides, experienced the least mean gains in reading readiness. Group C (five aides) mean gain scores fell between those of Group A and Group B. Analysis of variance shows these differences among groups to be statistically significant for Tests 1 to 4, but not for Test 5.

It is clear then, that although the design was relatively complex, and the analysis sophisticated, the Minneapolis experiment did not go very far. It did demonstrate the clear-cut increment in achievement contingent on using one aide in a kindergarten class for a readiness program. It also rather inadvertently indicated that too many aides may cause problems of supervision that actually interfere with effective teaching. This latter finding could be extended to the use of unprepared aides in any situation. But as an attempt to demonstrate the clear educational advantage in using aides, the experiment only scratched the surface. A great deal more needs to be done, and so far it would appear that the educational establishment has allowed a shocking neglect of research in this vital area. There are a multitude of theoretical and/or practical questions to be explored. The payoff in the use of teacher aides, relative to investment in other areas of our underfinanced educational system, is simply unknown.

Summary of Chapters 8 and 9

Chapters 8 and 9 (research oriented chapters) have tried to examine what empirical evidence is available concerning two secondary goals within the new careers concept: the development of personal mobility and the improvement of human services. We have examined data on the Minneapolis teacher aide program in an attempt to determine just how realistic these goals are. If a teacher aide program endorses the new careers concept, can it expect to reach these goals?

The chapters have tried to make two basic points. First, the major goals were reached by the Minneapolis teacher aide program. It can be shown that even before the establishment of a federally founded new careers program, the teacher aides in Minneapolis were making distinct contributions to the educational product. This was true in terms of the perceptions of teachers and school administrators. Both groups clearly perceived the utility of teacher aides and clearly cast them in something more than menial roles. It is significant of the new careers emphasis of the Minneapolis program that the school professionals felt that up to one quarter of the aide's time should be used in direct personal support for pupils. This represents the dawning of the idea that the aide can be used as a bridge to the community, especially to the ghetto community.

It was also obvious that the experience of working in a new careers program did produce profound changes in the self-concepts of enrollees. These changes are larger than any found in previous research with standardized instruments, although the changes are less for new careers personnel than for regular teacher aides. The changes in self-concept were accompanied by more ambiguous changes in aspirations for mobility and role orientation. It was hypothesized that these changes in behavior or intended behavior were causally connected to the prior changes in self-concept. Although these were the only aspects of personality that were measured in this study, it also appears from extensive observation that changes in attitudes, values, and opinions were also involved. These need to be examined in future studies.

The second point that these chapters mean to stress is that new careers is in fact a very complex problem area and, as of now, research is practically nonexistent. Research on the questions of personal change and the contributions to human service are difficult assignments, but it is incumbent on those who would advocate the new careers concept—in education and elsewhere—to take a hard look at its practicability. This can only be done by patient study and careful experimental design.

10 Implementing Teacher Aide Programs

It is recognized that communities outside the urban target areas may have teacher aide programs and that the new careers concept is not especially relevant for these communities. These communities may wish to hire housewives on a part-time basis to help with the many chores of the elementary classroom or the paper work of the secondary school. Political reasons may also militate against experimentation with new careers.

Although the implications for change in education are much greater with a new careers program, it is possible that the numerical majority of teacher aides in the country will actually be hired in the former, less adventurous type of program. The manpower crisis in education (see Pearl, 1968), while acute in the urban core, does have an impact on suburbia. The final two chapters will review the many aspects of teacher aide use, first, by providing information about the nonnew careers type of program, and then by concluding with a re-statement on new careers.

The authors have in no way meant to imply that new careers is the only model that can be used in the teacher aide area. There are many other possibilities. One of the few virtues of local control in American education has been the freedom of communities (from the New England small town to Ocean Hill-Brownsville) to experiment with new approaches to the multitude of education problems. It is hoped that work with teacher aides can imbue some of this spirit of experimentation. Perhaps the deepest implication of the whole new careers idea is that school role structure must have relevance to broader social conditions (see chapters 3 and 4 for an extended dis-cussion).

This chapter has been organized under a set of "problem" head-ings. All these topics have been dealt with earlier in the text, but this section will briefly bring them back into focus for a concentrated re-view with special emphasis on solutions for the nonnew careers vari-ety of program.

Who Is a Teacher Aide?

A teacher aide, under current programs, is a noncertified person working in some auxiliary capacity within the school. The relation-ship of aide to teacher is a variable one, ranging from doing busy work chores to actually assuming instructional tasks. It is clearly a stratified arrangement, with the teacher having final overall responsi-bility and with the teacher aide filling in where needed (although, as discussed throughout the text, there is room for experimentation with a full instructional responsibility for an aide in certain specific in-stances).

The past three or four years have seen a rapid increase in the number of teacher aides employed in American schools. Much of the increase has been financed by federal money appropriated for low-in-come areas. This has meant that the majority of teacher aides have been employed within these areas. However, what data exist indicate that the aide himself has not usually been a low-income person or even a resident of the school neighborhood. Many aides are middle-class housewives helping out in nearby poverty area schools. Another significant minority of teacher aides are suburban housewives, em-ployed in relatively affluent suburban schools on local money.

Certainly the employment of the middle-class teacher aide has tactical advantages. It drastically reduces the difficulty of recruitment and training. Most of these teacher aides are high school graduates, and many are college graduates. They are eager to work on a part-time basis and find the school day ideal because it coincides precisely with the hours when their children are not home. Many of these people are really volunteer-type workers.[1] They will work for a low wage because money is not of major importance to them in this job, and they will often seek the position on their own. It may be recalled that in one of the programs described in Chapter 5 the program administrator simply advertised the aide positions and then sat back to wait for the applications. Generally, this type of aide will work well with the teacher from the very beginning. Even without preservice training of any kind, this type of recruit can operate with minimum success in the middle-class schoolroom. She will not be motivated to compete with the teacher, and her value system is likely, although not necessarily, to be similar to that of the teacher. By and large, this will be a frictionless system, without major headaches for the administrator.

The one recruitment problem that has come to our attention involving the volunteer nonnew careers type of program is what might be called a decay-of-interest phenomenon. The middle-class volunteer is likely to become bored with the somewhat restrictive role after a three- or four-year period. Although the volunteer is not likely to aspire to be a teacher, he is likely to fade away to some other part-time job. One administrator of a teacher aide program (suburban type) commented to us that the typical career span of a teacher aide was three or four years. But because there seems to be a relatively large supply of volunteer types, especially under present demand, and because recruitment seems simple, even this turnover is likely to be only a minor nuisance for the administrator.

Salaries and Role Conflict
for Teacher Aides

Teacher aides have usually been paid a figure hovering slightly above the national legal minimum wage. In the average nonnew careers type of program, part-time people can generally be hired at a rate of $1.60 to $2.00 per hour. Although this is not a living wage (particularly at one-half time), the middle-class aide can subsidize

[1] Consistent with this aspect of recruitment, these types of aide programs will be referred to as volunteer-type programs in this chapter.

her own wages with family income. The main administrative tactic would seem to be making these wages adequate to cover the costs incurred (for example, baby-sitting, "mother's helper," or housekeeping services).

It is at this time a moot point whether or not raising the wages in a typical "volunteer" type of program would increase the quality of aide service. It is possible that in a loosely organized program it might actually decrease the quality of aide performance. If the wage reached a level comparable to a regular part-time job for semiskilled female labor (for example, $2.00 per hour), the aide position might attract a different kind of person, namely, lower-middle-class women under some family financial pressure. In the absence of an extensive preservice or in-service program (and this is the typical situation), such an individual, with lower average educational attainment, might not do as much for the teacher as her better educated, more intrinsically motivated volunteer counterpart. There will also be administrative problems attendant upon hiring someone for whom the job is more important than helping out.

Role Conflict

It is our experience that in the regular or volunteer-type of aide program, the major source of role conflict will occur not between teacher and aide but between aide and full-time noninstructional staff in the school. As a very practical (and sometimes touchy) problem, school clerical staffs, lunchroom workers, and others often view the entry of teacher aides with some alarm. These ancillary workers perceive, sometimes with justification, that the aides may threaten their job security. Even if the teacher aides or counseling aides do not immediately take work away from the regular ancillary staff, rumors and suspicions often grow to the effect that the future will see such encroachments on traditional job territories.

We do not wish to be alarmist about this problem. In schools and school systems with high morale, the likelihood of friction is slight. But in schools where morale is already a problem or where employee organizations have had a history of trouble with school management, the introduction of teacher aides may be viewed as a threat. It may even be viewed as a purposeful attempt to get cheap clerical labor. Civil service organizations or employee unions are very sensitive to perceived intentions of this sort. The authors are aware of several school systems where clerical staff have refused to cooperate with aides or have subtly sabotaged the well-intended but naïve intentions of aides to pitch in on school busy work. In one case, for example, office help refused to show aides how to operate any office equipment.

There is obviously no easy solution to this tricky little problem. One source of friction has been aide salaries that involve higher hourly rates than the regular school clerks. This is easily avoided by not pegging aide salaries above regular civil service levels. Another simple tactic is to make clear the functional distinction between the aides and other employees and, further, to make clear that the aides' clerical work is work previously done by the teacher, not by noninstructional staff. In any case, appropriate civil service or employee organizations should be consulted prior to the introduction of aides.

In the classroom, role conflict for the aide and/or teacher should be minimal under the volunteer-type aide program. Most of the problems of the new careers program are dealt with exhaustively in Chapters 3 and 4. It is perhaps worth repeating, however, that teachers have not been trained to work in a face-to-face relationship with another adult and that at least one observer (Neubacher, 1965) has noted that teaching may differentially select individuals predisposed to being alone in the work situation.

This latter is a somewhat complicated problem to which there is no immediate answer. However, a few simple rules should be followed in assigning aides to teachers. First, it should be obvious that teachers should be allowed to volunteer to use teacher aides. If a teacher is skeptical about using an aide, it would seem wise to let him operate without one for the first year, during which time the model of other teachers using aides will generally win him over to the idea. If an entire school seems resistant, let the school remain without aides but also let them know as directly as possible the benefits that teachers in a colleague school are deriving from employing aides. Such a tactic may be of increased importance in gaining support for a new careers program or in instituting experimental programs involving increased aide responsibility. With the skeptical teacher, one functioning model is often more effective than a hundred verbal arguments.

As a more subtle tactic aimed at reducing role conflict between an aide and a teacher, the authors would suggest something that does not seem to have been tried anywhere to date. That is, it is suggested that schools make some effort to match teachers and aides. Although the problems of matching may be most acute in a new careers program, some efforts at matching could be made even in the volunteer-type program. At the very least, one or two simple personality dimensions could be taken into account. Using abbreviated versions of basic personality tests (for example, the MMPI) it should be possible to match extrovert with extrovert and so on. At a minimum, it would seem wise to separate dramatically opposed personality types. The one consistently trouble-making combination that the authors have observed is the placement of an extrovert-like aide with an introvert-like teacher. Because most school systems give teachers batteries of personality tests, it should not be difficult for the schools to give the same tests to aides and to avoid some of the more obvious conflicts.[2]

Teacher Aide Duties

As indicated repeatedly throughout this text, there are a great many types of jobs that may be performed by a teacher aide. There are, also, great variations as to how much responsibility can, or should, be given to aides. Most of chapters 4 and 5 are devoted to a full explication of this topic. In these chapters three major types of aide roles are outlined—technical assistance role, supportive role, and supplementary role.

The preceding chapters have argued directly for an ambitious use of teacher aides, in line with the new careers concept. Here, however, the focus will be on the first two levels of role performance, the technical and the supportive roles.

There are also at least five different types of school placements open to aides: (1) elementary classroom, (2) secondary classroom or academic department (for example, modern language department), (3) library, (4) main (administrative) office, and (5) counseling or social work. The following is a brief discussion of possible assignments in each of these settings.

Elementary Schools

By far the greatest need and the greatest use of aides is in elementary school classrooms. Without returning to the thorny discussions of ambitious programs for aide use under the new careers idea it is nonetheless possible to provide a suggestive list of teacher aide duties under both the technical and the supportive aide role models.

---

[2] As discussed in chapter 5, we are well aware that the whole subject of pairing educational personnel for maximum effectiveness is a vast research area, only now getting even minimal attention.

A definitive list of potential duties under the technical assistance role would be many pages long; but the following should help any teacher in beginning to think about general areas in which an aide can be used. Ten general headings are followed by several examples in each area.

1. Attendance Records
   Taking daily attendance to office
   Marking daily attendance registers
   Balancing the register in pencil
   Marking attendance on report cards, permanent records, and transfer cards
   Checking class lists for trips, special purchases, and so on.
2. Report Card Clerk
   Preparing both duplicate and permanent report cards with name, grade, and so on
   Copying marks on permanent cards
   Checking cards in
3. Class Treasurer
   Collecting milk money, bank money, lunch money
   Keeping money records
   Being responsible for safekeeping of funds
4. Inventory Books and Supplies
   Helping teacher check materials and books used directly by pupils
   Checking all supplementary materials
   Acting as class librarian
   Making out various inventory and requisition forms
5. Monitor Lunch Program
   Collecting lunch money
   Supervising trip to lunch
   Sharing supervision of lunchroom
6. Class Health Officer
   Keeping health record on each child
   Checking daily for health problems
   Accompanying child to school nurse (or possibly home) when problem arises
7. Audiovisual Operator
   Operating any audiovisual equipment used in class
   Keeping list of sources for audiovisual materials
   Requisitioning audiovisual materials at teacher's direction
   Preparing and running off duplicater materials (stencils, mimeos, slides, transparencies)

Hand-preparing certain kinds of charts, or seeing to their preparation by school art department
8. Classroom Displays
   Making charts planned by teacher
   Preparing classroom displays (art work, book tables)
   Keeping bulletin board up to date
9. Grader
   Checking objective written work
   Assisting in checking routine seat work
   Monitoring programmed instruction techniques being used
10. Classroom Control
    Handling routine interruptions (for example, notes from other teachers and office phone calls)
    Assisting the teacher in reminding children of assignments
    Reporting lack of understanding of assignments
    Carrying out teacher-prescribed disciplinary action for minor infractions
    Assisting teacher with playground duties

The preceding list is obviously limited to highly technical types of jobs not usually classified as teaching. The supportive role for the aide would have the aide perform in areas usually considered to be teaching, while remaining clearly under a teacher's supervision. Any comprehensive list compiled of supportive role activities would also be quite long, but a partial list devised in the early stages of the Minneapolis teacher aide program may give some idea as to the range of the supportive role in the elementary school classroom (see Table 10–1). The list is broken down by subject matter areas, indicative of the involvement of the aide in the actual instructional process.

Table 10–1   Aide Duties in Supportive Role[a]

Subject Areas	Tasks
1. Reading	Flash card drill; making up reading games from reading manual; directing creative reading games, for example, puppet shows, card box TV, and skits; administering of group tests such as Metropolitan Reading Readiness.
2. Mathematics	Drilling with small group (3 or 4) of children; working with individuals for reinforce-

Table 10–1 (continued)

Subject Areas	Tasks
	ment; trouble-shooting for specific problems; engaging in number games with children.
3. Social Studies	Searching for discussion materials in magazines or books; putting reading text on tape for those who cannot read material; leading group discussions; assisting on field trips; helping in use of the library.
4. Writing-Spelling	Assisting child from desk to desk in mechanics; playing spelling games; helping child make charts; listening to stories, recording stories; helping child with dictionary; setting up and manning a listening table where child can tape stories; reading poems and so on.
5. Music	Playing musical instrument if talented; singing, teaching folk or camp songs; helping children with rhythm activities; building record library according to PTA (or other) list; working spontaneously with kids who like piano, and so on.
6. Art	Helping child assemble materials; helping with technical frustrations (for example, blunted crayons); discussing meaning of work *to* child, *with* child.
7. Physical Education	Replacing regular teacher in work with consulting PE teacher; organizing games; refereeing sandlot athletic contests.
8. Community involvement	Providing knowledge of family background of kids in room; home-visiting on emergency basis; recording community contact.

[a] The authors are especially indebted to Mrs. Gloria Florenz, who drew up the first draft of this list.

Secondary Schools

The use of aides in secondary schools is severely limited by the difficulty of the subject matter being taught. By necessity, the teacher aide program will be limited to a technical role except in a few special areas, for example, modern language, where a native speaker might be of great assistance in conducting a laboratory.

The most common use of teacher aides at the secondary level is to assign one or two aides to a single academic department in which they work for all teachers in the department. They may keep class records, do typing and duplicating work, grade objective examinations, or run errands for a teacher. In a well-organized system, the aide should be clearly identified as a sort of academic clerk for the department to whom students can come with certain requests (for example, materials in a physics laboratory) or to whom they may turn in routine or make-up assignments (to be relayed on to the teacher).

In at least one school (National Education Association, 1966), aides have been used to staff study centers attached to the main academic departments. These study centers are located adjacent to the office of the head of the department, thus making the aides strategically situated to give students routine help in getting materials or in making up work. Such a center can do a great deal to ease the increasing burden of resource development for secondary school staffs.

Still another school has used aides in conjunction with a modular type system. The system allows students a number of free hours per week, and the school has installed an aide in the study lounge–recreation complex where the students usually spend their free time. Technically in a supervisory position, the aide is also able to provide a contact between this free time and the classroom. The free time may be a quiet period in which a student may raise questions with the aide. If the question is a personal one the aide can deal with it on a person-to-person basis; if the question is an academic one, the aide may relay it to the appropriate teacher. In any case the aide is on the scene as a friend and informal counselor. Without the aide, the supervision of the lounge would devolve onto some teacher, thus taking up valuable professional time.

Library Aides

A relatively untapped dimension of aide use is that of library work. Schools may, and have, hired aides in this category under Title I of ESEA. The drastic shortage of trained librarians makes this an attractive area for schools to develop.

One of the better known library aide programs is the one begun in Portland, Oregon, in 1954.[3] In that year the Portland schools took over complete responsibility for the school libraries, and aides were hired to assist librarians. The program was expanded in 1962 under a

[3] Much of the following section is taken from an Administrative Leadership Service publication, *Teacher Aides* (1966).

statewide program to improve staff utilization in all of the state's schools. Later, resource centers were added to most elementary schools and aides were hired to manage these centers. Under this plan, materials, including library books, that are normally issued to teachers directly from the central depository, are issued to the school and managed through the materials center. This puts an important elementary school function into the hands of nonprofessionals. A partial list of duties for these resource center aides includes

1. Ordering audiovisual materials
2. Acting as custodian of instructional equipment
3. Making transparencies
4. Checking books in and out to students and/or rooms
5. Keeping file cards
6. Aiding the student or the teacher in locating information

There is no doubt that this creates a major responsibility for the resource center aide, and this model has not been widely imitated.

At the secondary level, the Portland schools have followed a more common pattern in developing a set of duties for the library aide:

1. Helping to guide students in use of library materials
2. Preparing charge desk for daily use
3. Taking attendance
4. Preparing magazines for circulation
5. Sending overdue notices and collecting fines
6. Filing circulation cards, catalog cards, and shelf list
7. Assisting in inventory
8. Reshelving books
9. Supervising study areas in the library

Administrative Assignments

Administrative duties are "snowballing" in practically all schools. Principals, like teachers, spend large amounts of time on busy work. Earlier chapters have dealt with some of the creative uses of aides for office work and have placed special emphasis on this type of job as a means of recruiting poor or minority group males to education. But there will probably be a need for at least one administrative aide in any school.

One may encounter some resistance on the part of the noninstructional staff toward an "intruder" when an aide is placed in the main office. Again, properly defined divisions of labor can probably avoid some of this difficulty. The administrative aide should, in most cases, restrict his duties to liaison work between office and classroom. A partial list of these duties would include keeping central office records on students and classrooms, supervising a morning milk program, looking after some student disciplinary problems, and running office errands to class or community. In general, however, strict limitations should be placed on the administrative aide role in a volunteer program.

Counseling and Social Work

A broad area that has been only marginally developed is the use of aides in counseling or school social work. This type of aide program is, again, of greatest relevance to a new careers type of program, where the aides are expected to help bridge the gap between school and community. But there is room for counseling aides in nonnew careers settings as well. Counselors, too, are burdened by increasing paper work, and the aide may help in the general handling of these clerical duties. A partial list of counseling or social work type functions is as follows:

1. Making sure all student files are up to date
2. Monitoring objective tests, especially group testing situations
3. Making routine home visits (especially if the aide is from the neighborhood)
4. Checking on absences or truants
5. Perhaps helping the professional to carry out small, practical pieces of research of value to local counseling goals

One other possible use of a mature and experienced counselor aide might be as a liaison between the counselor (or social worker) and the teacher. Usually, counselors hear from a teacher (unless the two are personal friends) only at a problem point. In routine counseling cases, counselors do not consult with the teacher(s) at all, nor is there a systematic follow-up even on direct referrals. On the other hand, many behavioral or academic difficulties are ignored by the teacher because he has no time to deal with them and such difficulties are not believed serious enough for referral of the child to counselors or other supportive staff. This situation might be improved by systematic contact of aide with teacher. Teacher comments on pupil problems, group hostilities, clique rivalry, or other problems might be mentioned to the aide while the incidents were still fresh in the teacher's mind. The aide might then make a routine recording of these comments either in the file records of individual students or in some sort of confidential log. In any case, more detailed information would be available to a counselor if and when problems did arise with a student. Using these notes, the counselor could get a more longitudinal view of his pupil-client.

Training and Supervision

Training and supervision are closely related problems in the strategy of using teacher aides. The broad area of training seems to break down into several major subtypes: (1) preservice training for aides, (2) in-service training for aides, and (3) preservice or in-service training for teachers and administrators.

Preservice Training

As far as we can tell, there has been very little preservice training for aides. What preservice training has existed has been of the orientation session variety—more social than technical in nature. At the same time, data from an ongoing research into the use of teacher aides in Minneapolis indicates that the major complaint on the part of teachers concerns the feeling that they have had to train their own aides. The teachers feel that much time is wasted in teaching aides to do mechanical chores (for example, operate a movie projector or run off a mimeograph) that the aide should have known before entering the classroom. It is our impression that this situation prevails nationally.

Preservice training should focus on technical or mechanical skills. Because time will almost certainly be limited for preservice work,[4] an effort should be made to train the aide as thoroughly as possible in the use of all basic equipment in the school. The rigidities of the school calendar make it difficult to have more than a few days of preservice training, and this time should be used to give the aide maximum technical competence. This training will make the aide of some immediate use to the teacher and, more important, will prevent the aide from being simply another burden for the teacher in the busy first days of school. This may seem elementary, but it has been overlooked by a number of programs.

There is one important exception to the notion that the preser-

[4] Most programs can expect to have little more than two or three days for a preservice program.

vice training should focus on mechanical skills. The preservice training should conclude (for example, on the final afternoon) with a thorough review of school policy and operating procedures. This also will spare the teacher the concern that the aide may commit some colossal faux pas on the first day of school. It will also assure greater security on the part of the aides. Again, teachers have often commented that they have had to take valuable class time to explain basic school policy to a bewildered aide.

In-service Training

Reversing what seems to be customary policy, we feel that general socialization to child behavior, classroom problems, learning material, and so on be avoided in preservice work (unless a great deal of time is available). Rather, these topics should become the core of in-service training. The main reason for this has already been given, namely, the lack of time in the typical preservice program. But it has also been observed that many well-meaning attempts to sensitize beginning aides to classroom problems, curriculum goals, and other educational topics are simply too much, too soon for inexperienced aides. By and large, even two weeks in class experience will familiarize the aide with these problems, thus providing the motivation and the knowledge base for a better, and certainly more efficient, training program. The aide will already have competency in the basic mechanical side of his job, he will have seen a class in action, he will have seen the teacher in the process of handling the common problems, and he will now be better prepared to learn formally the social and intellectual side of his job.

The precise content of such an in-service program, as well as its depth and extensiveness, cannot really be pinpointed. The limits are usually set by the extent of the school's meager resources for such training. The context is also determined, in part, by the social and economic context in which the school operates. Work in a target area school will certainly demand greater in-service training, especially if the aides themselves are middle class. However, a list of in-service training topics can be suggested here:

1. An elementary understanding of human development and child psychology (6 hours)
2. The social context of the school, neighborhood, and city (4 hours)
3. Teacher–teacher aide relations (2 hours)

4. Curriculum material, an elementary presentation or "familiarization" (4 to 6 hours) [5]
5. Some combination of group counseling and sensitivity training sessions (6 to 8 hours) [6]

This is obviously a minimum "core" curriculum for the in-service training of classroom aides. The time estimates are bare bone figures, meant to indicate the minimum requirement for adequate functioning at the technical assistance role level. The curriculum heavily emphasizes a brief retooling of the social and psychological skills of the aides. This reflects the feeling that, apart from being able to aid the teacher technically, the prime consideration of an in-service program should be to assure that the aides do no harm to the children in their frequent personal encounters (including, especially, discipline) and be trained to give positive assistance to the teacher's efforts to provide psychological and emotional support to the child. No matter how limited the formal functions of the aide, he will have repeated personal contacts with students. The first goal of in-service work should be to guarantee that he handle these effectively. Research indicates that aides get their greatest satisfaction from their personal relations with students, but there does not appear to be any systematic information on the quality of these interactions.

It is felt that the training subjects just listed are relatively self-explanatory and are within the capacity of the staff available within most school systems (for example, the director of the teacher aide program). However, a word should be said about the recommended group counseling or sensitivity sessions. These need not be fully developed sensitivity sessions in the technical use of this concept. The main goal of these sessions should include helping the aides to be aware of their own needs and helping them to recognize the relationship of these needs to the needs of pupils and other staff. This might provide the framework for bringing up such delicate subjects as potential resentment against aides on the part of other school staff, or questions of interracial or interethnic tensions within the school (and possibly within the staff). Obviously, the range of problems is going to be unique to each school, but it is always necessary for the aide to see his relationship (if any) to the problem or tension and to see how it might affect his work. These group sessions can be a starting point

---

[5] This will involve breaking the aide group by grade level and/or subject matter specialization.

[6] A very good reference on this is Pointer and Fishman (1968).

in this direction, although in comparison to more elaborate sensitivity training, questions of personality should be avoided and the discussion kept on a relatively abstract level. They should probably be called group counseling sessions and might be most effectively handled by someone who is outside the school system, yet familiar with its problems.

Training Supervisors

Certainly, the most overlooked aspect of training is the training of supervisors themselves. Very few aide programs have foreseen the need to prepare the teacher to use a teacher aide. This has led to a large amount of yearly confusion on the part of school personnel. Typically, the teacher has somewhat abruptly been handed an aide on the first day of school. We are even aware of a program where the aide informed the teacher as to his assignment! And it has been the exception, rather than the rule, for the teachers to have any formal preparation for using aides.

This is certainly a mistake. Even at the "technical aide" role level, teachers must be technically and psychologically prepared to use an aide. Not to provide this kind of preparation is to court inefficiency and interpersonal conflict in the classroom.

First of all, teachers should be maximally involved in planning an aide program. In most cases it would be wise to appoint (or elect) a steering committee of teachers and administrators (either at the school or district level) to set the general guidelines for the program. Clear channels of communications should likewise be established with the local professional organization(s). Although at the national level the UFT and the NEA have given strong support to the teacher aide idea, this has not always held for local affiliates. Where information about the program is scarce, one often finds a variety of semiofficial rumors. These rumors have commonly asserted potentially dangerous notions, such as that the teacher aides are really a cadre of potential strike breakers or the idea that the aides will allow a slow increase in pupil-teacher ratio. Because the situation regarding aides is a somewhat uncertain one, the local professional leadership has frequently been overly cautious, apparently guarding against the possibility that they might be caught off base at some future date. Good lines of communication and teacher involvement in planning, seem to be the only antidotes.

Beyond the planning stage all teachers scheduled to use aides should receive some prior preparation. As with aide training, time and training resources will of necessity be limited. But two or three workshop-like sessions would seem to be a minimum requirement. These sessions would ordinarily be organized and conducted by the director of the program, perhaps assisted by a teacher experienced in working with aides.

For purposes of this overview, the minimum pretraining for teachers should cover at least three major areas: potential uses for aides, legal and policy considerations of aide use, and, finally, some discussion of typical needs and abilities of the aides:

1. *Uses for teacher aides.* Teacher training sessions on aide use will certainly have to be broken down by functional area (for example, all lower grade teachers together). On their own, most teachers will think of only a small portion of potential uses for aides. In fact, left to his own devices, the teacher will tend to underuse the aide, partly out of uncertainty as to just what the aide's role includes. Teachers will also tend to cling to many busy-work tasks that could be assigned to an aide because the teacher has gotten so used to doing these tasks himself that it never occurs to him to unburden himself. These are sometimes jobs (for example, clean-up jobs) that punctuate the day for the teacher, but they are also jobs that consume valuable amounts of potentially creative time.

2. *Legal and policy considerations.* Legal problems of aide use and the general policy guidelines under which the program operates will have wide local variation. However, some of the standard problems have to do with the problem of legal liability (in most states the teacher will still be liable for all pupils at all times), the queston of what constitutes "teaching" (that is, what acts *must* be reserved for certified personnel), and what policy has been adopted on the necessity for the teacher's presence in the classroom. These formal requiremcnts should lead naturally into a definition of the teacher aide (or counselor aide, and so on) role. We hope that here some use could be made of the role distinctions as discussed in detail in this book. Specific local problems of role conflict can also be discussed at this point. It would be good to have a representative of the local professional association present for this discussion.

3. *Needs and abilities.* Our research into the Minneapolis teacher aide program indicates that teacher ignorance concerning the personal needs and abilities of aides is greater than might be

expected. Teachers generally tend to overestimate the technical skill of teacher aides and underestimate the fact that aides may have different needs and personalities from teachers. A remedy for this would be a clear exposition of the training received (or to be received) by the aides and the general educational background of the aide group. The latter should be accompanied, of course, by letting the individual teacher know the educational background and experience of the aide assigned to him.

Beyond these important pieces of information, this session might focus on the fact that research to date indicates that aides have high needs for either status or positive emotional relationships with children. And very often both needs are present. These needs sometimes go unnoticed by teachers whose needs (in the classroom, anyway) more often run to competent professional performance. The aide may not clearly understand or be able to respond to this teacher need, which often is perceived by aides as perfectionism.

In any case, the questions of human needs, role relationships, status, and the like should be discussed in a kind of open-ended session. This may not be too different from the group counseling previously prescribed for aides. This type of session can clearly be used to sensitize the teacher to the subtleties of working with another adult in a professional-to-nonprofessional relationship.

Summary

This chapter deals with the major practical problems of implementing teacher aide programs. It is recognized that not all teacher aide programs are new careers programs, nor should they be. The focus in this chapter has momentarily been directed at the problems that all aide programs share to some degree.

The problems covered here include (1) the definition of a teacher aide, (2) recruitment, (3) salaries, (4) role conflict, (5) aide duties, and (6) training and supervision. A few of the most troublesome areas for existing aide programs have been conflict between aides and other nonprofessional staff in the schools, personality adjustment of aide and teacher in the classroom, defining duties for aides, preparing the aide to do the technical side of his job with complete competence, and alerting teachers to the needs and limitations of aides. These potential trouble spots have all been mentioned at one or more points in our discussion.

11 Epilogue

There are not many new careers programs in education. There are, however, many teacher aide programs, and a substantial minority of these programs are evolving in the direction of new careers. Out of nearly 200,000 teacher aides who are employed in 1969–1970, projections indicate that something less than 10 percent are in anything like a new careers program. Yet a combination of factors makes it appear likely that most urban school systems, and some suburban or rural systems, will move toward the new careers idea in the near future (Riessman and Gartner, 1969).

One harsh statistic should illustrate the point. Preliminary data indicate that resignations of inner city school personnel rose dramatically in 1968 to 1969. This reverses a three-year trend of a declining resignation rate that began in 1964. Resignations and other forms of mobility among inner city teachers have been one of the major problems of urban school systems since the beginning of the century. This is one of the truisms of the war on poverty. Heightened salaries, special institutes, added prestige, and other factors seemed to have begun a reversal of this flight. A few skirmishes in the war on poverty were won, but the war on this front is now going badly again.

The cruel fact is that riots and perhaps a simple drying up of the antipoverty spirit (what Black leaders predicted all along) have ended what looked like a major breakthrough. The flight of white teachers to suburbia has begun again, apparently with renewed vigor. This is a complicated and unstable situation; but one conclusion is quite simple. If quality education is to be provided to the inner city, the nation cannot depend on the charity and martial spirit of white teachers rearmed by NDEA programs. Special institutes and "combat" pay may keep some, but it will not be enough. The urban schools must recruit more Black teachers, reservation area schools must recruit more Indian teachers, and so on. There is no avoiding this fact.

But where do the schools find these black teachers? Where do the schools find teachers for the impoverished white neighborhoods? Where are the special funds to come from now that the gold dust is gone from the poverty program? There are not enough young Negro college students to make a dent in the situation. This would be true even if a majority of these black students choose to go into teaching, which, of course, they will not do. There are dozens of other fields in today's job market, even for minority group youngsters.

The answer seems to lie in the large number of unemployed or underemployed young adults (aged 20 to 35) now fighting to make a living for themselves (and their families) in the tough world of the inner city. One thinks especially of the large mass of AFDC mothers, of large numbers of underemployed black males, and of a growing number of poor youth who have found employment through poverty programs but who can hardly be expected to make a career in the unstable world of government programs. These people can be recruited to education.

There is a great pool of talent here, much of it badly underutilized. Opportunity may have "knocked," but in the ghetto of the 1950s it knocked very briefly, one can be sure. There is no doubt that these people need a second chance to enter the world of higher education and the professions. That would be reason enough for new careers. But it is equally clear that the schools need these people as much as they need the schools. They are the new recruits—even if they are only "two year" teachers—to the frontiers of inner city education.

Putting aside for the moment the technical concerns with role and training, with mobility and new instructional forms, and putting aside all the talk, new careers boils down to the question of new teachers for new schools in a new inner city. It is to this reality that this book has tried to address itself. These are questions that most urban educators will confront very soon. It seems that there is only one way to go, and that is to go forward with new recruiting policies and new kinds of teachers. It is hoped that the preceding ten chapters have provided some forewarning, and, possibly, some foreknowledge.

Bibliography

Aald, V. "More Time to Think; English Composition Project," *Michigan Education Journal*, Vol. 41 (October 1963a), 19–20.

Aald, V. "Operation 1,000 Auxiliaries," *Times Educational Supplement*, Vol. 2499 (April 12, 1963b), 764.

Administrative Leadership Service. *Teacher Aides or Auxiliary School Personnel*. Arlington, Va.: Educational Service Bureau, Inc. 1966.

Alice, Sister Mary. "Teacher Aides: A Resource," *National Catholic Education Association Bulletin*, Vol. 56 (August 1959), 309–311.

Anderson, R. A. "Organizational Character of Education: Staff Utilization and Deployment; Sub-Professional and Paraprofessional Personnel," *Review of Educational Research*, Vol. 34 (October 1964), 458–459.

Anderson, Robert H. *Teaching in a World of Change*. New York: Harcourt, Brace & World, Inc., 1966.

Armstrong, Annilee. "Illini House, Volunteer Help for the Dropout Problem," *Illinois Education*, Vol. 53 (April 1965), 344–345.

Aronowitz, S. "Credentials: Useful or Not?" *New Careers Newsletter*, Vol. 2 (Spring 1968).

Atkinson, E. J. "Scope for Auxiliaries; Experimental Marking Scheme," *Times Education Supplement*, Vol. 2604 (April 16, 1965), 1177.

Attebery, Roland K., and Beverly Gibson. "Training Teacher Aides at Hanford," *California Education*, Vol. 3 (June 1966), 11–15.

Bailyn, B. *Education in the Forming of American Society*. New York: Vintage Books, 1960.

Bank Street College. "Profile of the New Careers Training Project at Institute for Youth Studies, Howard University," unpublished project report. New York: Bank Street College Study of Auxiliary Personnel in Education, 1967.

Barr, S. "Some Observations on the Practice of Indigenous Nonprofessional Workers," paper presented at the Program Meeting of the Council on Social Work Education (January 1966).

Bartlett, D. B. "Non-Teaching Assistants; A Southard Experiment," *Times Education Supplement*, Vol. 2615 (July 2, 1965), 29.

Becken, E. D. "Medford's Teacher Aides," *Oregon Education*, Vol. 40 (May 1966), 8–9.

Biddle, B. J., and E. Thomas. *Role Theory*. New York: John Wiley & Sons, Inc., 1966.

Blackman, E. B. "Lay Readers in 13th Grade English," *Improving College and University Training*, Vol. 12 (Autumn 1964), 243–245.

Blessing, K. R. "Use of Teacher Aides in Special Education: A Review and Possible Applications," *Exceptional Child*, Vol. 34 (October 1967), 107–113.

Bowman, Garda W., and J. G. Klopf. *Auxiliary School Personnel: Their Roles, Training, and Institutionalization*. New York: Bank Street College for the Office of Economic Opportunity, 1966.

Bowman, Garda W., and J. G. Klopf. *Careers and Roles in the American School*. New York: Bank Street College of Education for the Office of Economic Opportunity, 1967.

Branick, J. J. "How to Train and Use Teacher Aides," *Phi Delta Kappan*, Vol. 48 (October 1961), 61.

Braun, R. H., and J. Steffensen. "Grouping, Acceleration and Teacher Aides Experiments in Urbana Secondary Schools," *Bulletin of the National Association of Secondary School Principals*. Vol. 44 (January 1960), 305–315.

Brim, O. G. "Adult Socialization," in *Socialization and Society*, ed. J. A. Clausen. Boston: Little, Brown Company, 1968.

Brim, O. G., and S. Wheeler. *Socialization After Childhood: Two Essays*. New York: John Wiley & Sons, 1966.

Brody, Adele Cutler. "Career-Oriented Training: A Necessary Step Beyond Job Training." New York: New Careers Training Laboratory, 1967.

Bruner, J. *The Process of Education*. Cambridge: Harvard University Press, 1960.

Brunner, Catherine. "A Lap to Sit On—And Much More," *Childhood Education*, Vol. 43 (January 1962), 20–23.

Burke, Virginia M. "A Candid Opinion on Lay Readers," *English Journal*, Vol. 50 (April 1961a), 258–264.

Burke, Virginia M. *The Lay Reader Program: Backgrounds and Procedures.* New York: National Council of Teachers of English, 1961b.

Burke, Virginia M. "Lay Reader Program in Review," *Bulletin of the National Association of Secondary School Principals*, Vol. 46 (January 1962a), 261–268.

Burke, Virginia M. "Lay Readers for English Classes?" *NEA Journal*, Vol. 51 (January 1962b), 20–22.

Burkhardt, A. S. "Trained Volunteer and the Elementary Library," *American School Board Journal*, Vol. 150 (March 1965), 15–17.

Caplow, T. *The Principles of Organization.* New York: Harcourt, Brace & World, Inc., 1964.

Childe, V. Gordon. *Social Evolution.* London: C. A. Watts & Co., Ltd., 1951.

Clarke, Johnnie R. "Proposal for a Teacher's Aide Training Program: A Two-Year Program in a Community Junior College Can Fill a Vital Social and Classroom Need," *Junior College Journal*, Vol. 36 (May 1966), 43–45.

Clausen, J. A. (ed.). *Socialization and Society.* Boston: Little, Brown Company, 1968.

Clement, S. "More Time for Teaching," *Bulletin of the National Association of Secondary School Principals*, Vol. 46 (December 1962), 54–59.

Cohen, E. "Labor Department Sets New Guidelines for New Careers," *New Careers Newsletter*, Vol. 2 (Spring 1968), 6–7.

Collis, N. "Non-Teacher," *New York State Education*, Vol. 54 (May 1967), 22–23.

Corwin, R. *A Sociology of Education,* New York: Appleton-Century-Crofts, 1965.

Cremin, Laurence. *The Transformation of the Schools: Progressivism in American Education, 1876–1957.* New York: Vintage Books, 1961.

Curry, J. "Two Birds Uncaged," *Times Education Supplement*, Vol. 2696 (January 20, 1967), 187.

Cutler, M. H. "Teacher Aides Are Worth the Effort," *Nation's School*, Vol. 73 (April 1964), 67–70.

Davies, D. "The Teacher and Her Staff," keynote address by national telephone hookup to National Commission on Teacher Education and Professional Standards, 1967.

Davis, D. "The Fenville Teacher Aide Experiment," *Journal of Teacher Education*, Vol. 13 (June 1962), 189–190.

Deason, J. "What They Say about Teacher Aides," *School Executive* 77 (December 1957), 59–60.

DeBernardis, A. "New Challenge for Community Colleges," *Educational Screen A.V. Guide,* Vol. 44 (December 1965), 34–35.

DeLara, Lane E. "Teacher Aides in the Junior High Schools," *Clearing House,* Vol. 42 (December 1967), 234–237.

Denemark, G. W. "Teacher and His Staff," *National Education Journal,* Vol. 55 (December 1966), 17–20.

Diederich, Paul B. "Research Report: College-Educated Housewives as Lay Readers," *Bulletin of the National Association of Secondary School Principals,* Vol. 47 (April 1963), 201–211.

Dohorty, Eugene N. "Princeton Township Lay-Corrector Program," *English Journal,* Vol. 53 (April 1964), 273–276.

Edalfelt, R. A. "Teacher and His Staff," *Virginia Journal of Education,* Vol. 60 (April 1967), 11–13.

Effhirm, A., and S. Aronowitz. "Power for the Paraprofessional in the Ghetto," paper presented at First Conference, National Council on New Careers, Detroit, Michigan, June 4–7, 1968.

Egerton, John. "Quasi Teachers: A Growing Breed," *Southern Education Report,* Vol. 4 (February 1966), 2.

Emmerling, Frank C., and Kanawha Z. Chavis. "Innovations in Education: 'The Teacher Aide,'" *Educational Leadership,* Vol. 24 (November 1966), 175–184.

Erickson, A. G. "Helena Reports on High School English Teacher Aide Program under Title I, ESEA," *Montana Education,* Vol. 43 (September 1966), 26–27.

Erickson, E. *Summary Report: Teacher and Teacher Aide Studies, Phase VI.* Grand Rapids, Michigan: Grand Rapids Educational Studies Center, 1968.

Esbensen, T. "Should Teacher Aides Be More than Clerks?" *Phi Delta Kappan,* Vol. 47 (January 1966), 237.

Falk, R. F. "A Theoretical Extension and Test—The Durability of Changes in Self-Concept," unpublished M.A. thesis. San Francisco: San Francisco State College, 1966.

Felton, Nadine. *Career Incentive Plan for Higher Education of Non-Professionals.* New York: New Careers Development Center, 1967.

Ford, Paul M. "Lay Readers in the High School Composition Program: Some Statistics," *English Journal,* Vol. 50 (November 1961), 522–528.

Foster, Robert E. "In Slow Gear: Volunteer Teacher Aides," *Instructor,* Vol. 74 (September 1964), 136–137.

Freund, J. "Time and Knowledge to Share: Project for Academic Motivation," *Elementary School Journal,* Vol. 65 (April 1965), 351–358.

Freyman, L. "A+ for Our Lay Readers," *NEA Journal,* Vol. 53 (November 1964), 19–20.

Geston, J. "Aides for the Teacher," *North Dakota Teacher,* Vol. 46 (January 1967), 26–27.

Goldstein, David H. "Teacher Aides: The Indianapolis Plan May Lend Itself to Your School," *Instructor,* Vol. 76 (October 1966), 31–32.

Goralski, Patricia J. and F. V. Hayen. *Teacher Aide Program.* Minneapolis: Minneapolis Public Schools, 1967.

Goralski, Patricia J., and F. V. Hayen. *Teacher Aide Program: 1967–1968.* Minneapolis: Minneapolis Public Schools, 1968.

Gouldner, A. *Patterns of Industrial Bureaucracy.* New York: The Free Press, 1954.

Grayson, Jan. "Teacher Aides: Mother," *Elementary School Journal,* Vol. 62 (December 1961), 134–138.

Green, D. H. "Value of an Attendant in a Classroom for the Trainable Mentally Handicapped," *National Catholic Education Association Bulletin,* Vol. 63 (August 1966), 472–473.

Greenberg, Barry. *Review of Literature Relating to the Use of Non-Professionals in Education.* New York: New Careers Development Center, 1967.

Greenshields, H. J. "Big Timbers Teacher-Helper Plan," *The American School Board Journal,* Vol. 104 (April 1942), 20.

Gross, N., W. S. Mason, and A. W. McEachern. *Explorations in Role Analysis.* New York: John Wiley & Sons, Inc., 1958.

Haber, A. "Issues Beyond Consensus," unpublished paper presented to First National Conference on New Careers, Detroit, Michigan, 1968.

Haney, J. "Teachers' Responsibilities," *Wyoming Education News,* Vol. 31 (November 1964), 2.

Hartley, James. *New Careers for Non-Professionals in Education.* Educational Resources Information Center, February 1968.

Hayen, F. V., and Pat Goralski. *Teacher Aide Program.* Minneapolis: Public Schools Special School District #1, 1967.

Heinemann, F. E. "Defining Duties of Aides," *Minnesota Journal of Education,* Vol. 44 (November 1963), 19.

Henderson, P. B. "Quality Education through the Use of Instructional Aides," *Arizona Teacher,* Vol. 55 (January 1967), 10–12.

Herman, W. L. "Teacher Aides; How They Can Be of Real Help," *Grade Teacher,* Vol. 84 (February 1967), 102–103.

Higham, Jean Starr. "Lay Reader Program Is One Answer for Improving Student Writing," *Montana Education,* Vol. 42 (November 1965), 15–16.

Hinmon, D. E. "Morris Experiments with College Students as Teacher Aides," *Minnesota Journal of Education,* Vol. 46 (April 1966), 17–19.

Hodge, O. "Assignment of the Teacher Aide," *Oklahoma Teacher,* Vol. 47 (February 1966), 10–11.

Johnson, P., and W. O. Nesbitt. "Some Conclusions Drawn from the Snyder, Texas, Project," *Bulletin of the National Association of Secondary School Principals,* Vol. 44 (January 1960), 63–75.

Johnson, William H. "Utilizing Teacher Aides," *Clearing House,* Vol. 42 (December 1967), 229–233.

Journal of Teacher Education. "Bay City, Michigan, Experiment: A Cooperative Study for the Better Utilization of Teacher Competencies:

Symposium," *Journal of Teacher Education,* Vol. 7 (June 1956), 100–153.

Kennedy, G. "Preparation, Orientation, Utilization and Acceptance of Part-Time Instructors," *Junior College Journal,* Vol. 37 (April 1967), 14–15.

Kennedy, L. A. "Help-Help-Help," *Oklahoma Teacher,* Vol. 48 (January 1967), 29–30.

Kilroy, W. J., Jr. "Bonus in the Classroom," *Massachusetts Teacher,* Vol. 45 (May 1966), 14–15.

Kinch, J. W. "A Formalized Theory of Self-Concept," *American Journal of Sociology,* Vol. 68 (January 1963) 481–486.

Kolker, Harriette B. "Some Answers to Some Questions on the Lay Reader Program," *English Journal,* Vol. 52 (January 1963), 51–54.

Kowitz, G. T. "Problems in Teacher Utilization," *American School Board Journal,* Vol. 138 (February 1959), 24–26, 56.

Kozol, J. *Death at An Early Age: The Destruction of the Hearts and Minds of Negro Children in the Boston Public Schools.* Boston: Houghton Mifflin Company, 1967.

Krueger, Paul H. "Some Questions on the Lay Reader Program," *English Journal,* Vol. 50 (November 1961), 529–533.

Lamberth, E. L. "Helping Teachers in Norfolk," *American School Board Journal,* Vol. 149 (September 1964), 16.

Lane, W., R. Corwin, and W. G. Monghan. *Foundations of Educational Administration.* New York: Crowell-Collier and Macmillan, 1966.

Lawson, E. H. "Role of the Auxiliary: Teaching in the Truest Sense," *Times Education Supplement,* Vol. 2587 (December 18, 1964), 1137.

Leggatt, T. W. "The Use of Non-Professionals in Public Education: A Study in Innovation," Doctoral dissertation, University of Chicago, 1966.

Liebert, Lisa. *New Careers and Model Cities: A Partnership for Human Renewal.* New York: New Careers Development Center, 1967.

Lord, P. "Taking a Less Rigid View: Jobs for Auxiliaries," *Times Education Supplement,* Vol. 2583 (November 20, 1964), 931.

Lynton, Edith. "Concepts and Practices in the Education Training and Utilization of Subprofessional Workers," *ERIC* (May 1967).

Lyon, H. C. "Introduction to Success: Teenage Trainees Working with Preschool Youngsters," *American Education,* Vol. 3 (May 1967), 5–7.

McClure, A. "How I Help the Teacher," *Catholic School Journal,* Vol. 63 (November 1963), 30.

MacLennan, B. W. "New Careers as Human Service Aides," *Children,* Vol. 13 (September 1966), 190–194.

Manchester, C. "St. Paul Teacher Aide Program, 1967–1968," program report to St. Paul Public Schools, St. Paul, Minnesota, 1968.

Martin, M. "Aide in Action," *Arizona Teacher,* Vol. 54 (March 1966), 25.

Meltzer, B. N. "Mead's Social Psychology," in *Symbolic Interaction,* eds. J. Manis and B. N. Meltzer, Boston: Allyn and Bacon, Inc., 1968.

Miller, S. M., and F. Riessman. "The Working Class Subculture; A New View," *Social Problems*, Vol. 9 (Summer 1961), 86–97.

Miller, W. W. "Clerical Help," *NEA Journal*, Vol. 52 (November 1963), 32.

Mondale, Senator Walter. "The Full Opportunity and Social Accounting Act of 1967," *Congressional Record*, Vol. 113 (February 1967).

Morse, Arthur D. *Schools of Tomorrow—Today*. New York: Doubleday and Company, 1960.

Mott, P. E. *The Organization of Society*. Englewood Cliffs, N. J.: Prentice-Hall, Inc., 1965.

National Association of Secondary School Principals. *Locus of Change: Staff Utilization Studies*. Washington, D.C.: National Education Center, 1962.

National Education Association. *Paraprofessional Tasks. Innovations for Time to Teach*. Washington, D.C.: National Education Association, 1966, 113–147.

National Education Association. "Teacher Aides in Large School Systems," *NEA Research Bulletin*, Vol. 45 (May 1967a), 37–39.

National Education Association. *Classroom Teacher Speaks on His Supportive Staff*. Washington, D.C.: National Education Association, 1967b.

National Education Association. *Auxiliary School Personnel*. Washington, D.C.: National Education Association, 1967c.

Naylor, Naomi. "Curriculum Development Program for Pre-School Teacher Aides," *ERIC*, ED 013-122 (February 1968).

Nelson, Gaylord. "Teacher Aide Bill," *Congressional Record*, Vol. 113 (January 30, 1967a).

Nelson, Gaylord. "S.721: Teacher Aide Program Support Act of 1967," *The National Elementary Principal*, Vol. 46 (1967b), 40–44.

Nelson, L. "Changing Concepts of Teacher Leadership," *Education Leader*, Vol. 21 (December 1963), 177–182.

Neubacher, James. *The Use of the Teacher Aide in Inner City Schools*. Minneapolis: Training Center for Delinquency Prevention and Control, University of Minnesota, 1965.

New Careers Newsletter. "New Laws with New Careers Opportunities," *New Careers Newsletter*, Vol. 2 (Spring 1968), 17–18.

Newcomer, K. "How Would You Like an Assistant Teacher?" *School and Community*, Vol. 50 (May 1964), 23–24.

Noar, Gertrude. *Teacher Aides at Work*. Washington, D.C.: National Commission on Teacher Education and Professional Standards, 1967.

North, M. "Dear Miss North," *Pennylvania School Journal*, Vol. 114 (March 1966), 317.

Otterness, June, *et al.* "Teacher Aides in Minnesota," *Minnesota Journal of Education*, Vol. 44 (November 1963), 20.

Park, Charles B. "The Teacher-Aide Plan," *Nation's Schools*, Vol. 56 July 1955a), 45–55.

Park, Charles B. *A Cooperative Study for the Better Use of Teacher Competencies.* Mount Pleasant, Mich.: Central Michigan University, 1955b.

Parris, Judith. "Using the Extra Hands," *Times Education Supplement,* Vol. 2509 (June 21, 1963), 1360.

Parris, Judith. "Part-Time Teaching," *Times Education Supplement,* Vol. 2510 (June 28, 1963), 1413.

Pearl, Arthur. "New Careers, One Solution to Poverty," unpublished paper, 1966.

Pearl, Arthur. "New Careers and the Manpower Crisis in Education," in *Up From Poverty,* eds. F. Riessman and H. I. Popper. New York: Harper & Row, Publishers, 1968a.

Pearl, Arthur. "Strategy for Implementing a New Careers Design," paper for Center for Community Planning Department of Health, Education, and Welfare, Washington, D.C., 1968b.

Perkins, Bryce. "How to Use Teacher Aides Effectively," *Getting Better Results from Teacher Aides, Substitutes and Volunteers.* Englewood Cliffs, N.J.: Prentice-Hall, Inc., 1966, 33–48.

Petrich, Paul. "English Lay Reader Program at Hanover High School," *Bulletin of the National Association of Secondary School Principals,* Vol. 44 (October 1960), 113–119.

Pino, E. C. "Teacher Aides Are In," *Grade Teacher,* Vol. 83 (May 1966), 183–185.

Pointer, Avis Y., and J. R. Fishman. *New Careers: Entry-Level Training for the Human Service Aide.* Washington, D.C.: New Careers Development Program, University Research Corporation, 1968.

Pope, L., and R. Crump. "School Drop-Outs as Assistant Teachers," *Young Children,* Vol. 21 (October 1965), 13–23.

Rademacher, Elizabeth. "A Training Program for Teacher Aides," unpublished manuscript, University of Oregon, 1968.

Riessman, Frank. "Aim for the Moon," *Ohio School,* Vol. 44 (April 1966a), 20–21.

Riessman, Frank. "New Developments in the New Careers Movement," New York: New Careers Development Center, 1966b.

Riessman, Frank. *Are Welfare Recipients Employable?* New York: New Careers Development Center, 1967a.

Riessman, Frank. *Issues in Training the New Nonprofessional.* New York: New Careers Development Center, 1967b.

Riessman, Frank. *Training the Nonprofessional.* Newark, N.J.: Scientific Resources Incorporated, 1967c.

Riessman, F., and A. Gartner. "The Instructional Aide: New Developments," *Social Policy,* Vol. 5 (January 1969) published by New Careers Development Center, New York.

Riessman, F. and A. Pearl (eds.). *New Careers for the Poor.* New York: The Free Press, 1965.

Riley, R. A. "Volunteer Teacher Aide Program Tried in Dixie School District," *California Education,* Vol. 1 (January 1964), 25–27.

Rioux, J. W.   "At the Teacher's Right Hand," *American Education*, Vol. 2 (December 1965a), 5–6.

Rioux, J. W.   "Here Are Fourteen Ways to Use Non-Teachers in Your School District," *Nation's School*, Vol. 76 (December 1965b), 42.

Rose, A. M. (ed.).   *Human Behavior and Social Processes*. Boston: Houghton Mifflin Company, 1962.

Rutherford, E.   Unpublished and untitled manuscript proposing a cooperative educational experiment between San Jose State College and the San Jose Public Schools, 1967.

Samter, E. C.   "Teacher Aide: An Aide in Teaching?" *New York State Education*, Vol. 51 (October 1963), 21.

Samuel, H. E.   "What Teachers Think," *District of Columbia Education Association Newsletter* (September–October 1965), 1–2.

School Management.   "If You're Thinking about Using Teacher Aides," *School Management*, Vol. 2 (July 1958), 27–29, 60–63.

School Management.   "How Aides Can Improve a Physical Education Program," *School Management*, Vol. 6 (July 1962), 57–58.

Schriuner, A. W.   "Value of Teacher-Aide Participation in the Elementary School," *Arithmetic Teacher*, Vol. 10 (February 1963), 84–87.

Shipp, Mary D.   "Teacher Aides: A Survey," *The National Elementary Principal*, Vol. 46 (May 1967), No. 6, 30–33.

Smelser, N.   "Systems Theory and Social Development," in *Political Development and Social Change*, eds. J. L. Finkle and R. W. Gable. New York: John Wiley & Sons, Inc., 1966.

Smith, A.   "Utilization of Advanced Physics Students in the Fourth Grade," *School Science and Mathematics*, Vol. 66 (February 1966).

Smith, L. M., and W. Geoffrey.   *The Complexities of an Urban Classroom*. New York: Holt, Rinehart and Winston, 1968.

Soles, S.   "Teacher Role Expectations and the Internal Organization of Secondary Schools," *Journal of Education Research*, Vol. 57 (January 1964), 227–238.

Stafford, C.   "Teacher Time Utilization with Teacher Aides," *Journal of Education Research*, Vol. 56 (October 1962), 82–88.

Stinnett, T. M.   "A Master Teacher in Every Classroom," *Educational Leadership*, Vol. 14 (April 1957), 435–440.

Stoddard, G. D.   "Creativity in Education," in *Creativity and Its Cultivation*, ed. H. L. Anderson. New York: Harper & Row, Publishers, 1959.

Stoddard, G. D.   *The Dual Progress Plan*. New York: Harper & Row, Publishers, 1961.

Strauss, A.   *George Herbert Mead on Social Psychology*. Chicago: University of Chicago Press, 1964.

Sutherland, Olive.   "I Use an Assistant Teacher," *Agricultural Education Magazine*, Vol. 37 (November 1964), 118–119.

Swift, D. F., and I. Rootman.   "Self-image and Role Perception of Teachers: Towards a Typology," *Canadian Education Research Digest*, Vol. 4 (March 1964), 5–16.

Thompson, Margaret. *Contamination of New Careerists by Professionalization.* Minneapolis, Minnesota: New Careers Research, University of Minnesota, 1969.

Thompson, S. D. "Emerging Role of the Teacher Aide," *Clearing House,* Vol. 37 (February 1963), 326–330.

Trump, J. Lloyd, and Dorsey Barnham. "Focus on Change—Guide to Better Schools." Chicago, Ill.: Rand McNally & Company, 1961.

Tumin, Melvin. "Teaching in America," *Saturday Review* (October 21, 1967), 77–79, 84.

Turney, David T. *Secretaries for Teachers.* Nashville, Tenn.: Department of Education, George Peabody College for Teachers, 1962a.

Turney, David T. "Secretarial Help for Classroom Teachers," *Education Digest,* Vol. 28 (December 1962b), 24–26.

Twist, Dwight E. "Improving Instruction Through More Effective Utilization of Certified Personnel." San Diego, Calif.: San Diego Unified School District, 1967.

U.S. Department of Health, Education, and Welfare, Office of Education. *Staffing for Better Schools.* Washington, D.C.: Government Printing Office, 1967.

Valdez, R. F. "Noon-Duty Assistant Programs," *National Education Association Journal,* Vol. 53 (April 1964), 63.

Valette, Rebecca M. "Young Mother in Academe," *Liberal Education,* Vol. 51 (October 1965), 379–381.

Waller, W. *The Sociology of Teaching.* New York: John Wiley & Sons, Inc., 1932.

Weisz, V. C., and H. J. Butler. "Training Teachers' Aides at Garland," *Junior College Journal,* Vol. 36 (April 1966), 6–7.

White, L. A. *The Evolution of Culture.* New York: McGraw-Hill, Inc., 1959.

Wiley, Wretha. *Designing Jobs and Careers in Model Cities Program.* New York: New Careers Development Center, 1967.

Wilson, H. C. "On the Evolution of Education," in *Essays on the Social Systems of Education,* ed. B. J. Biddle. Columbia, Mo.: University of Missouri Press, 1966.

Yankelovitch, D. *A Study of the Nonprofessional in CAP.* Washington, D.C.: Office of Economic Opportunity, 1966.